Ready Reckoner for Hospitality, Tourism and Hotel Management

Ready Reckoner for Hospitality, Tourism and Hotel Management

FAQ
Frequently Asked Questions

GULSHAN SONI
Lecturer BCIHM & CT
M.Phil Tourism Management,
Executive MBA, MSci HM & CT,
Diploma in Training & Development, (M.H.R.D.)
G.H.O.T.P (J.P. Hotels Ltd.)

KANISHKA PUBLISHERS, DISTRIBUTORS
NEW DELHI-110 002

KANISHKA PUBLISHERS, DISTRIBUTORS
4697/5-21 A, Ansari Road, Daryaganj
New Delhi-110 002
Phones : 2327 0497, 2328 8285
Fax : 011-2328 8285
E-mail: kanishka_publishing@yahoo.co.in

Ready Reckoner for Hospitality, Tourism and Hotel Management

First Published 2009

ISBN 978-81-8457-142-4

PRINTED IN INDIA

Published by Madan Sachdeva for Kanishka Publishers, Distributors, 4697/5-21A, Ansari Road, Daryaganj, New Delhi-110 002, Typeset by Sunshine Graphics, Delhi, and Printed at Rajdhani Printers, Delhi.

Preface

The aim of this book is to cover the basic as well as the advance management knowledge necessary for those involved in hospitality sector at different levels. This book provides a framework for an individual to build further studies and to increase there appetite for knowledge.

This book has been primarily designed to be a Ready Reckoner for students preparing for placements, interviews, young professionals looking forward to career enhancement/ promotion / career change.

This book is designed to serve as a practical guide for Training managers, Operations managers, HR managers, and Executives. This book will be prove to be very interesting and fruitful for their reference and will increase their knowledge.

This book contains more than 5,000 questions and well over 8,000 answers. As a result of the increase in competition and complexity of hospitality as well as sophisticated demand of hospitality employees, this book will help professionals, to be more knowledgeable.

The inspiration to write this book came from the hospitality industry itself as no such book on question and answer pattern is available on the subject. This book is developed by the help of many existing managers in luxury hotels of India. This book contains relevant questions and answers on current trends in hospitality.

This book will not only fascinate the professionals but will also be perfectly suited to those just starting out in this highly glamorous hospitality world. The technical information on hospitality becomes easily available through this book.

I find this book a source of inspiration, and each page will awakens a longing to pick up the telephone and talk to me. Its is work that I value most sincerely and one that from now on, will not be far from me.

I express my heart-felt gratitude to the management of Banarsidas Chandiwala Institute of Hotel Management and Catering Technology in general and Sh. Bhuwan Mohan Ji, Secretary, Shri Banarsidas Chandiwala Sewa Smarak Trust Society in particular, for their motivation and encouragement to undertake this relatively less explored but highly poignant area of hospitality. I also extend my thanks to Principal Mr. R.K. Bhandri, Deputy Director Administration Mr. Pradeep Gupta, Professor R.K. Sinha, Associate Professor Gautam Chaterjee, Sr. Lecturer Bhupesh Kumar, Lecturer S.K. Beri, (BCIHM & CT), for their altruistic support.

I would like thanks to the Mr. Madan Sachdeva and Mr. Vivek Chaturvedi of Kanishka Publishers, Distributors for there persistence and support. Finally, I would like to thanks to all my friends and my well wishers.

I heartily invite suggestion and feedback for further improvement of the book.You can contact me on.

E-mail: sonigulshan@rediffmail.com

Gulshan Soni

Contents

Introduction

This book has been developed after understanding the problems that professional and students faced in operations /interviews. This book has been developed in mind that there is no such reckoner is available in the market to guide the students as well as professionals. Ready Reckoner for hospitality is developed to meet the needs of industry professional and students. It would also be a significant tool for managers and supervisors in assisting them in efficient running of hospitality operations.

This is a sincere effort to write this treasure of professional voculabary for the hospitality industry professional. This book covers all the sector of hospitality and has encompassed all the platform of the hospitality industry may it be housekeeping, environment studies, frontoffice, airlines, food production, food and beverage service management and has not left behind any area for the benefit of the hospitality fraternity at any level, may it be skilled craftsman, or inefficient supervisors or a management oriented manager or director of the organization.

In coming years I want to make this book as an encyclopedia for hospitality professional and my aim is that it was first necessarity for all hospitality professionals for at any level. In coming edition you will get more question and answer in this book according to current industry trend and with upcoming new subjects.

Hence, this book is expected to be a catalyst for the growth and development of experienced professional in this field.

AUTHOR

CHAPTER

1

Food and Beverage Equipment

Q1. The size of tablecloth required to fit a table approx 76cm (2'6") square is___?

Ans. 54 inches × 54 inches i.e. 137cm ×137cm.

Q2. The size of a fish plate is ___?

Ans. 20cm (8 inch) diameter.

Q3. The capacity of a demy tasse is___?

Ans. 905 c.l. (3½ oz).

Q4. The most suitable glass for service of champagne is ___?

Ans. The flute, the tulip, the saucer–in the order.

Q5. Which of the following has only two prongs.

(*a*) Oyster fork

(*b*) Pastry fork

(*c*) Snail fork

(*d*) Fruit fork

Ans. Snail fork.

Q6. The capacity of a Hi ball glass is___?

Ans. 8 oz.

Q7. The capacity of a Beer Goblet is___?

Ans. 7:10-12oz.

Q8. The capacity of a Cocktail glass is___?

Ans 2-3oz.

Q9. The capacity of a brandy balloon is___?

Ans. 8 oz.

Q10. The capacity of a Liqueur glass is___?

Ans. 6 oz.

Q11. The polivit method is used to___?
Ans. Polish Silver.

Q12. Describe the polivet method.
Ans. EPNS silver is kept in a tank of hot water with a sheet of aluminium foil and an acidic agent to polish silver.

Q13. A coaster is a___?
Ans. Glass mat.

Q14. Indicate four factors which determine that a wine glass is suitable for tasting wine.
Ans. It should be plain and clear; have a stem, a slight incurring lip and should allow the wine to breathe.

Q15. How could you judge, by use of a glass, if you have been poured a 60 ml shot of brandy balloon?
Ans. Lie the glass on its side–the brandy should reach the lip of glass, but not spill.

Q16. The standard size of a square napkin is___?
Ans. 18 inches × 18 inches or 20 inches × 20 inches.

Q17. The standard height of a chair is___?
Ans. 3 ft.

Q18. China ware is made of___?
Ans. Silica, Soda ash and China clay.

Q19. Standard size of a side plate is___?
Ans. 6¾ inch dia.

Q20. The capacity of a tea-cup is___?
Ans. 6 2/3 oz.

Q21. The bud-vase ashtray and cruet set are collectively termed as___?
Ans. The central appointments.

Q22. The knife that doubles as a fork is___?
Ans. Cheese Knife.

Q23. The fork that doubles as a knife is___?
Ans. Pastry fork.

Q24. The bowl in which breakfast cereals are served is called a___?
Ans. Nappy bowl.

Q25. The bowl in which juice is kept chilled on a Room Service tray is called___?
Ans. A Supreme bowl.

Q26. The spoon that accompanies a knickerbockers Gory is ___?
Ans. A parfait spoon.

Q27. The container for castor sugar accompanying grapefruit is___?
Ans. A Sugar dredger.

Q28. Soup is served out of a___?
Ans. Soup tureen.

Q29. The petite marmite bowl is made out of earthenware because___?
Ans. It has to be over-proof.

Q30. A swizzle stick is used to___?
Ans. Stir drinks.

Q31. Size of salver for serving?
Ans. 12 inches diameter (round).

Q32. Size of salver for clearing?
Ans. 20 inches diameter (round).

Q33. Size of coffee pot?
Ans. ½ pint and 1 pint.

Q34. Size of Hot milk jugs?
Ans. ½ pint and 1 pint.

Q35. Size of cold milk jugs?
Ans. ½ pint and 1 pint.

Q36. Size of entrée plate?
Ans. $9^3/_8$ and 10 inches diameter.

Q37. Size of tea pot?
Ans. ½ pint,1 pint,1½ pint, 2 pint.

Q38. Size of sweet plate?
Ans. 7 inch & 8½ inch diameter.

Q39. Size of soup plate?
Ans. $8^3/_8$ inch diameter.

Q40. Size of joint plate?
Ans. 10 inch diameter.

Q41. Size of coffee cup?
Ans. 8-10 oz.

Q42. Size of cereal/ salad plate?
Ans. 5 inch & 7½ inch diameter.

Q43. Standard time of serving poached fish after ordering?
Ans. 20 minutes after order.

Q44. Standard time of serving grilled Steaks after ordering?
Ans. Underdone (rare done): 10 min.
Medium done: 15 min.
Well done: 20 min.

Q45. Standard time of serving grilled fish/ fried fish after ordering?
Ans. 10-15 min.

Q46. Standard time of serving fried potatoes after ordering?
Ans. 20 min.

Q47. Standard time of serving grill tomatoes after ordering?
Ans. 10 min.

Q48. Standard time of serving lamb chop after ordering?
Ans. 20- 25 min.

Q49. Standard time of serving grilled Prawns after ordering?
Ans. 10-15 min.

Q50. Standard time of serving Pasta after ordering?
Ans. Par boiled 5-8 min.
Otherwise: 15-20 min.

Q51. Size of Demitasse cup?
Ans. 3½ Oz.

Q52. Composition of glassware used in hotels?
Ans. Its contains 15 per cent sodium oxide (soda), 72 per cent silica (sand), 9 per cent CALCIUM OXIDE (LIME) and 4 per cent minor ingredients.

Q53. Standard size of beer tankard?
Ans. ½ pint.

Q54. Standard size of water goblet?
Ans. 10 oz.

Q55. Standards size of red wine glass?
Ans. 7 oz.

Q56. Standards size of white wine glass?
Ans. 5½ oz.

Q57. Standards size of old fashioned?
Ans. 9 oz.

Q58. Standards size of champagne saucer?
Ans. 6 oz.

Q59. Standards size of Tom Collins glass?
Ans. 12 oz.

Q60. Standards size of beer goblet?
Ans. 10-12 oz.

Q61. Standards size of juice glass?
Ans. 5 oz.

Q62. Standard size of slip cloth?
Ans. 36 inches × 36 inches.

Q63. Standard size of buffet cloths?
Ans. Minimum Size By 6 inch × 12 inches.

Q64. Standard size of chair?
Ans. From floor to seat height 18 inches
From floor to straight rest side 3 inch, Width is 18 inches.

Q65. Standard size of square table cover for 2 pax in?
Ans. 2ft 6 inch ×2ft 6 inch.

Q66. Standard size of square table cover for 4 pax?
Ans. 3ft × 3ft.

Q67. Standard size of rectangular table cover for 4-6 pax?
Ans. 2'6 inch × 4'6 inch.

Q68. Standard size of Tea napkin?
Ans. 6 inch × 6 inch.

Q69. Standard size of snacks napkin?
Ans. 8 inch × 8 inch.

Q70. Standard size of breakfast napkin?
Ans. 12 inches ×12 inches.

Q71. Standard size of lunch/ dinner napkin?
Ans. 20 inches × 20 inches or 28 inches × 28 inches.

Q72. Standard size of round table for 4 pax?
Ans. 1m (3') in diameter.

Q73. Standard size of round table for 8 pax?
Ans. 1.52m (5') in diameter.

Q74. Serviettes are also know as___?
Ans. Napkins.

Q75. What is food?
Ans. Food means any articles used as food or drink for human consumption other than drugs and water.

Q76. Standard size of Tea spoon?
Ans. 6 inch (152mm).

Q77. Standard size of dessert spoon?
Ans. 7½ inch.

Q78. Standard size of Soup spoon?
Ans. 6½ inch.

Q79. Standard size of Ice cream spoon?
Ans. 5³/₈ inch.

Q80. Standard size of demitasse spoon?
Ans. 4½ inch.

Q81. Standard size of table spoon?
Ans. 8½ inch.

Q82. Standard size of dinner fork?
Ans. 8½ inch.

Q83. Standard size of salad fork?
Ans. 7 inch.

Q84. Standard size of oyster fork?
Ans. 5 inch.

Q85. Standard size of Table fork?
Ans. 8½ inch.

Q86. Standard size of fish fork?
Ans. 6½ inch.

Q87. Standard size of dinner knife hollow handle?
Ans. 8½ inch.

Q88. Standard size of dinner knife?
Ans. 9 inch.

Q89. Standard size of butter knife?
Ans. 6½ inch.

Q90. Standard size of butter spread?
Ans. 6 inch.

Q91. Standard size of table knife hollow handle?
Ans. 8½ inch.

Q92. Standard size of table knife?
Ans. 8½ inch.

Q93. Standard size of fish knife?
Ans. 7½ inch.

Q94. Measurement of 1 Tea spoon?
Ans. 5gm.

Q95. Measurement of 1 table spoon?
Ans. 15gm.

Q96. 1 cup water equals___ml?
Ans. 240ml.

Q97. 1 cup of pulses equals___gm?
Ans. 200gm.

Q98. 1 cup of cream equals___ml?
Ans. 240ml.

Q99. 1 cup of granulated sugar equals___gm?
Ans. 200gm.

Q100. 1 cup of refined oil equal___ml?
Ans. 220ml.

Q101. Standard size of soup spoon?
Ans. $6^{3}/_{8}$ inch.

Q102. Standard size of dessert spoon?
Ans. 7 inch.

Q103. Standard size of service spoon large?
Ans. $9^{7}/_{8}$ inch.

Q104. Standard size of coffee/demitasse spoon?
Ans. $4^{1}/_{3}$ inch.

Q105. Standard size of sundae spoon?
Ans. 7 inch.

Q106. Standard size of ice cube spoon?
Ans. 7½ inch.

Q107. Standard size of soup laddle?
Ans. 12 inches.

Q108. Standard size of salad service spoon?
Ans. 10 inches.

Q109. Standard size of pastry fork/knife?
Ans. $5^{3}/_{8}$ inch.

Q110. Standard size of serving fork large?
Ans. $9^3/_8$ inch.

Q111. Standard size of carving fork?
Ans. 9½ inch.

Q112. Standard size of snail/shell fish fork?
Ans. $5^3/_8$ inch.

Q113. Standard size of steak knife?
Ans. $8^7/_8$ inch.

Q114. Standard size of joint/dinner knife?
Ans. $9^5/_8$ inch.

Q115. Standard size of fish knife gourmet sauce spoon?
Ans. $6^7/_8$ inch.

Q116. Standard size of soup plate?
Ans. $8^3/_5$ inch diameter.

Q117. Standard size of fish plate/meat plate?
Ans. 8 inch dia.

Q118. Standard size of entrée plate?
Ans. $9^3/_5$ inch dia.

Q119. Standard size of dessert/sweet plate?
Ans. 8 inch dia.

Q120. Standard size of side/b&b/quarter plate?
Ans. $6^3/_5$ inch or 7 inch dia.

Q121. Standard size of tea saucer?
Ans. 5 inch dia.

Q122. Standard size of demitasse saucer?
Ans. 4 inch dia.

Q123. Capacity of soup bowl?
Ans. 10oz.

Q124. Capacity of tea cups?
Ans. $6^2/_3$ inch.

Q125. Capacity of coffee cup?
Ans. 7oz.

Q126. Capacity of demitasse?
Ans. 3½ oz.

Q127. Standard Cover size per pax?
Ans. 24 inches × 18 inches.

Q128. Size of waiter's cloth?
Ans. 26 inches × 26 inches.

Q129. Standard size of ashtray?
Ans. 13.6 cms($5^3/_8$")

Q130. In which dish boil eggs is served?
Ans. Oeuf sur la pla.

CHAPTER

2

Food and Beverage Production

Q1. What is Food?

Ans. Its means any article used as food or drink for human consumption other than drugs and water.

Q2. How much calories in 90gm of cooked T-bone steak?

Ans. 168 approx.

Q3. How much calories in 90gm of cooked porter house steak?

Ans. 180 approx.

Q4. Beef is good source of___?

Ans. Protein and iron.

Q5. Veal is good source of___?

Ans. High in proteins and vitamin b.

Q6. How much calories in 90gm of cooked roast lamb leg?

Ans 162.

Q7. Lamb is good source of___?

Ans. High in protein, iron and zinc.

Q8. How much calories in 90gm of cooked pork spare ribs?

Ans. 337.

Q9. How much calories in 90gm of fresh ham (pork leg)?

Ans. 183.

Q10. How much calories in 90gm of cured ham regular?

Ans. 151.

Q11. How much calories in 90gm of cured ham extra lean?

Ans. 123.

Q12. How much calories in 90gm of cooked fresh tuna grilled?
Ans. 118.

Q13. How much calories in 90gm of cooked sole?
Ans. 99.

Q14. How much calories in 90gm of cooked calamari fried?
Ans. 149.

Q15. How much calories in 90gm of cooked lobster?
Ans. 83.

Q16. How much calories in 90gm of cooked chicken breast w/o roast?
Ans. 142.

Q17. How much calories in 90gm of cooked chicken breast with skin?
Ans. 193.

Q18. How much calories in 90gm of cooked drum stick w/skin?
Ans. 112.

Q19. How much calories in 90gm of cooked turkey breast w/o skin?
Ans. 115.

Q20. How much calories in 90gm of cooked turkey thigh w/o skin?
Ans. 138.

Q21. How much calorie in 28.3gm of cheddar cheese?
Ans. 114.

Q22. How much calorie in 28.3gm of Emmental cheese?
Ans. 107.

Q23. How much calorie in 28.3gm of parmesan, grated cheese?
Ans. 129.

Q24. How much calorie in 28.3gm of feta cheese ?
Ans. 75.

Q25. How much calorie in 28.3gm of edam cheese ?
Ans. 101.

Q26. How much calorie in 28.3gm of muenster cheese?
Ans. 104.

Q27. How much calorie in 28.3gm of mozzarella cheese?
Ans. 80.

Q28. How much calorie in 1 cup of whole milk?
Ans. 149.

Q29. How much calorie in 1 cup of fat free (skim) milk?
Ans. 86.

Q30. How much calorie in 1 cup of chocolate milk?
Ans. 158.

Q31. How much calorie in 1tsb whipping cream?
Ans. 44.

Q32. How much calorie in 1tsb heavy cream?
Ans. 52.

Q33. How much calorie in 1tsb light cream?
Ans. 29.

Q34. How much calories in 1tbs olive oil?
Ans. 119.

Q35. How much calorie in banana bread 1 slice?
Ans. 196.

Q36. How much calorie in 1 cup of cooked whole wheat pasta?
Ans. 174.

Q37. How much calorie in 1 cup of cooked chow mein?
Ans. 237.

Q38 How much calorie in 1 cup long grain white rice?
Ans. 205.

Q39. How much calorie in 1 cup long grain wild rice?
Ans. 166.

Q40. How much calorie in chicken Caesar salad 1 standard serving?
Ans. 450.

Q41. How much calorie in cheese burger 1 standard serving?
Ans. 330.

Q42 How much calorie in medium fries 1 standard serving?
Ans. 450.

Q43. How much calorie in fried shrimps (6-8)?
Ans. 454.

Q44. How much calorie in fried oyster (6)?
Ans. 368.

Q45. How much calorie in 2tbs cheddar cheese dip?
Ans. 60.

Q46. How much calorie in 2tbs guacamole dip?
Ans. 60.

Q47. How much calorie in 2tbs salsa dip?
Ans. 9.

Q48. How much calories milk chocolate in 30gm?
Ans. 144.

Q49. How much calories white chocolate in 30gm?
Ans. 153.

Q50. How much calories in 1 teaspoon in granulated sugar?
Ans. 16.

Q51. What is steaks?
Ans. Is a slice of beef varying in thickness usually taken from fillet, rump.

Q52. What is entrecote steak?
Ans. These are taken from the deboned sirloin without the fillet from this comes minute steak, sirloin steak and double sirloin steak. Entrecote steak with bone weighing 650gm is T-bone and porter house steak i.e. sirloin steak.

Q53. From entrecote which steaks are come___?
Ans. There are 3 steaks
Minute steak: 100gm 1cm thick

Sirloin steak: 150gm 1.5cm thick
Double sirloins: 250-300gm 2.5cm thick.

Q54. What is beef steak?
Ans. This is head of the fillet the first slice. Its normally grilled.

Q55. What is chateau brand?
Ans. This is a double fillet steak take from the shoulder of the fillet 3.5 to 10cm thickness and average weight of 340gm to 1 kg.

Q56. What cooking method is best for chateau brand?
Ans. Its is generally served grilled at a temp. of 204.5°c.

Q57. Garnishes of chateau brand and which sauced is served?
Ans. Garnished with chateau potatoes and served with Colbert sauce or maitre d hote butter.

Q58. What are tornadoes?
Ans. A round barrel shaped steak cut from the lower middle of the beef fillet. Its 2-3cm thick and weight approx 100gm.

Q59. What is fillet mignon?
Ans. These are made from the tail end of the fillet. All fats are removed. The weight varies according to the weight of the fillet.

Q60. Common method of cooking steaks?
Ans. Steaks are generally grilled or sautéed.

Q61. Common serving method of steak?
Ans. Steak are generally served according to their dones.
Rare
Medium
Full done.

Q62. What is the cooking temp of steaks?
Ans. For thicker steaks lower temp. is 325°F used.

Q63. In five spice berriès which of flavours come___?
Ans. Clove, cardamom, pepper, star anise, fennel.

Q64. What are the six basic flavour are___?
Ans. Sweet, sour, bitter, spicy, pungent and salty.

Q65. What is pimento?

Ans. Also called Jamaica pepper and all spices, pimento is the aromatic berry of a small tropical tree. In aroma and flavour its resemble a mixture of cinnamon, nutmeg, and clove.

Q66. What is pimiento?

Ans. Is a sweet tasting red pepper shape like a heart and are sold fresh, canned or bottled in brine and stuffed in green olives. A large red, heat shaped sweet pepper that measure 3 to 4 inches long and 2 to 3 inches wide.

Q67. What is mould?

Ans. A furry growth, consistency of very small fungi, which grows on food such as meat, cheese, bread and preserves that are kept in warm, moist condition.

Q68. What is Chantilly?

Ans. Cream beaten to the consistency of a mousses, sweetened and flavoured with vanilla or other flavours called Chantilly.

Q69. What is crudités?

Ans. Raw vegetable or fruit cut into little sticks or battened served as an horsd'oeuvre and accompanied by cold sauce are knows as crudités.

Q70. What is five spice powder?

Ans. A mixture of five Chinese spices: star anise, clove, fennel, cinnamon and Sichuan pepper. Its widely used in Chinese cooking.

Q71. What is chaud-froid?

Ans. A dish that is prepared as a hot dish but served cold.

Q72. Mention the varieties of mustard?

Ans. There are three varieties such as

Black mustard

Brown mustard

White or yellow mustard.

Q73. Dijon mustard is famous mustard from___?

Ans. France.

Q74. Dijon mustard prepared from?
Ans. Its prepared with verjuice or wine must and white wine, or leans mustard with wine vinegar.

Q75. What is English mustard?
Ans. Its is available in fine powder consisting of white mustard with turmeric added.

Q76. Explain term leaven?
Ans. Loosely, any substance that can produce fermentation in dough.

Q77. Difference between cake and gateaux?
Ans. Cake can be large or small, light or rich, where cake can remain fresh for several days. e.g., fruit cake. Gateaux is generally used for fancy cake, but light preparations, often with fresh decoration such as chocolate cake.

Q78. What is conti?
Ans. The name given, in classic French cookery to dressing made from lentils.

Q79. French name of truffle ?
Ans. Pied montese.

Q80. Mention the types of stews?
Ans. There are 4 types.
Ragout
Navarin
Blanquette
Fricassee.

Q81. Ideal temperature for storing eggs?
Ans. 35 to 45°F.

Q82. Ideal temperature for storing ice cream?
Ans. 10°F.

Q83. Ideal temperature for storing fruit and vegetable?
Ans. 40 to 45°F.

Q84. Ideal temperature for storing meat?
Ans. 32 to 36°F.

Q85. Ideal temperature for storing fish?
Ans. 30 to 34°F.

Q86. Explain term HACCP?
Ans. Hazardous Analysis Critical Control Point.

Q87. What is croissant?
Ans. A crescent shaped roll generally made with leavened dough.

Q88. Name the different varieties of oil?
Ans. Bergamot oil, cassia oil, cinnamon oil, clove leaf oil, clove bud oil, coriander oil, corn mint oil, dill oil, garlic oil, ginger oil, lemongrass oil, peppermint oil, lime oil, nutmeg oil.

Q89. What is fonds de cuisine?
Ans. Basic kitchen stock.

Q90. What is Estouffade?
Ans. Brown rich stock.

Q91. To finish a sauce with butter is know as___?
Ans. Monter au beurre.

Q92. Standard cooking time for chicken stock?
Ans. 2 hours.

Q93. Standard cooking time for brown stock?
Ans. 6hrs.

Q94. Correct storage temperature of stocks?
Ans. 1°c-4°c.

Q95. Correct service temperature of hot sauce is___?
Ans. 85°c.

Q96. One litre of soup gave___of entrée portions?
Ans. 5.

Q97. What is the holding temperature range of hot emulsion sauce?
Ans. 30°c to 37°c.

Q98. Diable is derviate of___?
Ans. Demi glace.

Q99. Vin blanc is derviate of___?
Ans. Fish veloute.

Q100. The ratio of water in cooking pasta___?
Ans. 10:1 (water:pasta).

Q101. When making pulao what is the ratio of water?
Ans. 1 to $1^1/_3$

Q102. Polenta made from___?
Ans. Corn meal.

Q103. Farinaceous include___?
Ans. Rice and pasta.

Q104. Explain term court-bouillon?
Ans. A well flavoured poaching liquid for fish.

Q105. French term commis de cuisine means___?
Ans. Assistant cook.

Q106. Explain term confit?
Ans. Salted meat of pork, duck, goose or turkey which is cooked in own fat. Its may be served hot or cold.

Q107. Culinary term used for under cooked pasta?
Ans. "Al dente".

Q108. In which ways vegetable can be purchased?
Ans. Fresh, canned, frozen, fresh processed, dried/pickle.

Q109. When we are making fresh pasta why dough must be rested?
Ans. For relax the gluten.

Q110. Explain dashi?
Ans. Dashi is stock used in Japanese cuisine.

Q111. Type of dashi stocks?
Ans. Four type of dashi stocks:
Kelp-dashi
Shitake dashi
Bonito dashi
Dashi-jako-dashi.

Q112. What is hoisin sauce?
Ans. Athick brownish sauce made from soya bean, chillies garlic and spices.

Q113. Explain term kebab?
Ans. Meat/vegetable mixture coated on a skewer or could be shallowed fry.

Q114. What is mignonette pepper?
Ans. Coarsely ground or crushed peppercorn knows as mignonette.

Q115. Ajino moto is also know as___?
Ans. MSG (monosodium glutamate).

Q116. Explain nargisi kofta?
Ans. Mince meat with blend of Indian spices and coated around boil egg and deep fryied and put in curry know as nargisi kofta.

Q117. Explain sauerkraut?
Ans. Shredded and pickled the white cabbage is know as sauerkraut.

Q118. Explain poories?
Ans. Type of Indian bread. Its round and small in size and always deep fried.

Q119. What is Zarda?
Ans. A sweet pulao served at the end of a meal.

Q120. Explain term sashimi?
Ans. Slice of raw fish, seasoned with soya sauce, horseradish and ginger. Its famous dish of Japanese cuisine.

Q121. Difference between rechauffe and rechauffer?
Ans. Rechauffe means: reheated warm food and rechauffer means: to reheat and warm up.

Q122. Explain term biryani?
Ans. Indian classical rich dish prepared with rice and any meat or vegetable. There are two type of briyanis. Kacchi and pacchi briyani.

Q123. To hang meat so as to tenderize is know as___?
Ans. Mortifier.

Q123. To coat a dish or mask a dish with sauce knows as___?
Ans. Napper.

Q124. "Farniture" in french means to___?
Ans. Garnish.

Q125. Explain the term gratinate?
Ans. To colour under a salamander or oven knows as gratinate.

Q126. What is antipasto?
Ans. First course of a meal in Italian cuisine, usually denotes starters.

Q127. Explain term al dente?
Ans. Its is used to describe the point of pasta cooking its means "on the teeth" in Italian.

Q128. What is agar- agar?
Ans. A natural vegetable gelatin. A variety of dried seaweed resemble vermecilli noodles and soaked in water before use.

Q129. Difference between marinade and marinate?
Ans. Marinade means a mixture of oil, wine and other ingredients and marinate means to soak in marinade mixture knows as marinate.

Q130. Explain Nori?
Ans. Its is basically used in Japanese cuisine in SUSHI. It is a type of seaweed. Best quality nori is purple black.

Q131. Nori is rich in___?
Ans. Iodine.

Q132. How can we improve the flavour and texture of nori?
Ans. Toasting improve the flavour and texture of nori.

Q133. Food safety programme based on which international certificate?
Ans. HACCP.

Q134. Mention the goal of HACCP?
Ans. 100 per cent "safe food".

Q135. HACCP was developed by___?
Ans. NASA and Pillsbury company.

Q136. Principles of HACCP are outline by whom?
Ans. The 7 principles of HACCP is outlined by the Food and Agriculture Organization of the United Nations in Codex Alimentarius.

Q137. Explain term hazard?
Ans. A biological, chemical or physical agent that may contaminate food and pose a risk to the safety of the food.

Q138. What is CCP?
Ans. Critical Control Point is appoint where bacteria is contaminated with food.

Q139. Name some name of fish variety?
Ans. Flounder, flathead, bully mullet, bar cod, ocean trout, gold band snapper, king fish, parrotfish, silver dory, sardines, pilchard, ling, pearl perch.

Q140. Name some shell fish and crustaceans?
Ans. Arrow squid, lobster, mussels, prawns, scallop, mud crab, blue swimmer crab.

Q141. Name some standard term for degree of doneness of beef and lamb?
Ans. Very rare, Rare, Medium rare, Medium, Welldone, Very welldone.

Q142. Mention name of some lettuce?
Ans. Iceberg, Butter, Mignonette, Red coral, Green coral, Red oak, Green oak, Cos, Rocket, Radicchio, Lola Rosa, Red sails, Pirate, Baby red bibb, Baby red romaine, Brune d' hiver, Argula, Escarole, Belgian endive.

Q143. Mention some mushroom name?
Ans. Shitake, Black Fungi, Enoki, Shimeji, Oyster, White Fungi, Swiss brown.

Q144. Mention some herbs name?
Ans. Lemon balm, Marjoram, Fennel, Rue, Yarrow, Curry leaves, Nettle, Chives, Tarragon, Bergamot, Rosemary, Savory, Oregano, Sage, Thyme, Basil.

Q145. The ideal temperature of dry storage?
Ans. 15° to 18°c.

Q146. Turning vegetable to gave desire shaped is knows as___?
Ans. Barrel.

Q147. Coarsely cut root vegetable is know as___?
Ans. Mireporx.

Q148. Uniform cut of vegetable is known as___?
Ans. Paysanne.

Q149. What is bouquet garni?
Ans. The bundle of herbs and vegetable impart flavour to stock and sauce referred as bouquet garni.

Q150. Explain term zest?
Ans. The coloured outer skin from citrus fruit.

Q151. Explain term segments?
Ans. The fillets of citrus fruit with no skin.

Q152. Whipped egg white and sugar is knows as___?
Ans. Meringue.

Q153. Roasting juices is also know as___?
Ans. Jus roti.

Q154. At what Temperature roasting is start___?
Ans. 200°c.

Q155. What is trussing needle?
Ans. A long needle used for trussing poultry.

Q156. Corn starch is also used to lighten cake and pastry at what ratio___?
Ans. 1 part of corn starch to 4 part of flour.

Q157. What is corn starch?

Ans. Corn starch is highly refined and pulverized starch made from the corn.

Q158. How pasta can be classified into categories?

Ans. It can be classified according to ingredients and preparation. There are basically two methods:
Factory produce
Fresh/home made pasta.

Q159. Alimentary pasta includes?

Ans. Macaroni, Spaghetti, Farfel a. Those are factory produce are called alimentary.

Q160. How pasta can be classified according to there use?

Ans. The four basic types are classified as___.
Pasta for soup
Pasta for boiling
Pasta for baking
Filled pasta.

Q161. Name some name of pasta which are used for soup?

Ans. Penette, Stelline, Risoni, Conchigilettes.

Q162. Name some pasta for boiling?

Ans. This group include: Macaroni, Rigatoni, Penne, Eliche (spirals).

Q163. Name some filled pasta?

Ans. Cannelloni, Ravioli, Manicotti, Capilleti (little hats).

Q164. Mention type of noodles?

Ans. The types of noodles are as follows:
Bean thread noodle
Shrimp noodle
Soba noodle
Somen
Udon.

Q165. What is polenta?

Ans. This is north Italian porridge or mush usually made for corn meal (maize). However it can be made from barley meal and in certain areas from chestnut.

Q166. What is gnocchi?

Ans. Gnocchi are small dumplings made from flour, semolina, potatoes, and or choux paste. It's a type of pasta.

Q167. What is Spaetzle?

Ans. Its is a type of pasta. Its is mixture of flour, eggs and cream. Which is formed into small dumplings which are poached in boiling water.

Q168. What are the different shapes of pasta classification?

Ans. Long, tubular, flat, short.

Q169. Name the pasta name which are stuffed while pasta is on raw stage?

Ans. Ravioli.

Q170. Name the pasta name which are stuffed while pasta is partial cooked?

Ans. Cannelloni.

Q171. What is the composition of milk?

Ans. Its contain a minimum of 3.25 per cent of butter fat, 8.5 per cent of milk solid, and 88 per cent of water.

Q172. What is raw milk?

Ans. Raw milk is solid in some place which has not been pasteurized or homonized.

Q173. What is fortified milk?

Ans. Commonly in these have Vitamin A and/or B and possible extract non milk fat.

Q174. What is skim or non milk?

Ans. Has almost or all of fat removed its contains less than 0.5 per cent of fat.

Q175. Why does a layer of cream form on surface of milk?

Ans. Milk has major 5 constituents from those fat is the lightest as it has a very low density (around 9gm/ml), less than even of water. Cream is that portion of milk, which is rich in fat when ever milk is stored undisturbed for along period of time in a container, there is tendency of fat to rise to the top and form a creamy layer, as it's the lightest constituent.

Q176. What are the five major constituents of milk?
Ans. Water, fat, protein, lactose and mineral.

Q177. Heavy whipped cream contained ___ per cent of butter fat?
Ans. 36 to 40 per cent.

Q178. Light whipped cream contained___ per cent of butter fat?
Ans. 30 to 36 per cent.

Q179. Light cream contained___per cent of butter fat?
Ans. 18 to 30 per cent.

Q180. Butter contains how much fat___?
Ans. 80 per cent.

Q181. Butter is purchased commercially in which forms?
Ans. Patties (individual serving)
Pints (1 pound block)
Tubs or bulb (40 to 60 pound weight).

Q182. Cheese is composed of what three major components?
Ans. Water, fat, protein.

Q183. Mention type of stocks?
Ans. There are three types
White stock
Brown stock
Vegetable stock.

Q184. What are the basic steps for preparing stocks?
Ans. There are 4 methods
Start with cold liquid
Allow natural clarification
Skim carefully
Simmer, don't boil.

Q185. Skimming is also know as___?
Ans. Depouiller, Ecremer.

Q186. What is Remouillage?
Ans "Second wetting" after draining away the first stock, more water is added and mixture is skimmer again.

Q187. What is court bouillon?

Ans. A flavourful poaching liquid used for fish and shell fish.

Q188. What are the three elements of court bouillon?

Ans. Aromatic and spices, salt, liquid.

Q189. What is stock?

Ans. Stock is termed as "fond" means a liquid for making sauce, stew and soups. The word fond means foundation. Its is base of cooking.

Q190. Soups are classified into___?

Ans. Soups are classified into followings categories:

Clear

Thick

Specialty.

Q191. Clear soups are classified?

Ans. Broths, consommé, Essence, jelly soup.

Q192. Thick soup are classified as?

Ans. Purees, Coulis, Bisque, Vegetable soup, Cream soup, Veloute.

Q193. Which are neutral sauces?

Ans. Sauces made up of non meat are non as neutral sauces.

Q194. What are the essential points of good sauce?

Ans. Certain are the essential point of good sauce

Texture

Body

Colour

Consistency.

Q195. What contribution of sauces in a food?

Ans. There are certain qualities it will added on a food such as;

Its gives flavour

Its give moisten to food

Richness

Appearance

Interested and appetite appeal.

Q196. Explain term liason?

Ans. Is the French term for any mixture used for thickening or binding of sauce, soups, or other culinary preparation.

Q197. Milk and cream are not simple liquid but emulsifying of fat globules in water the emulsifying agent is___?

Ans. Casein.

Q198. What are the five physical properties to making a sauce?

Ans. The five physical properties are as follows:
Viscosity
Texture
Colour
Luster
Opacity.

Q199. What is de pouillage?

Ans. Its means removal of all the fat and impurities in the stocks or sauces.

Q200. Mention the two classification of mother sauces?

Ans. There are two classification.
White
Brown.

Q201. Mention the name of hot mother sauces?

Ans. There are basic six mother sauce:
Béchamel
Tomato
Espagnole
Veloute
Hollandaise
Béarnaise.

Q201. Difference between hollandaise and béarnaise?

Ans. Hollandaise flavour with lemon juice and béarnaise flavoured with vinegar, shallots and tarragon.

Q202. Explain term Re-montage?

Ans. It's a process to repair a broken emulsion sauce. (curdling of sauce to repair it).

Q203. What is beurre blancs?

Ans. Beurre blancs is a sauce originally from Loire valley it was made excellent with local butter and muscatel wine.

Q204. Mention the name of the 4 basic ingredients used in beurre blancs?

Ans. The four basic ingredients are as follows:

White wine

Vinegar

Shallots

Butter.

Q205. What is beurre Noistte?

Ans. Butter heated gently to a light brown colour so it gives a nutty aroma.

Q206. What is beurre meuniere?

Ans. Its occur when butter reaches the point of beurre noistte and the cooking is finished with dash of lemon juices and chop parsley.

Q207. Mention name of compound butter?

Ans. Ail butter, Anchovies butter, bercy butter, beure rouge butter, Colbert butter, homard butter.

Q208. Mention some derivatives of demiglaces?

Ans. Piquant, Diable, Robert, Lyonnaise, Bordelaise, Charcuteire.

Q209. Mention some derivates of veloute?

Ans. Allemande, Aurora, Aurora for fish, Supreme sauce, Fine herbs, Bercy, Chivery, Normande, Diplomat.

Q210. Mention some derivatives of béchamel?

Ans. Scotch egg, Soubise, Mornay, Lobster sauce.

Q211. Mention some derivatives of tomato sauce?

Ans. Portuguese, Provencal, Bretonne, Italienne.

Q212. Mention some derivatives of hollandaise?

Ans. Noisette, Moussline, Maltaise, Moutare.

Q213. Mention some derivatives of béarnaise?

Ans. Choron, Fayot.

Q214. Mention name of cold mother sauces?
Ans. Mayonnaise.

Q215. Mention some derivates of mayonnaise?
Ans. Cambridge, Russe, Tartor, Gloucester, Genoise, Andalouse.

Q216. Most Salad are classified into?
Ans. Salad are classified as follows:
Fruits
Vegetable
Leafy
Meat
Seafood
Gelantine.

Q217. What are the parts of salads?
Ans. Salads contain mainly four parts:
Base
Body
Dressing
Garnish.

Q218. Mention the type of salads?
Ans. There are primarily 3 types:
Simple
Compound
Combination.

Q219. Mention the name some vegetable leafy green salads?
Ans. César salad, Danicheff, Tropical vegetable salad.

Q220. Mention the name of fruit salads?
Ans. Woldroff salad, Diplomat, Fedora, Florida, Banana pecan.

Q221. Mention name of some rice based salads?
Ans. Andalousina, Maharaja.

Q222. Mention name of some chicken based salad?
Ans. Beat rice, Bressaine, Toska, Fanchedde.

Q223. Mention some name of sea food salad?
Ans. Alibaba, Mikado, Pernollet, Parisian.

Q224. Explain term acidify?
Ans To add lemon juice or vinegar to cooked item.

Q225. Explain term Agar-agar?
Ans Is made from seaweed and used as a setting and agent for jellies and cold pudding when ordinary gelatin is not permitted.

Q226. The terms used for baked in oven are known as___?
Ans Au four.

Q227. Explain term Aspic?
Ans Its is transparent savoury jelly generally made for seasoned stock. Its used as a coating or garnish for meat or fish to make moulds of meat, fish or games.

Q228. Explain the term Horsd'oeuvres?
Ans The term horsd' which translates from French word "outside the meal" is universally recognized.

Q229. Explain term dot?
Ans Small bits of butter, cheese, cream etc. over the surface of a dish before baking or grilling.

Q230. Explain term dust?
Ans To sprinkle with fine sugar, dried milk or with flour are knows as dust.

Q231. The name given to the crispy skin of pork after roasting is know as___?
Ans Crackling.

Q232. Starches achieves maximum viscosity at___temperature?
Ans 212°c.

Q233. What is slurry?
Ans Addition of water to starch know as slurry (as in Chinese cooking).

Q234. Mention the names of leavenings agents?
Ans Baking soda, Baking powder, Yeast.

Q235. Cold sandwich are grouping into___?
Ans Its grouping into two such as: Open sandwich, Closed sandwich.

Q236. The finest caviar come from the sea____?
Ans. Caspian Sea (around 98% of the world caviar comes from this sea).

Q237. Mention the types of caviar?
Ans. There are three varieties of caviar:
Beluga
Ossetra
Sevruga.

Q237. Which is the most expensive caviar?
Ans. Beluga is the most expensive. The eggs are light to dark in colour.

Q238. How we categorized the types caviar?
Ans. We categorized caviar according to size, colour and spices of sturgeons fish.

Q239. How we categorized caviar according to there method of processing?
Ans. Following are the methods of caviar processing are as follows:
Fresh caviar
Pressed caviar
Pasteurized caviar
Frozen caviar.

Q240. Different between spreads and dips?
Ans. Spreads are offer more solid mixture which needs to spread with a knife and dips is a mixture that is loose or soft to cling a item which dip into it.

Q241. Anti Pasto is famous international horsd 'oeuvre from?
Ans. Italy.

Q242. Tapas is famous international horsd 'oeuvre from?
Ans. Spain.

Q243. Zakuski is famous international horsd 'oeuvre from?
Ans. Russia.

Q245. Sushi is famous international horsd 'oeuvre from?
Ans. Japan.

Q246. What is gluten?
Ans. Gluten is insoluble nitrogenous part of wheat flour.

Q247. What is the primary function of yeast?
Ans. The primary function of yeast is to change sugar into Co_2, so the dough in which its generated aerated.

Q248. Time required for soft boil eggs is___?
Ans. 3 to 5 min.

Q249. Time required for hard boil eggs is___?
Ans. 10 min.

Q250. Name of types of meringues?
Ans. There are two types:
Soft meringues
Hard meringues.

Q251. For soft meringues___sugar is required for each egg white?
Ans. 2 tbs.

Q252. For hard meringues___sugar is required for each egg white?
Ans. ¼ cup.

Q253. Oyster cruet include?
Ans. Cayenne pepper, peppermill, chilli vinegar and Tabasco.

Q254. What is Sapago?
Ans. Green coloured hard cheese from Switzerland.

Q255. Parmesan is also is known as___?
Ans. Parmigiano, reggiano.

Q256. Explain term savoury?
Ans. A savoury is a salt item served on varying shapes of toast such as:
Tartlettes
Barquettes
Bouchees.

Q257. Mention some name of pasta?
Ans. lasagne, ravioli, spaghetti, capelleti, fettuccini, bucatini, macaroni, penne, farfalle, rigatoni, gnocchi, vermicelli, tagliatelli, tortellini.

Q258. What is pesto?
Ans. Its is an Italian sauce.

Q259. Mention 5 international recognized ingredients of pesto?
Ans. Basil, Parmesan cheese, Olive oil, Pine nut, Garlic.

Q260. What is salami?
Ans. A charcuterie product originating in Italy now made in many countries. It takes the form of a fat sausages made from the finely minced pork (or mixture of meats) inter spread with pieces of fat.

Q261. What fagioli means?
Ans. Means white haricot beans.

Q262. What alla pizzailoa indicates in Italian dishes?
Ans. Its indicates that the dish contains beef or veal sorted in very hot oil and simmered with tomatoes, garlic and herbs.

Q263. Italian cruet set includes?
Ans. Grated parmesan cheese, Pepper mill, Chilli flakes and Oregano.

Q264. Chakriphool is also knows as___?
Ans. Star Anise.

Q265. Accompainents served for Irish stews?
Ans. Worcestshire sauce and pickled red cabbage.

Q266. Scrambled eggs garnished with a trellis of anchovies and studded with capers is called___?
Ans. Scotch wood cook.

Q267. Rock salt is also knows as___?
Ans. Fat salt.

Q268. Term grossel means?
Ans. Grossel means fat salt or also knows as rock salt.

Q269. Gelatin obtained from sturgeon fish know as?
Ans. Isinglass.

Q270. Differentiate between marzipan and frangipane?
Ans. Marzipan is almond paste used for coverings cakes and pastry and frangipane is an pastry cream made with milk, sugar,

flour, eggs, and butter, with either crushed macaroons or with grounded almond and used for various dessert.

Q271. Differentiate between broiler chicken and spring chicken?
Ans. The difference between in there weights. Broiler chicken weight 750gm–1 kg and spring chicken weight 350gm-450gm.

Q272. Mention the name of heat transfer?
Ans. It can be transfer by three methods:
Conduction
Convection
Radiation.

Q273. The basic ingredients for sweet and short pastry?
Ans. Flour, fat and sugar.

Q274. What is the ratio of flour, fat and sugar in sweet and short pastry?
Ans. 1:2:3.

Q275. Mention the name of different types of pastries?
Ans. The different type of pastries are as:
Short pastry/ sweet short pastry
Puff pastry
Hot water pastry
Chox pastry.

Q276. What are basic ingredients for making pastry?
Ans. Flour, butter and egg.

Q277. What qualities in bread flour?
Ans. In bread flour high protein content with good gluten strength and high water holding capacity.

Q278. What is ghee?
Ans. Clarified fat is called ghee.

Q279. What is chipolata?
Ans. Small fresh sausages, about 2cm in diameter. They are eaten fried or grilled italian origin.

Q280. What is chinois?
Ans. A conical strainer with handle.

Q281. Explain term 'food poisoning'?
Ans. The term food poisoning is used to describe any illness that results from ingesting contaminated food or drink.

Q282. What is food danger zone?
Ans. The bacteria that commonly cause food poisoning generally grow and mulitiply at temperatures between 50°F and 145°F (10°c to 63°c), with an optimum the same as that of the human body-98°F (37°c) is called food danger zone.

Q283. ___Bacteria is widely linked to poultry and other meats?
Ans. Salmonella.

Q284. Salmonella mainly founds in___?
Ans. Poultry Eggs.

Q285. What is the golden rule for reheat food?
Ans. Reheat left overs only once, and make sure the internal temperature reaches 160°F.

Q286. What is the ideal temperature of poaching?
Ans. The temperature of the liquid for poaching is 93-95°c.

Q287. Explain term broiling?
Ans. Cooked without oil and fat in pan.(jeera bhunaoo)

Q288. Normal frying temperature for deep frying?
Ans. 160 to 190°c approx.

Q289. Explain term barding?
Ans. This the covering of food items of meat, poultry or game and in some case fish, with thin slice of fat bacon or salted pork.

Q290. Explain term bouquet garni?
Ans. Its consists of aromatic vegetable and herbs and other flavouring determines by the requirement of the dishes.

Q291. What bouquet garni do___?
Ans. A bouquet garni is a very useful means of adding flavour to a cooking liquid.

Q292. Explain term chiffonade?
Ans. This refers to finely shredded vegetables leaves such as spinach, lettuce etc.

Q293. Explain term disgorging?
Ans. Removal of unwanted matter from food mainly removal of blood from brains, sweetbreads and calf heads, so as to whiten them.

Q294. Fine herbs refers to____?
Ans. Its refers to fresh herbs usually Parsley, Chervil, Tarragon and Chives.

Q295. Explain term larding?
Ans. Larding is the process for inserting strips of pork fat or fat bacon into joints or cuts of meat which are deficient in fat.

Q296. Explain term lardons?
Ans. These are baton–shaped pieces cut from the streaky bacon.

Q297. Explain term pluches?
Ans. Term generally applied to term for sprigs of parsley or blanched chervil for garnished a dish.

Q298. Royale refers to____?
Ans. Its refers to an egg custard mixture cooked and cut in various shapes for soups garnish.

Q299. Mention some name of consommé soup?
Ans. Consommé de volaille (chicken consommé), consommé Carmen, consomme burnoise, consomme Colbert, consomme royale, consomme diane, consomme xavier.

Q300. Mention some spaghetti preparation?
Ans. Spaghetti Carbonara, Spaghetti Milanaise, Spaghetti Napolitaine, Spaghetti Sicilienne.

Q301. Mention name of some round white fish?
Ans Bass, Bream, Cod, Haddock, Hake, Snapper.

Q302. Mention name of some oily fish?
Ans. Eel, Trout, Salmon, Trout, Herring, Sardine, White bait.

Q303. Mention some name of flat white fish?
Ans. Brill, Halibut, Lemon sole, Turbot, Dover sole.

Q304. What gastronomy mean?
Ans. The art and science of eating food.

Q305. Yeast is killed at a temperature___?
Ans. 136°F (58°c) or above.

Q306. What is food cost?
Ans. The cost of the material that go directly into the production of the menu.

Q307. What is food cost percentage?
Ans. The ratio of the cost of food served to the food sales during a given period.

Q308. Formula of food cost per cent?
Ans. Food cost percentage= foodcost/sales.

Q309. Several parts of knife?
Ans. Parts of knife are as follows:
Tip
Bolster
Spine
Tang
Rivets
Heel
Cutting edge.

Q310. What is seasoning?
Ans. An item added to enhance the natural flavours of a food without dramatically change it taste: salt and pepper are most common seasoning.

Q311. What is flavouring?
Ans. An item that adds a new taste to a food and change its natural flavour. Flavouring includes herbs, spices, vinegar and condiment.

Q312. What is aromatic?
Ans. An item that enhance the natural aromas of a food.

Q313. What is condiment?
Ans. Traditionally any item added to dish for flavour, include herbs, spices and vinegars; now also refers to cooked or prepared flavouring such as prepared mustards, relish, bottled sauces and pickled.

Q314. Mention type of vinegar?

Ans. Types of vinegar are as follows:

Wine vinegar
Malt vinegar
Rice vinegar
Distilled vinegar
Cider vinegar
Flavoured vinegar
Balsamic vinegar.

Q315. Mention the method of heat transfer?

Ans. The method of heat are as follows:

Conduction
Convection
Radiation
Microwave cooking.

Q316. The process of cooking sugar is know as..........?

Ans. Caramelization.

Q317. Mention name of dry heat cooking methods?

Ans. Dry heat cooking methods are as follows:

Broiling
Grilling
Roasting and baking
Sautéing
Pan frying
Deep frying.

Q318. Mention name of moist heat cooking methods?

Ans. Moist heat cooking methods are as follows:

Poaching
Simmering
Boiling
Steaming
Stewing.

Q319. What is stock?

Ans. As tock is flavoured liquid; a good stock is key to great soup or braised dish the French appropriate called FOND means base.

Q320. What is sauce?

Ans. A sauce is thickened liquid used to flavour and enhance other foods. A good sauce adds flavours, moisture, richness and visual appeal.

Q321. What is onion brulee?

Ans. Burnt onion, made charring onion halve; used to flavour and colour stocks and sauces.

Q322. Explain term barding?

Ans. Barding is the process covering the surface of meat or poultry with thin slice of pork fat.

Q323. What is curing salt?

Ans. Curing salt is mixture of salt and sodium nitrate.

Q324. What is sausages?

Ans. Sausages are forced meats stuffed into casing.

Q325. Mention the names of types of sausages?

Ans. The type of sausages are as follows:
Fresh sausages
Smoked or cooked sausages
Dried or hard sausages.

Q326. Mention the types of yeast?

Ans. There are three types:
Compressed yeast
Active dry yeast
Instant yeast.

Q327. What is proofing?

Ans. The final rise of shaped yeast product just prior to baking.

Q328. What is profitroles?

Ans. A small baked around of éclair paste filled with ice cream and top with chocolate sauce.

Q329. What is éclairs?

Ans. Baked fingers of éclairs paste filled with pastry cream; the top is than coated with chocolate glazed or fondant.

Q330. Eclairs paste is also knows as___?
Ans. Pate a choux.

Q331. What is gum paste?
Ans. A smooth dough made of sugar and gelatin; it dries relatively slowly, becoming very firm and hard. The paste can be coloured and rolled out, cut and shapped.

Q332. Explain mireporx?
Ans. A mixture of coarsely chopped onions, carrots, leeks, celery used to flavour stocks, stews and food.

Q333. What about the ratio of vegetable in mireporx?
Ans. Generally a mixture of 50 per cent of onion, 25 per cent carrot and 25 per cent of leeks and celery.

Q334. ___is a type of hard wheat milled into semolina flour which is used for making pasta?
Ans. Durum.

Q335. What is emulsification?
Ans. The process by which generally unmixable liquid are forced into a uniform distribution.

Q336. What is dumplings?
Ans. Any variety of smail starches products made from dough or batter that are simmered or steam: can be plain or filled.

Q337. Explain chutney?
Ans. A sweet and sour condiment made of fruits or vegetables cooked in vinegar and spices; some what chutney are reduce to puree.

Q338. What is aspic?
Ans. A clear jelly usually made from a clarified stock thickened with gelatin; used to coat food, especially charcuterie items or garnish food.

Q339. ___Principle protein found in eggs?
Ans. Albumen.

Q340. Explain term basting?
Ans. Moistening food during cooking with melted fat, pan drippings or other liquids to prevent drying.

Q341. ___is Italian ice cream?
Ans. Gelato.

Q342. ___to soak food in a liquid usually alcoholic , to soften them?
Ans. Macerate.

Q343. Difference between jam and marmalade?
Ans. Jam is a fruit gel made from fruit pulp and sugar while otherwise marmalade is a citrus jelly that also contains unpeeled slices of citrus fruit.

Q344. The consistency of liquid, usually a sauce, that will coat the back of a spoon know as___?
Ans. Nappe.

Q345. Explain term Mise-en-place?
Ans. Refers to preparation and assembly of all necessary ingredients and equipment.

Q346. Explain term pilaf/ pualoo?
Ans. A cooking method of rice in which the rice are lightly sautéed in hot fat and then in hot liquid is added; the mixture is simmered without stirring until liquid is absorbed.

Q347. What is relish?
Ans. Cooked or pickled sauce usually made with vegetables or fruits and often used as an accompaniments.

Q348. The tall hat cap wear by chef knows as___?
Ans. Toque.

Q349. Crumbly mixture of fat, flour, sugar and some times nuts and spices; used to top baked goods know as___?
Ans. Streusel.

Q350. To soak a food in hot liquid in order to extract the flavour or impurities or to soften texture knows as___?
Ans. Steeps.

Q351. The seasoned rice used for sushi knows as___?
Ans. Zushi.

Q352. What is vinegar?
Ans. A thin sour liquid used as preservatives, cooking ingredients and for cleaning solution know as vinegar.

Q353. Mention the name of Chinese cooking region/school?
Ans. The Southeastern – Canton (Guangdong, TeCheow)
Western – Szechuan (sometimes called Chungking)
Northeastern – Peking (or Shantung)
Central – Honan (and Shanghai) and
East Coast – Fukien (Fujian).

Q354. What is hundred year eggs?
Ans. An egg that has been preserved with a coating of lime, ashes and salt before being buried for 100 days.

Q355. What is Baklawa?
Ans. Dessert of layered pastry filled with nuts and steeped in honey-lemon syrup–usually cut into triangular or diamond shapes.

Q366. Arabic omelet is know as___?
Ans. Ejje.

Q367. What is Moutabel?
Ans Eggplant dip made with tahina, olive oil and lemon juice.

Q368. What is daikon?
Ans. Much used in Japanese and Chinese cooking. It has a similar taste and texture to ordinary radish and is grated and added to stewed dishes or mixed with finely chopped chilies as a relish.

Q369. In Indonesian cooking culinary terms for cooked in vinegar, soy sauce and garlic knows as___?
Ans. Adobo.

Q370. Explain term pasteurization?
Ans. The process of heating a liquid to a prescribe temperature for specific period of time in order to destroy pathogens bacteria.

Q371. lobster roe is called?
Ans. Roe.

Q372. Temperature of caramelisation___?
Ans. 160-180°c.

Q373. How we convert Fahrenheit into Celsius?
Ans. C°= (f°-32)×5/9.

Q374. What are the different grade of eggs?
Ans. The grade of eggs are as follows:
AA
A
B.

Q375. What is gumbo?
Ans. A creole soup or stew thickened with okra is called gumbo soup.

Q376. What is approximate yield from a whole cooked chicken?
Ans. 50 per cent.

Q377. Which helps to milk is curdle?
Ans. Rennin enzymes helps milk to curdle.

Q378. Main parts of Sandwich?
Ans. Spread, Filling and the Accompliments.

Q379. Emulsifying agent in Mayonnaise?
Ans. Egg yolk.

Q380. Which vitamins lost during cooking?
Ans. Vitamin C, vitamin B1 and vitamin B2.

Q381. What is pH?
Ans. It is the hydrogen –ion concentration of a liquid.

Q382. Explain salt peter?
Ans. Its a potassium nitrate used to preserve meat.

Q383. In meat curing salt peter gives the characteristic of___?
Ans. Pink colour to meat.

Q384. Explain term 'surf and turf'?
Ans. It's a combination of red meat and sea food goes long in one plate with there sauces.

Q385. Lavash bread from which country?
Ans. Turkey.

Q386. Mention the types of cakes?
Ans. They are divide into three separate groups:
Batter cakes
Foam cakes
Chiffon cakes.

Q387. Mention the type of dough used in making pastry?
Ans. They are basic 4 types:
Sweet dough
Pie pastry dough
Puff pastry dough
Cookie dough.

Q389. Explain term Bavarian cream?
Ans. A cold dessert made from eggs custard stiffened with gelatin mixed with whipped cream and some times fruit puree.

Q390. Jacket potatoes in French called___?
Ans. Pomme de terra chemine.

Q391. Explain term vol-au-vent?
Ans. A round case puff pastry (6-8inch dia), having a pastry bid. Its filled after baking and served hot as starter.

Q392. Two harmful bacteria that common in food?
Ans. Bacillus Cereus and Staphylococcusaureus.

Q393. Which Bacteria may found in fried rice and meat?
Ans. Bacillus cereus.

Q394. Which Bacteria may found in undercooked eggs or poultry?
Ans. Salmonella, Campylobacter jejuni.

Q395. Mention the types of sausages?
Ans. Types of sausages are as follows:
Frankfurt sausages
Chipolata sausages
Strasbourg sausages
Mortadella.

Q395. Mention some varieties of onion?
Ans. White onion, spring onion, yellow onion, pink and red onion.

Q396. Mention some varieties of potatoes?
Ans. Apollo, Bea, Resy, Bintje, Grenaille, Urgent, Ostara.

Q397. Mention some name of parsley varieties?
Ans. Flat and Curly.

Q398. Mention some name of pears variety?
Ans. William, Conference, Comice, Passé Crassane.

Q399. Mention some name of tomatoes variety?
Ans. Marmande, Roma, Monfauet hybrid.

Q400. Mention the name of apple variety?
Ans. Calville, Belle de Boskoop, Golden delicious, Granny smith.

CHAPTER

3 The Menu

Q1. Who is credited with first having started the practice of using menus?

Ans. The Duke of Brunswick.

Q2. What factor would you need to consider when planning a menu?

Ans. *(a)* Availability of supplies

(b) Assess your market

(c) Balance from light to heavy and back to light

(d) Ensure the food value

(e) Avoid clashes of colour or repetition of colour

(f) The uniform should be uniform.

Q3. Give six examples of hors-d' oeuvres?

Ans. Caviar, Seafood cocktail, Melon Frappe, Smoked Salmon, Oysters, Pate' de foie gras.

Q4. Give six examples of potages (Soup)?

Ans. *(a)* Lobster Bisque (Bisque d' homard)-thick lobster soup

(b) Petite Marmite-beef and chicken flavoured consommé

(c) French Onion Soup-soup a' l' oignon-clear soup with sautéed golden onion; garnished with a cheese toast

(d) Consommé Celestine-clear soup garnished with savory pancakes

(e) Consommé julienne-garnished with strips of root vegetables

(f) Tortue Claire-clear turtle soup.

Q5. When a clear soup is pleased on a menu where should it appear?

Ans. Consommé is always the first soup to be mentioned.

Q6. Name seven international soups?

Ans. *(a)* Minestrone-Italian–Rice vegetable broth with the flavour of tomato garnished with cheese

(b) Scotch Broth–Scotland-Veg and Mutton broth with pearl barley

(c) Oxtail Soup- England-Rice beef soup

(d) Bortsch–Russia – Beetroot and duck flavoured consommé

(e) Mulligatawny–India–Curry flavoured with coconut milk garnished with rice

(f) French Onion soup–France–Onion flavoured consommé

(g) Kartoffel Zouppe-Germany-Potato Soup.

Q7. Name three egg dishes (Qeufs)?

Ans. *(a)* Spanish Omelets with onions /tomatoes/capsicum

(b) Mushroom Omelets

(c) Oeufs Florentine- poached eggs on a bed spinach.

Q8. Name Three pasta Dishes (farineaux)?

Ans. *(a)* Spaghetti Bolognaise –with rich beef mince sauce Ravioli–Pasta envelopes-filled with a Varity of stuffing's.

(b) Cannelloni-Large tubes of pasta, filled with stuffing.

Q9. Name 4 Fish dishes (poisons)?

Ans.

1. Sole meunier, re: Shallow fried in butter.
2. Sole cobert: Breadcrumb it and deep fried.
3. Darne de saumon grille: Grilled salmon cutlet with béarnaise sauce.
4. Sole Veronique: poached in white wine 7 garnished with white grapes.

Q10. What are entre'es?

Ans. They are generally small, well garnished dishes which come ready to serve from the kitchen. They always accompanied by a rich sauce.

Q11. What purpose do sorbets serve on a French menu?

Ans. They act as a 'rest' between courses.

Q12. What is the difference between a frappe and a sorbet?

Ans. A sorbet is a frozen fruit juice or wine, often with whipped egg white served as a break is a French classical juice or liqueur poured over crushed ice.

Q13. What are Releve's?

Ans. Releve's are large butchers joints which require carving in the restaurant, these are usually roasted.

Q14. Give two example of Releves?

Ans. Roast leg of pork with apple sauce
Roast ribs of beef with horseradish sauce.

Q15. Salad served as an accompaniment to roti or roast dishes. Is also served in a___?

Ans. Crescent shaped or kidney shaped dish placed at the top left hand corner of the cover.

Q16. Give five examples of legume dishes?

Ans. Puree de pommes-creamed potatoes
Petit pois au buerie- green peas tossed in butter
Tomatoes grille'- grille tomatoes
Choufleur mornay- cauliflower with cheese sauce.
Crepes Verdu-Think Pancakes Stuffed with Vegetables.

Q17. What is menu?

Ans. The menu means range of food items served in an establishment including there organization into a number of course.

Q18. Mention types of menu?

Ans.
1. A la carte menu
2. Table d' hote
3. Set menu
4. Carte du jour
5. Cycle menu.

Q19. Classify the type of salads, with examples of each?

Ans. Its classified into followings:
1. Simple salads
2. Tossed salads
3. Composed salads.

Q20. On the basis of their uses the salads are classified into:

Ans.
1. Appetizer salad
2. Side salad
3. Main dish salad
4. Custom based salad
5. Dessert salad.

Q21. Give three examples of items to be found on a cold buffet (buffet froid)?

Ans. Poulet roti-roast chicken
Galantine de vollaille
Mayonnaise de poison-fish mayonnaise.

Q22. Which is lighter–a soufflé or mousse and why?

Ans. Soufflé it incorporates more beaten eggs white, uses less cream and gelantine than a mousse.

Q23. Give three names of classic sweet (entremets) dishes?

Ans. Crepes suzette-pancakes in rich orange sauce.
Peche Melba–peach halves with vanilla ice cream and raspberry jam.
Omelets Norvigieme-Baked Alaska-layers of sponge cake and ice cream topped with meringue and baked.

Q24. What is welish rarebit?

Ans. A savoury tit-bit of cheese flavoured with ale on toast and gartinate.

Q25. Give the features of a table d'hote menu?

Ans. Fixed number of course
Choice within most courses
Selling price is fixed for the whole menu
Dishes provided with all be served at a set time.

Q26. Name the Famous Dish invented by the chef of Napoleon the Great?

Ans. Chicken Marengo.

Q27. Name the Famous Indian Dal Made from five Lentils?

Ans. Dal Panchratan.

Q28. What is French name for snails?

Ans. Escargots.

Q29. Italian word for sandwich?

Ans. Panini.

Q30. French word for waffle?

Ans. Gaufre.

Q31. What will be temperature of table water?
Ans. 7°c to 10°c.

Q32. What the other term for omelet's?
Ans. Baveuse.

Q33. The light meal taken by French people between meal knows as___?
Ans. Gouter.

Q34. Small croutons of bread also know as___?
Ans. Snippet.

Q35. Standard weight of tea bag?
Ans. 2gm.

Q36. Continental breakfast includes?
Ans. It is light breakfast includes:
Breakfast rolls (brioche bread, croissant, muffins or toast),
Preserves (jam, jelly or marmalade)
Tea or coffee.

Q37. English breakfast includes?
Ans. This includes heavy breakfast:
Fruits (stewed or fresh)
Cereals (porridge, oatmeal, corn flakes etc.)
Bacon, ham, sausages
Eggs to order
Breads (muffin, brioche, toast, croissant etc.)
Preserves (jam, jelly or marmalade)
Beverages (tea, coffee, milk, juices etc.)

Q38. What is table d' hote menu?
Ans. A fixed number of courses /limited choices of dishes is called table d' menu.

Q39. Standard layout of table d' hote menu includes?
Ans. Water goblet, dessert fork, joint knife, soup spoon, side knife, dessert spoon, fish fork, napkin, side plate, joint fork, fish knife.

Q40. What is a la carte menu?

Ans. An a la carte menu is defined as.

1. Individual order for each course
2. Individual cooking time for each dish
3. Individually served
4. Individually priced.

Q41. What is menu planning?

Ans. Menu planning is process of planning and scheduling intake meals for general or specific individual requirements.

Q42. In balance diet the ratio of energy distribution of carbohydrate, protein and fat?

Ans. 7:1:2.

Q43. Mention the principles of planning a menu?

Ans. Following are the principles are as follows:

- Meeting nutritional requirement
- Meal, pattern must fulfill client needs
- Meal planning should save time and energy
- Meal plan should give maximum nutrients
- Economic consideration
- Planned menu should provide variety
- Menu should give satiety
- Availability of foods
- Type of operation
- Location
- Capability of staff.

Q44. What is buffet menu?

Ans. Buffets is general are food displays. They are shows of culinary skill as well as food presentation. Buffet menu are always be skillfully prepared.

Q45. The beverage menu can be segmented into___?

Ans. They are segmented into followings:

- Pre dinner beverages
- Dinner beverages
- Dessert beverages
- Cheese beverages
- Lunch beverages
- Breakfast beverages.

Q46. Simple four course food and beverage menu?

Ans.

Food	*Beverage*
Asparagus in virgin olive oil and basil	Sauvignon blanc
Green tagliatelli with venison sauce	
Braised lamb with vegetables	Beaujolais nouveau
Tarte tatin	Gewürztraminer

Q46. Mention five course menu with matching wine?

Ans.

Food	*Beverage*
Consommé	Madeira
Char grilled barramundi with lemon leaves	Marsanne
Fricandeau of veal	Pinot Noir
Cheese, Mild cheese	Hermitage
Chocolate pate with vanilla sauce	Semillon

Q47. Mention four course menu with non alcoholic beverage?

Ans.

Food	*Beverage*
Fresh artichoke bottoms filled with white mushroom	Grape fruit and carrot juice
Sorrel soup with fresh cheese	Unsweetened apple cider
Spring vegetable with beurre blanc and fresh herbs	Unsweetened grape juice
Rhubarb compote with raspberries	Camomile

Q48. Which aspects direct influence food cost control?

Ans. Food cost control aspects are follows:

- Food and beverage operational policy
- Preparation and product techniques
- Raw material pricing and buying criteria
- Storage and safe keeping of raw material
- Expected return on investment.

Q49. How we calculate individual menu items food cost per cent?

Ans. Individual food cost = food cost of the menu item/selling price of the menu item×100.

Q50. How we calculated for all over all food cost per cent?

Ans. Overall food cost = total food cost of item sold/total sales revenue × 100.

Q51. How we calculate selling price of menu item (according to food cost % method)?

Ans. Selling price of menu item = food cost of menu item/over all food cost per cent × 100.

Q52. How we calculate selling price according to (prime factor method)?

Ans. Selling price = (food cost+ labour cost)/food and labour cost per cent 100.

Q53. Design a children menu?

Ans.

Items	*Price Rs.*
Hamburger on bun (French fries & pickle)	100
Peanut butter & jelly (served with fresh fruits)	150
Chicken sandwich on bun (with French fries)	125
Grilled cheese sandwich (served with smiley's)	125
Cup of soup	75
French fries	75
Tossed salads	50
Pasta in cheese sauce	125
Chocolate milk	50
Soft drink	50
Ice cream	50
Pastry	50

Q54. What DBML stands?
Ans. Diabetic meal.

Q55. What VLML stands?
Ans. Vegetable lacto meal.

Q56. What BLML stands?
Ans. Blond meal.

Q57. What KSML stands?
Ans. Kosher meal (juices).

Q58. What LFML stands?
Ans. Low cholesterol meal.

Q59. Mention the types of juices?
Ans. The types of juices are as:
- Vegetables–celery, cucumber, tomato
- Root vegetables: carrots, beet roots
- Greens: parsley, kale,
- Fruits: grapes, apple
- Herbs: fennel, peppermint
- Wheat grass: spirulina (a blue green sea algae)
- Cruciferous vegetable: broccoli, cabbage.

Q60. Mention the types of water?
Ans. The types of water are as follows:
- Spring water
- Purified water
- Mineral water
- Sparkling bottled water
- Artesian water
- Well water
- Municipal/tap water.

Q61. Mention name of some international spring water company?
Ans. Name are as follows:
- Dasani
- Evian
- Poland spring
- Arrow head
- Deer park

- Ice mountain
- Ozarka
- Zephyrhills.

Q62. What is Evian?

Ans. Well know brand of spring water, comes from a source in the northern French alps. The water is collected from an aquifer that is fed by snowmelt and rainfall. Other than filtration from ground sand and clay, no other purifying process is used to produce this bottled water.

Q63. Explain tonic water?

Ans. Tonic water is carbonated beverage that derives its somewhat bitter taste from the addition of Guinine. Its is usually flavoured with lemon or lime, lots of sugar and often contains caffeine.

Q64. Explain carbonated water?

Ans. Its also know as sparkling water, fizzy water and seltzer, is plain water into which carbon dioxide gas has been dissolved and is the major defining component of most soft drinks.

Q65. The process of dissolving carbon dioxide gas in water /soft drinks is called___?

Ans. Carbonation.

Q66. In past soda water is also know as___?

Ans. Club soda.

Q67. What is mineral water?

Ans. Is a water containing minerals or dissolve substance that alter its taste or give it therapeutic value.

Q68. What is syrup?

Ans. A syrup is a thick, viscous liquid, containing a large amount of dissolved sugars, but showing little tendency to deposits crystals. The viscosity arise from the multiple hydrogen bonds between dissolve sugar, which has many hydroxyl groups, and the water.

Q69. Mention some syrup names?

Ans. The followings are as follows:

- Agave nectar syrup

- Barley malt syrup
- Birch syrup
- Brown rice syrup
- Chocolate syrup
- Corn syrup
- Fruit syrup
- Golden syrup
- Inverted sugar syrup
- Maple syrup
- Sugar beet syrup
- Palm syrup
- Kithul treacle syrup
- Sorghum syrup.

Q70. Mention the breakfast menu for diabetes?

Ans. Breakfast menu for diabetes person are as follows:
(360 calories, 52.5gms carbohydrate)
1 slice toasted whole wheat bread with 1 teaspoon of margarine
¼ cup of cottage cheese
½ cup oat meal
½ cup skim milk
½ small banana
(Remember to drink 8oz. of water with each meal).

Q71. Mention the lunch menu for diabetes?

Ans. Lunch menu for diabetes person are as follows:
(535 calories, 75 carbohydrates)
1 cup of vegetable soup with 6 crackers
1 turkey/chicken sandwich (2 slice of whole wheat bread and 1 ounce turkey/chicken and 1 ounce of low fat cheese,1tsp mayonnaise)
1 small apple. .
Remember to drink 8oz. of water with each meal.

Q72. Mention the dinner menu for diabetes?

Ans. Dinner menu for diabetes person are as follows:
(635 calories, 65gms of carbohydrate)
4 ounce of broiled chicken breast with some herbs
$^{2}/_{3}$ cup cooked brown rice
½ cup of cooked carrots

1 small whole grain dinner roll with I tsp of margarine
Tossed salad with 2 tablespoons low fat salad dressing
1 small slice angel food cake or unsweetened canned apricot.

Q73. Mention the breakfast menu for lacto-vegetarian persons?

Ans. The lacto-vegetable meal are as follows:

- Orange -1 medium
- Cottage cheese-1/4 cup
- Whole-grain toast, 2 slices
- Margarine, 1 teaspoon
- Skim milk, 1 cup.

Q74. Mention the lunch menu for lacto-vegetarian people?

Ans. The lacto-vegetarian lunch meal are as follow:

- Split –pea soup,1 cup
- Sesame or whole–grain crackers, 6
- Part-skimmed cheese slice,1 slice
- Tomato and cucumber salad
- Salad dressing, 1 tbs
- Baked apple
- Skim milk, 1 cup.

Q75. Mention the breakfast menu for high blood pressure peoples?

Ans. Breakfast menu for high blood pressure peoples are as follows:

- Orange juice 6 oz.
- Skim milk 8 oz.
- 1 cup cheerios cereal
- 1 medium banana.

Q76. Mention the lunch menu for high blood pressure peoples?

Ans. Lunch menu for high blood pressure peoples are as follows:

- Sandwich (2 slice whole wheat bread,1tbsp light mayonnaise, 3oz. broiled chicken breast, 1oz part skim mozzarella cheese, 2 romaine lettuce wedges)
- Raw vegetables (5 carrots, 5 celery sticks)
- 8 oz. skim vegetables
- ½ cup fruit cocktail in light syrup.

Q77. Mention the dinner menu for high blood pressure peoples?

Ans. Dinner menu for high blood pressure peoples are as follows:

- 3 oz. herbed baked cod

- 1 cup wild rice
- 1 cup steamed medley: broccoli, cauliflower, carrots
- 1 tbsp light Italian dressing
- 1 small whole whet dinner roll
- 1 tsp low –salt soft margarine
- ½ cup sliced strawberries.

Q78. Mention the snack menu for high blood pressure peoples?

Ans. Snack menu for high blood pressure peoples are as follows:

- ¼ cup dried raisins
- ½ cup unsalted mixed nuts
- Calorie free beverage.

Q79. Mention the low cholesterol breakfast menu?

Ans. Low cholesterol Breakfast menu are as follows:
Whole –grain cereal with non fat milk and fruit.

Q80. Mention the low cholesterol lunch menu?

Ans. Low cholesterol lunch menu are as follows:

- Mediterranean salmon salad with bread, fruit and yoghurt
- 1 cup sauté green vegetables
- ½ cup of other vegetables; cooked, raw (chopped).
- ½ cup of vegetables juice.

Q81. From where most expensive meal in the world?

Ans. The Dome restaurant in Bangkok, in Thailand offer most expensive meal in the world. (cost is $30,000 not including tax).

Q82. Name the modern French menu with English names and examples?

Ans.

French	*English*	*Examples*
Hors d' oeuvres	Appetizers	Melon with port, rémoulade, oysters, smoked salmon, shrimp cocktail
Potage	Soup	Vicchychoisse, Consommé julienne, crème of tomato soup
Poisson	Fish	Grilled fish lemon butter, Sole de bonne femmme

Contd...

French	*English*	*Examples*
Entrée'	First meat dish	Braised Agneau
Releve'	Main meat dish	Chateaubriand, grilled pepper steak, saddle of agneau
Sorbet	Flavoured ice	Champagne sorbet, sorbet vanilla
Roti	Roast of game birds	Roast chicken
Legumes	Vegetables	Legumes of paprika, vegetable fricassee
Entremets	Sweet dish	Crepe suzette
Savoureux	Savory	Cheese and cracker
Dessert	dessert	Fruits and Nuts, Jellied fruit

CHAPTER

4 Cheese

Q1. What is Cheese?

Ans. Cheese is made from milk, with the addition of a starter (bacteria) and rennet to help curdle the milk. The solids (cured) separate from the water (whey) and are packed into moulds to mature and become cheese. The degree of pressure to which they are subjected determines the type of cheese.

Q2. How are cheese broadly classified?

Ans. Hard; Semi – hard; soft or cream and blue.

Q3. Name five English cheeses.

Ans Cheddar, Cheshire, Lancashire, Derby, Leicester and Stilton.

Q4. Cheddar is classified as a___cheeses?

Ans. Hard.

Q5. Caerphilly comes from___?

Ans. Wales.

Q6. Name three French Chesses.

Ans. Brie, Camembert, Roquefort.

Q7. Name three Italian cheeses.

Ans. Gorgonzola, Parmesan, Bel Paese.

Q8. Match the following with the country of origin.
Emmental, Gouda, Gruyere, Edam, Danish Blue?

Ans. Switzerland, Holland, Switzerland, Holland, Denmark.

Q9. Roquefort is the French cheese made from___?

Ans. Ewe 's milk (i.e. Sheep's milk).

Q10. The cover for Cheese on a classic French menu is___?
Ans. Side plate, Side knife, Small fork.

Q11. What are the accompaniments for cheese?
Ans. Cruet (Salt, pepper and mustard)

- Butter in a butter dish
- Radishes sticks on ice
- Caster sugar for cream cheese
- Assorted Cheese biscuits
- Celery.

Q12. Give four important factors when steering cheese?
Ans. Cool, dark place, good air circulation, correct packaging, store away from foods which absorb flavours.

Q13. Name two cheeses used in cooking?
Ans. Parmesan and Cheddar.

Q14. What is the fondue?
Ans. A Swiss specialty, where in a copper pot of melted cheese and wine is kept upon a burner and guests dip pieces of dry bread into the mixture on special long forks.

Q15. How is Blue Cheese formed?
Ans. By skewering certain types of cheese with copper wires to inject it with a kind of penicillin.

Q16. The cover of cheese is___?
Ans. The cover of cheese:

- Side plate
- Side knife
- Sometimes small fork.

Q17. Mention name of fresh cheese?
Ans. Cottage cheese, Ricotta, Mozzarella, Cream cheese.

Q18. Mention name of soft cheese?
Ans. Bel paese, Brie, Camembert, Carre' de l'est, Munster, Feta.

Q19. Mention name of semi hard cheese?
Ans. Edam, Emmenthal, Derby, Cheddar, Cheshire.

Q20. Mention name of Hard cheese?

Ans. Parmesan, Provolone, Pecorino.

Q21. Mention name of blue cheese?

Ans. Danish blue, Dorset blue, Blue Cheshire, Blue de bresse, Stilton, Roquefort, Gorgonzola.

Q22. Hard cheese contain how much moisture and milk fat?

Ans. Its contain not more than 43 per cent moisture and Not less than 42 per cent milk fat of dry matters.

Q23. Skimmed milk paneer contain how much moisture and milk fat?

Ans. It shall contain more than 70 per cent of moisture and milk fat contain is not more than 13 per cent of the dry matter.

Q24. Processed cheese contain how much moisture and milk fat?

Ans. Its contain not more than 47 per cent moisture and Not less than 40 per cent milk fat of dry matters.

Q25. How processed cheese are made?

Ans. Processed cheese and processed cheese spreads are prepared from one or more varieties of cheese, the mix being heat treated with an emulsifying salt to prevent separation of the fat and the protein.

Q26. Processed cheeses contain how much water?

Ans. Its contain higher contain of water from 48-60 per cent.

Q27. What is whey?

Ans. Whey is the greenish liquid which exudes from the curd and it contain the albumen and globulin.

Q28. What is the average composition of whey?

Ans. Average composition of whey in per cent:

- Water: 93.5
- Fat: 0.30
- Lactose: 5
- Albumen and globulin: 0.75.

Q29. Meaning of albumen and globulin?

Ans. Albuminous means proteins, Proteins which Coagulated by heat it called globulin.

Q30. What is casein?

Ans. Chief protein constituent of milk. Coagulated by action of rennet or by acids.

Q31. What is pitched curd?

Ans. Curd that settle in the whey.

CHAPTER

5 Tea and Coffee

Q1. Name the major tea producing countries of the world?
Ans. China, India, Ṣri Lanka, Kenya.

Q2. Name some special tea blends?
Ans. Assam – strong and full bodied
Darjeeling – delicate mallow flavoured
Ceylon – blend gold with good flavour
Jasmine – fragrant and scented flavour
Lapsang Scouchong – a smoky, pungent perfumed tea from China
Orange Pekoe – Slightly fruity aroma and flavour.

Q3. What are Herb teas?
Ans. These are fruit flavoured and herb infused green teas, served without milk or sugar and full of aroma and flavour.

Q4. Give example of herb teas.
Ans. Camomile, Peppermint, Rosehip, Mint etc.

Q5. Give Example of fruit teas.
Ans. Cherry, Lemon, Blackcurrant, Mandarin Orange.

Q6. In India , what percentage of tea is grown in Darjeeling?
Ans 2 per cent–Assam grows 72 per cent-74 per cent. The rest is from scattered areas.

Q7. What Forms does tea come in?
Ans. Leaf, CTC (cut turned curried) and Dust.

Q8. Describe the method of making a good pot tea?
Ans. First use boiling water to swirl out clean the pot. This keeps the pot hot. Add roughly one teaspoon of tea leaves per cup of tea required. Add boiling hot water to the leaves in the pot.

Cover the pot and allow to brew infuse for 3-4 minutes before serving. Clean out pot and spout after use.

Q9. What is Chinese Tea?

Ans. Green Tea, Served without milk or lemon in special Chinese tea-cups. These are shaped like a tulip and have no handles.

Q10. What is Russian Tea?

Ans. Tea is made in normal way. But no milk is added. A wedge of lemon is offered separately and the tea is served in glasses which stand in a silver holder with a handle. Sugar may offered.

Q11. How would you make iced tea?

Ans. Make a strong decoction of tea and pour it into a tall tumbler full of ice. Serve lemon wedge and sugar syrup separately. Garnish with lemon slice and mint springs.

Q12. What are the most important spices of coffee called?

Ans. Coffee Arabica and coffee Robusta. Arabica accounts for 755 of World Production.

Q13. What are the different degrees of roasting coffee beans?

Ans. Light or pale – suitable for mild beans
Medium – Gives a stronger flavour for well define coffees
Full roasting–gives a bitter taste–popular in Latin countries
High roasting – Accentuates the strong bitter aspects of coffee, much of the original flavour is last.

Q14. How would you make good coffee?

Ans. Use freshly roasted and ground coffee. Use boiling water with the correct measure of coffee. Do not boil the coffee. Add milk separately.

Q15. What is cona coffee?

Ans. Cona is a brand name associated with the vacuum infusion method of coffee production. The cona has chambers. The lower bowl is filled with warm water up to the water level indicated . The filter is placed in the upper bowl and the required amount of coffee grounds added. The upper bowl is then set in the lower bowl and the water is heated. As the water reaches boiling point it rises into the upper chamber and infuses with the coffee grounds. On reducing the heat, the coffee liquid passes back into the lower bowl, leaving the grounds in the upper bowl.The upper bowl is removed and cleaned and the coffee in the lower bowl is used for service.

Q16. How does the service of South Indian coffee differ from the normal service?

Ans. In normal service, the coffee is served from a coffee pot and milk from a creamer. In South Indian coffee. The coffee decoction is drawn from a filter and is so rich that the coffee is served in the creamer and the milk in the coffee pot.

Q17. What is roasted coffee?

Ans. Its means properly cleaned green coffee which has been roasted to a brown colour and has developed its characteristics aroma.

Q18. What is ground coffee?

Ans. Its mean the powder product obtained from the roasted coffee only and shall be free from husk.

Q19. What is jasmine tea?

Ans. Green (unoxidised) tea that is dried with jasmine Blossom and produce a tea with a fragrant and scented flavour.

Q20. What is early grey tea?

Ans. Its blend of Darjeeling and China tea flavoured with oil of bergamot (aromatic herb).

Q21. What is after noon tea?

Ans. Its a blend of Darjeeling and high grown Ceylon tea to produce a refreshing and light tea.

Q22. What is morning Tea?

Ans. Its is a blend of Assam and Kenya tea to make a bright and, flavour some and refreshing tea.

Q23. What are the common degrees of coffee roasting?

Ans.
- Light roasting or pale roasting
- Medium roasting
- Full roasting
- High roasting.

Q25. What are the character tics of good coffee?

Ans. Its should have

- Good flavour
- Good aroma
- Good body
- Good colour when milk or cream is added.

Q26. What is café Latte?

Ans. Shot of espresso plus hot milk.

Q27. What is Instant coffee?

Ans. Coffee made from processed powder.

Q28. What is cappuccino?

Ans. Espresso coffee topped with steamed froth milk, often finished with sprinkle of chocolate powder.

Q29. Give two well known brands of de-caffeinated coffee?

Ans. Caffeine, a stimulant in coffee is removed to made de-caffeinated coffee. "Cafe Hag" in Europe and "Sanka" in America are two well known brands.

Q30. How would you make Irish Coffee?

Ans. In a wine glass or Irish coffee glass place a teaspoonful of sugar. Leave the spoon in to conduct the heat and add piping hot strong black coffee. Dissolve the sugar and add one measure of Irish whiskey. Finally float double cream on the top of the coffee over the back of a spoon. Do not stir. Sprinkle brown sugar on the cream. In some cases the rim of the glass may be coated in caramel.

Q31. Name some other types of specialized coffee.

Ans. Monks Coffee – Benedictine is used
Russian Coffee – Vodka
Calypso Coffee – Tai-Maria
Jamaican Coffee – Rum
Highland Coffee – Scotch whisky
Seville Coffee – Cointreau.

Q32. French coffee is flavoured with____?

Ans. French coffee flavoured with chicory.

Q33. Name of the world most expensive coffee bean?
Ans. Kopi Luwak coffee bean.

Q34. Which is certified organic coffee?
Ans. Kalani coffee.

Q35. What is specialty of Kopi Luwak coffee bean?
Ans. Its also know as Civet coffee, is coffee that is made from coffee berries that have been eaten by and passed through the digestive track of the Asian palm civet. The civet eat the berries but beans pass through their system undigested.

Q36. Kopi Luwak coffee bean eaten by which animal?
Ans. Its eaten by Asian forest animal called civet.

Q37. Which fruit is used substitute of coffee?
Ans. Fig is used.

Q38. Flavouring agents in Turkish coffee___?
Ans. Vanilla pod.

CHAPTER

6 Wine

Q1. Name the major wine production countries of the world.
Ans. France, Italy, Germany, Spain, Portugal, USA.

Q2. Name the main wine producing region of France.
Ans. Bordeaux, Burgundy, Cotes du Rhone, Loire Valley Alsace, Champagne, Beaujolais.

Q3. Name four other regions which product wine?
Ans. Jura; Provence; Languedoc; - Rousillon; Savoy.

Q4. Which are the grape varieties common to Bordeaux?
Ans. Red-Cabernet Sauvignon, Cabernet Franc, Malbec; Petit Verdot and Merlot.
White- Sauvignon Blanc, Muscadelle, Semillon.

Q5. Which is the British term for Bordeaux Red Wines?
Ans. Claret.

Q6. Name the five famous wine producing regions of Bordeaux?
Ans. Graves; Pomerol; St. Emilion, Sauternes.

Q7. Name some famous wines from Medoc?
Ans. Chateau Lafite: Chateau Mouton–Rothschild, Chateau La Four, Chateau Margaux.

Q8. Name some famous wines from Graves?
Ans. Chateau Pape Clament, Chateau Haut Bailly, Chateau Haut Brions.

Q9. Name some famous wines from St. Emillion?
Ans. Chateau Cheval Blanc, Clos fourtet, Chateau Av___.

Q10. Which type of wines is Sauternes famous for?
Ans. Sweet white wines.

Q11. What is noble rot?
Ans. The term used for the withering of the Semillon grapes which intensifies the sweetness and flavour. It is caused by a mould known as noble rot which forms on the grapes in the autumn.

Q12. Name some famous dessert wines from Sauternes?
Ans. Chateau d'Yquem, Chateau la Tour Blanche, Chateau Clemens, Chateau de Rayne Vigneau.

Q13. How can you distinguish between a dry white wine and a dessert wine on sight?
Ans. The dessert wines are a golden yellow hue, the dry wine would be a faint yellow.

Q14. Name the wine growing districts of burgundy?
Ans. Cote de Nuits and Cote de Beaune, Chalonnaise, Maconnaise, Beaujolais, Chablis.

Q15. Give examples of wines from each of the districts?
Ans. Cote De Nuits–Chambertin, Musigny
Cote de Beaune–Pommard, Volnay, Puligny-Montrachet
Chaonnaise–Givry, Mercurey, Rulley
Maconnaise–Pouilly-Fuisse
Beaujolais–Broully fleunie, Margon St. Amour
Chablis–Grand Crus-Chablis Moutonne
Premier Crus–Monts de Milleu, Fourchaume.

Q16. Name some famous wines from the Cotes du Rhone?
Ans. Chateauneur-de-Pape; Cote Rotie, Hermitage (Red), Chateau Grillet, Clarrette de Die (White), Lavel (Rose).

Q17. Give examples of wines from the Loire valley?
Ans. Pouilly Fume, Anjou, Muscadet, Sancerne.

Q18. What is the service temperature of red wines?
Ans. 18 -22 degree C.

Q19. What is the service temperature of white and rose wines?
Ans. 10-12 degree C.

Q20. What is the service temperature of champagne?
Ans. 6-8 degree C.

Q21. What do the following terms used in connection with champagne mean?

Ans. *(a)* Brut, *(b)* Extra Sec, *(c)* Sec, *(d)* Demi-Sec, *(e)* Doux, *(f)* Magnum, *(g)* Jeroboam, *(h)* Rehoboam, *(i)* Methuselah, *(j)* Nebuchadnezzar, *(k)* Cuvee, *(l)* Rose.

Q22. Name some famous champagne shippers?

Ans. G.H. Mumm; Charles Heidsieck; Krug; Lanson; Veuve Clicquot-Ponsardis; Taittinger; Moet and Chandcn, Pol Roger; Perrier-Jouet.

Q23. Name some premier champagnes?

Ans. Moet and Chandon- Dom Perignon
Heidsieck- Diamant Bleu
Lanson- Black Label
Taittanger- Comtes de Champagne.

Q24. How could you tell a Bordeaux wine from a Burgundy on sight in the bottle?

Ans. Bordeaux bottle is a square shouldered green bottle, the Burgundy comes in slope shouldered bottle, dark green for reds olive for whites.

Q25. Give the characteristics of a German wine bottle?

Ans. It is slope sided with a long neck. It is always brown for Rhine wine and Breen for Mosels.

Q26. Name some famous German wines?

Ans. Liebfraumilch, Berncasteler Doctor, Liefin Schlohberg; Berendt Berncasteler.

Q27. Name some famous Italian wines?

Ans. Asti Spumante (sparkling sweet white wine), Chianti Classico, Ruffino Riserva Ducale, Marsala Chiarli Lambrusco, Vino Cortese Secco, Borolo.

Q28. What are fortified wines?

Ans. They are still wines that are made in the normal way but then have extra alcohol added to them. This increases the alcoholic content, stops further fermentation and improves the keeping Quality of the wine.

Q29. Name some fortified wines?
Ans. *(a)* Sherry, *(b)* Port, *(c)* Madeira, *(d)* Marsala.

Q30. Name the famous sherry producing regions of spain?
Ans. Jerez, San Lucar de Bamarreda, Porto Santa Maria.

Q31. What are the different styles of sherry?
Ans. *(a)* Fino–A very pale light dry wine with a delicate aroma. Alcoholic Content -15 degree.
(b) Amontillado–An aged fino- dry taste.
(c) Manzanilla–A fino that has been aged at Snalucar de Barrameda. It is pale, dry and crisp with a fruit bitter after taste.
(d) Oloroso–A dark gold wine with plenty of body and a nutty flavour. Content 18 degree.
(e) Palo Oloroso–A rare oloroso with a body and colour of an oloroso, but the dryness of an Amantillado.

Q32. Explain the Solera System?
Ans. A solera is a series of casks, stacked one on top of another in a pyramid three-four casks high. The younger sherry is placed at the top and the older at the bottom. As wine is drawn off from the bottom, the lower casks will be filled from these above lower case so that young sherry in continually blended with old sherry. The finished wine is fortified with brandy.

Q33. Name the grapes used is sherry manufacture?
Ans. Pedro Ximinez, Moscatel, Palamino.

Q34. Name some famous sherry brands?
Ans. Tio Pepe–Gonzalez Byass
Carols and Javier De Terry–501 Fino
Garveys–San Patricio
Duff Godon–E1 CID
Harveys–Bristol Cream.

Q35. What is port?
Ans. Fortified wine from Portugal–particularly produced around the valley of Douro.

Q36. Name some famous ports?
Ans. Foncesca's Tawny Port.

Cockburn's – Port-Vintage Character
Graham's – Five Crowns Churchills
Taylor's – Reserve.

Q37. What are the different types of port?

Ans. *(a)* Vintage- the wine of a single exceptional year
(b) Late Bottled Vintage- Similar wine, bottled when mature
(c) Crusted – Good, but not vintage port
(d) Tawny- Of a tawny (light brown) colour due to the fact it has been stored in wood for many years–smooth and light.
(e) Ruby- A dark, rough wine aged in wood for a short period.
(f) White-From white grapes–drier than red–an aperitif.

GENERAL QUESTIONS ON WINE

Q38. Wines which accompany fish dishes are normally___?

Ans. Dry and white- the sharp flavour of the wine gives a good balance and harmony to light textured and oily flesh of fish.

Q39. Examples of wines which may be suggested to accompany fish are?

Ans. Chablis (Burgundy)
Pouilly-fuisse (Burgundy)
Meursault (Burgundy)
All Alsace Wines
Muscadet (Loire Valley)
Hocks (Germany)
Steinwein (Germany).

Q40. Almost all red wine harmonize well with___?

Ans. Lamb and Beef.

Q41. Name some example of red wines from French?

Ans. St. Julien (Bordeaux)
Pauillae (Bordeaux)
St. Emilion (Bordeaux)
Pomerol (Bordeaux)
Medoc (Bordeaux)
Nuit St. Georges (Burgundy)
Beaune (Burgundy).

Q42. Which wine would you serve with appetizers?

Ans. Dry white or rose water.

Q43. White meats such as veal and pork may be served with___?
Ans. Medium white wine.

Q44. Sweets and desserts may be accompanied by ___wines.
Ans. Sweet white wines e.g. Sauternes, Barsac etc.

Q45. Stilton and other cheeses blend well with___wine.
Ans. Port.

Q46. After dinner you could serve___?
Ans. Brandies and liqueurs with coffee.

Q47. Name some famous rose wines.
Ans. Anjou Rose, Cabernet d' Anjou, Travel Maters rose.

Q48. What does the term vinde Pays signify?
Ans. These French wines are from large district areas of France. The are the typical wine of a region having an alcoholic strength not less then specified by the district committee.

Q49. What does the term VDQS signify on a wine?
Ans. Vine De limit 's de Quality suoeriever are exceilent second quality wine f France produced by specified vineyards and districts. Under strict regulations.

Q50. What is AOC?
Ans. This is a geographical guarantee on France labels for quality wine from a define area. All areas and districts have their own Appelletion Controlees, which ensure that all wines they pass from the region conform to their standards.

Q51. Name some famous verities of wine producing grapes?
Ans. Black–Cebernet Sauvignon–(Bordeaux, Loire Valley)
Pinot Noir (burgundy), (Champagne)
Gamay–(Beaujolais)
Grenache–(Chateauneuf–du pape–Rhone valley)
White–Semillon–Sauternes
Sauvignon–Pouilly Surdoire and Bordeaux
Chardonnay–Champagne, Burgundy
Riesling–Germany and Alsace.

Q52. How are Rose wines produced?
Ans. By three method: either from red grapes fermented on the

skins for up to 48 hours or by mixing red and white wines together or by pressing grapes so that some colour is extracted.

Q53. What are aperitifs?

Ans. Aperitifs are drinks had before meals to stimulate the appetite.

Q54. Name some types of aperitifs?

Ans. Sherry, Vermouth, Bitters, Pastis.

Q55. What are vermouths?

Ans. Vermouths are aromatized wines which have been fortified. The basic wine is of ordinary quality and blended is a set style. Other ingredients include unfermented grape juice, various flavourings (herbs, roots, bark flowers and quinine) and sugar as sweetening.

Q56. What are the main types of vermouth?

Ans. Dry and Sweet.

Q57. Name some dry Vermouth?

Ans. Martini Dry
Cinzano Dry
Cham be'ry
Noilly Prat.

Q58. Name some sweet vermouths?

Ans. Cinzano Bioanco
Cinezano Red
Martini Sweet Red
Noilly Prat Red
Punt E Mes.

Q59. How should vermouths be served?

Ans. Frappe' (ie on crushed ice).

Q60. Name some famous bitters?

Ans.
- Amer Picon–A very black and bitter France apertif, usually consumed with grenadine or casts to make it more palatable.
- Angostura–Takes it name from a town in Venezuela, but is now made in Trinidad, Brownish red, used mainly as a flavouring agent.

- Campari–A Pink bitter sweet Italian aperitif with a slight flavour of orange peel and quinine. Served with soda or orange juice or frappe.
- Frenet Branca–The Italian version of the Amer Picon. Served with water or Soda.

Q61. Name some famous pastis?

Ans.
- Ouzo – Greek – almost like a aniseed flavoured brandy
- Pernod – French – a clear liquid obtained by distillation of oils turns milky when iced water is added
- Ricard – French – Like all pastis, has an aniseed flavour
- Suze – French – Produced by Pernod firm. Golden yellow colour with a bitter sweet after taste orange and caramel is added.

Q62. Is brandy a wine or a spirit?

Ans. Brandy is a spirit distilled from wine.

Q63. What is Cognac?

Ans. Cognac is brandy produced in the Cognac region of Franch, north of Bordeaux.

Q64. Name the six region of Cognac.

Ans. Grande Champagne, Petite Champagne, Borderies, Fine Bois, Bons Bois, Bois Ordinaries.

The First Two areas are the classical areas. Together they produce a brandy known as fine champagne. This must contains at least 50 per cent of the grapes from each of the regions.

Q65. What is a "Angle's Share"?

Ans. When Cognac is being heated, a great deal evaporates. This is called the Angle's Share. It is estimated that as much Cognac is lost as is drunk each year in France.

Q66. What do the labels VSOP & X.O signify on cognac labels?

Ans. VSOP- Very Special Old Pales are aged in Oak barrels for 5 Years, Xo are foe 40.

Q67. How should brandy be served?

Ans. In a brandy snifter at room temperature. The guest would normally warm it to the degree required him self.

Q68. Mention the names of wines which are generally served with fish pates?

Ans. Light dry whites without over fruit are best such as Chablis, Muscadet, Alsace pinot blanc.

Q69. Mention the names of wines which are generally served with smoked salmon?

Ans. Needs a hefty wines (strong) such as Pinot Gris, Cote de Beaune.

Q70. Mention the names of wines which are generally served with deep fried mushroom?

Ans. These are best with medium bodied simple red such as; cotes du rhone.

Q71. Mention the names of wines which are generally served with pasta?

Ans. Pasta really best with Italian wines such as Vernaccia, Barbera, Arneis.

Q72. Mention the names of wines which are generally served with lobster?

Ans. When its served in hot as main course its require heavy wine such as; Chardonnay, Alsace Pinot Gris.

Q73. Which is the world's largest producer of wine?

Ans. Italy.

Q74. What is AC?

Ans. Appellation Controlee.

Q75. Boredeaux red wine made from which grapes?

Ans. Malbec, cabernet sauvignon, cabernet franc, merlot.

Q76. Boredeaux sweet white wine made from which grapes?

Ans Muscadelle, Semillon.

Q77. Loire wine made from which grapes?

Ans. Folle blanche, melon de Bourgogne.

Q78 . Champagne wine made from which grapes?

Ans. Pinot Noir, chardonnay.

Q79. Burgundy wine made from which grapes?
Ans. Chardonnay, pinot-noir.

Q80. Bordeaux-dry white wine made from which grapes?
Ans. Muscadelle, Semillon.

Q81. ___the roman god of wine?
Ans. Bacchus.

Q82. The study of grapes know as?
Ans. Ampelography.

Q83. Standard size of wine bottle?
Ans. 75cl.

Q83. ___Wine has longest shell life?
Ans. Madeira.

Q84. Explain term aroma?
Ans. The scent of a wine frequently used interchangeably with the word "bouquet" especially young wines. Usually refers to the particular smell of the grape variety. The word "bouquet" is usually restricted to describing the aroma of a cellar aged bottled wine.

Q85. What austere describes?
Ans. Austere describes high-acid wines.

Q86. A huge bottle that holds 16 standard bottles know as___?
Ans. Balthazar.

Q87. Explain the term blanc de blanc?
Ans. Meaning a white wine made with of grapes, such as champagne made of chardonnay.

Q88. Explain the term banc de noir?
Ans. White wine made from red grapes, such as sparkling wines made from pinot noir, blanc de noirs often have a pale pink colour.

Q89. Explain term blush?
Ans. A pink coloured wine made from red grapes.

Q90. What Chene refers?
Ans. Its refers to oak.

Q91. If in bottle mention chene what its means?
Ans. Its means aged in oak barrels.

Q92. Explain terms zinfandel?
Ans. Its means a spicy California special red wine.

Q93. What limousin refers?
Ans. Its describe a type of oak cask from Limoges, France.

Q94. Average size of wine bottle?
Ans. 75cl.

Q95. Explain term 'petillant'?
Ans. Sparkling wine with the pressure of four atmosphere is called petillant.

Q96. Bacchus is the___god of wine?
Ans. Roman.

Q97. ___the name of the alcoholic beverage which was used to toast the American declaration of independence?
Ans. Madeira wine.

Q98. What pH indicates in wine?
Ans. Its indicates chemical measurement of the acidity in a wine.

Q99. Low pH value indicates what in wines?
Ans. Low pH values wines are better candidates for aging.

Q100. What is Made Wine?
Ans. Wines that are made from grape concentration and not from fresh grapes is called made wine.

Q101. Explain tannic/tannin?
Ans. Some young reds wines mouth puckery sensation, due to skin and stalk of the grapes as well as the oak barrels.

Q102. Explain the term bouquet?
Ans. Often used interchangeably with word aroma. The complex of aromas that develops with age in fine wines; in general young wines may not have not bouquet.

Q103. Explain term body?
Ans. The weight and texture of a wine. Often refers to alcohol

content. Taster's palate usually due to from a combination of alcohol, glycerin and sugar content. Commonly expressed as full-bodied, medium–bodied, or light-bodied.

Q104. How to read a wine label?

Ans.

Q105. Explain the composition of wine?

Ans.

Components	*Proportion/litre*
Water	700-900ml
Carbon-dioxide	0-50cc
Sulphur-dioxide	80-200mg
Ethanol	8.5-15 per cent by volume
Acetaldehyde	.0005-.5gm
Ester	.5-1.5gm
Acetic Acid	.3-0.5gm
Residual sugar	.8-180gm

Q106. Explain term pruning?

Ans. During the growth of wines a process of cutting the unwanted vegetative parts of the wine is undertaken for a better product and operation is called pruning.

Q107. Ideal storage temperature of barrel in cellar is___?

Ans. 13°c and humidity above 75 per cent.

Q108. French wines are graded according to?

Ans. The French wines are grade as follows:

- A.O.C.
- VDQS
- Vin de table
- Vin de payee.

Q109. Mention names of port wines?

Ans. The port wine are as follows:

- Vintage
- Crusted
- Ruby
- Tawny
- White port.

Q110. Mention the name of popular region of Portugal wine?

Ans. The popular region for wine growing are as follows:

- Tawny
- Minhao
- Dao
- Douro
- Lisbon.

Q111. Mention the Italian quality control categories?

Ans. Italian wines is controlled by law made after 1963, control categories are as follows:

- Denominazione Semplice (DS)
- Denominazione di Origine Controllata (DOC)
- Denominazione di Origine Controllata e Garantita (DOCG).

Q112. Mention the wine region of Italy?

Ans. The wine region of Italy are as follows:

- Piedmont
- Lombardy

- Veneto
- Alto Adige
- Tuscany
- Sicily
- Campania.

Q113. Mention some Italian wine?

Ans. Barolo, Boco, Barbera, Bonarda, Luyana, Albana, Marsala, Bianco, Chianti, Kalterer.

Q114. Mention the German wine quality control categories?

Ans. Quality control is indicates by___

- Lindwein
- Dutscher tafel wine
- Qualititats wein Bestimmter Anbaugebiete (QBA)
- Qualitatswein mit Pradkat (QmP).

Q115. What grapes varieties used for German wines?

Ans. Riesting, Sylvaner, Muller-thurgan etc.

Q116. Mention the wine region of German?

Ans. The wine region of German wines are as follows:

- Mosel-saar-Ruwer
- Rheingau
- Rheinpfalz
- Nahe Rheinhesseu
- Badeu
- Ahr
- Franken.

Q117. German sparkling wine knows as___?

Ans. Sekt.

Q118. U.S. is the worlds___largest wine producer?

Ans. Fifth.

Q119. Mention the wine producing areas of USA?

Ans. The wine producing areas of USA are as follows:

- California
- Oregon
- Washington
- New York

- Maryland
- Virginia.

Q120. Name some Indian varieties of wines?

Ans. Varieties of Indian wines are as follows:

- Bosca sherry
- Bosca vermouth
- Bosca Riesling
- Riviera white
- Riviera red
- Golconda white
- Golconda ruby
- Bosca rose
- Marque de pompedour.

Q121. What the serving temperature of young red wine?

Ans. 16°c.

Q122. How you read a wine label thoroughly?

Ans.

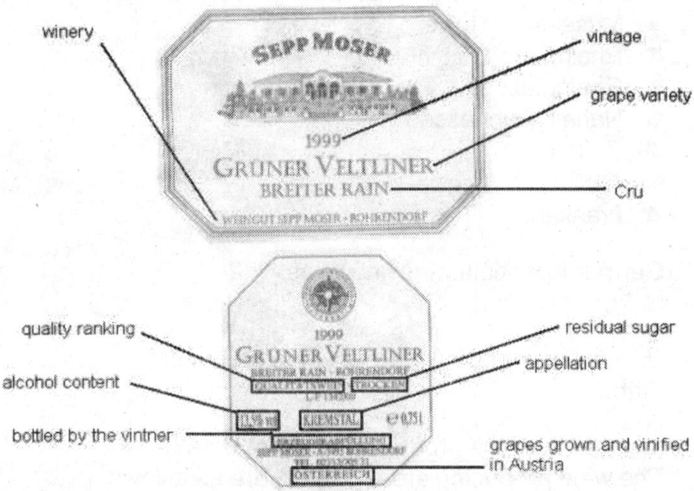

CHAPTER

7 Beer

Q1. What is beer?

Ans. A fermented drink deriving its alcohol content from the conversion of melt sugar into alcohol with brewer's yeast.

Q2. Which are the main categories of beer?

Ans. Top fermented, Wheat beers, Bottom fermented.

Q3. Name some top fermented beers?

Ans. Mild Ale, Pale Ale, Bitter Ale, Porter, Stout.

Q4. Name some wheat beers?

Ans. Weizenbier, Weisse, Gueuze – Lambic.

Q5. Name some bottom fermented beer?

Ans. Pilsner, Vienna, Munchener, Dortmunder, Bolk.

Q6. What do the terms Lager and Ale signify?

Ans. Lager is a generic term for bottom fermented beers, and ale is a generic term of all top fermented beers.

Q7. What are the main ingredients used in the manufacture of beer?

Ans. Malt i.e. malted barley, Hops – the flower of what used to be a wild weed, Sugar, Brewers yeast used foe fermenting the beer.

Q8. Name some famous beer brewers?

Ans. Anheuser Busch (USA), Schlitz (USA), Heineken (Holland), Mille (USA), Pobst (Denmark), Tooheys (Australia), Fosters (Australia), Swan (Australia), Budwelser (USA), San Meguel (Spain).

Q9. Explain the following terms associated with beer manufacture. Fining, Grist, Malting, Pitching, Racking, Sparging, Wort?

Ans. Fining–Substance added to beer to clear and brighten it.

- Girst–Malt crushed in rollers.
- Malting–Process or converting starch to sugar in the cereal prior to crushing in the rollers.
- Pitching–The addition of yeast to the wort in the fermenting.
- Priming–A solution of sugar and hope added to beer to develop the condition of beer.
- Racking–Running off a beer from one cask to another leave the sediment behind.
- Sparging–Grains left in the Mash tun are washed off with hot water to extract the final sugar.
- Wort–The Mash Plus hops and sugar, boiled together.

Q10. What is draught beer?

Ans. Beer served straight from the barrel.

Q11. What are the traditional size of the barrel?

Ans. 1 Pin–20.45 liters (4½ gallons)
1 Firkin–40.91 liters (9 gallons)
1 KEG–45.56 liters (10 gallons)
1 Kilderkin–81082 liters (18 gallons)
1 Barrel–163.65 liters (36 gallons)
1 Hogshead–245.48 liters (54 gallons).

Q12. What is the service temperature of beer?

Ans. 13 degree to 15 degree c.

Q13. Which country is Highest consumer of beer annually?

Ans. Germany with approx 150 liters per capita per annum.

Q14. How is beer served?

Ans. In tankards or tall glasses, Customers should be asked if they like their beer with a had.

Q15. Standard alcoholic content of beer?

Ans. Its varies according to type but usually between 3.5-10 per cent AV.

Q16. What are strong ales?

Ans. Strong ales colour between pale and brown and taste between dry and sweet. Alcoholic content also varies.

Q17. What are the main ingredients of beers?

Ans. The ingredients of beer as follows:

- Grains
- Water
- Hops and spices
- Yeast.

Q18. Brewing process includes which steps?

Ans.
- Mashing
- Clarification
- Filtration
- Fermentation
- Maturation
- Filtration
- Pasteurization.

Q19. Which is commonly used grain for malting?

Ans. Barley.

Q20. Mention the names of types of malt?

Ans. Type of malts are as follows:

- Filtration
- Pale malt
- Amber and brown malt
- Crystal malt
- Chocolate malt
- Black malt.

Q21. What hops do in beer?

Ans. The cone of the hops plant were originally added to beer as preservative. They prevent the brew from going sour. But also bring a characteristics bitter flavour and aroma to the drink.

Q22. Mention types of hops?

Ans. Bramling cross, Crystal, Cascade, Fuggles, Huller, Perle, saaz. and so on.

Q23. What yeast do in beer?

Ans. Without yeast, malt, hops and water will never make a beer. Its transformed the hopped cereals solution into a potent drink, hiding a magic beneath a living cloak of froth and foam.

Q24. In bottom fermented beer which yeast is used?
Ans. Saccharomyces Carlsbergensis.

Q25. Mention the styles of beer?
Ans. Ale, Alt, Bock, Dortmunder, Chillibeer, Lager, Ice beer, Pilsner, Porter, Stout, Witbier, and so on.

Q26. Most expensive and strongest beer in the world ?
Ans. Samuel Adams/Boston Beer Company Utopias world strongest and most expensive beer in world cost ($100).

CHAPTER

8 Sprits

Q1. The process of producing sprits is known as____________?

Ans. Distillation. The principle of distillation is that they ethyl alcohol vaporizes at a lower temperature (78 degree C) than water (100 degree C).

Q2. What are the two main method of production spirits?

Ans. The pot still and the coffee still (or patent still).

Q3. What are the main features of the pot still?

Ans. The spirit produced in the manner will contain many impurities. These impurities all take time to mature with in the spirit it self and as a result, distiller must by law mature all pot still spirits for a minimum of all pot still spirits have to be distilled twice. All pot still spirits have to be distilled twice. All pot still at a very high alcoholic strength and have to be diluted to an acceptable drinking strength.

Q4. What are the main features of the coffee still?

Ans. 1. Only one distillation is required to produce an acceptable marketable product

2. A stronger spirit is produced than by the pot still method

3. A very pure spirit is extracted.

Q5. Explain the term alcoholic wash?

Ans. It is the fermented liquid which may have a cereal, sugar cane or grape base, used in distillation to obtain a marketable production.

Q6. In the process of distillation of a spirit what are:

A: Heads B: Hearts C: Tails?

Ans. A: Heads in spirit given off first in the distillation process and cannot be used in the final product.

B: Hearts is the bulk of the spirits given off during distillation.

C: Tails: is the last part of the spirit given off in the distillation process and also can't use.

Q7. Whichever method of distillation is used the end product brandy, rum, gin etc. will be colourless. State true or false.

Ans. True: Any necessary colour will be achieved either by the addition of caramel or from the wood of the casks in which it is matured.

GIN

Q1. What is Gin?

Ans. Gin is a spirit distilled in a patent (Coffey) still to remove all its impurities and then flavoured with plant extracts by steeping them in the pure spirit. This flavoured spirit is re-distilled in a pot still to give the final product.

Q2. What are the main flavouring agents in Gin?

Ans. Juniper Berries and Coriander seeds.

Q3. What are the various types of Gin?

Ans. There are two types of gin

- English gin
  London dry gin
  Plymouth gin
- Dutch genever.

Q4. Name Ten brands of Gin?

Ans. Booths finest, Beefeaters, Gordons, Squires, Gilbeys, Tanqueray, Bombay sapphire, Belgravia, London dry gin, Gilbert, Coates, Barkleys, Squires, Boodles.

Q5. What would you serve if you were asked for a G&T?

Ans. Gin and Tonic water.

Q6. What is tonic water?

Ans. Aerated water flavoured with guinine.

Q7. Which tonic is used specially for gin?

Ans. Schweppes tonic.

Q8. Name some Indian gin?

Ans. Blue lag, high society, blue bull, forbes dry gin.

RUM

Q1. What are the various type of rum?

Ans. There are three types of rum.

- Light-cleared coloured-smooth tasting
- Medium-golden coloured-Not as smooth tasting
- Heavy- dark coloured-rich and full bodied.

Q2. What is the main flavourings agent in the manufacturing of rum?

Ans. Molasses which drawn from the sugar cane.

Q3. Which are the main rum producing country in the world?

Ans.
- Cuba,
- Puertorico,
- Jamaica,
- Trinidad.

Q4. How is rum served?

Ans. Its may be had with iced water or Warm water, topped with cola (cuba libre) and its also used in many cocktails and fruit punch.

Note: The best dark rum and aged rums particular, should be served straight, unchilled, as digestives.

Q5. Name some famous brand of rum?

Ans. Captain Morgan, Wood's 100, Bacardi, Mount gay Lambs, Havana club.

Q6. Why was a daily 'TOT' of rum an naval tradition for many years?

Ans. Rum contains Vitamin C and was served with Lemon. Thus preventing scurvy (disease cause by vit c) amongst sailors.

Q7. Rum is the best accompaniments to___?

Ans. Fruits of all kinds.

Q8. What is rum?

Ans. Rum is spirit made from the fermented by products of sugar cane is called rum.

Q9. Name some white rum?
Ans. Bacardi, Bacardi lemon, Rom Rico, White diamond, Daiquiri.

Q10. Name some Jamaicans rums?
Ans. Captain Morgan, Lemon hart, Myons.

Q11. Name some Demerara rum?
Ans. Old jack dark, Lambs navy rum.

BRANDY

Q1. What is brandy?
Ans. Is a spirit made by distilling wines or the fermented mash of fruits, which is than suitable aged in oak barrel.

Q2. What is cognac?
Ans. Cognac the royal family of brandy. Word is made by the distillers of cognac regions.

Q3. All brandy is cognac explain this statement?
Ans. No, all cognac is brandy but all brandies are not cognac. Cognac is regions 7 word derived from cognac distillers.

Q4. What is AC?
Ans. Means Appellation Cognac.

Q5. AC allows which types of grapes?
Ans. Its allows three types of grapes:
- St.emillion (ugmi blance)
- Folle blanche
- Colombard.

Q6. Cognac is divided in how much regions?
Ans. Its divided into seven sub-divisions:
- Grande champagne
- Petit champagne
- Borderies
- Fine bois
- Bons bois
- Bois ordinaries
- Bois communs dits a terroir.

Q7. What does star denote in brandy?
Ans. Star denote the age of brandy. Certain qualities of brandy by marks such as

- One star
- Two star
- Three star.

Q7. Who started star system?
Ans. Jas Honnessy originated this system in 1865 to distinguished qualities of brandy.

Q9. How we gave three star to brandy?
Ans. Those are over 15 years old are get three star rated.

Q10. Explain CEFVSV POX?
Ans. Full forms as follows:

- C: cogna
- E: especial
- F: fine
- V: very
- S: superior
- V: very
- P: pale
- O: old
- X: extra.

Q11. What V denotes in brandy?
Ans. Its denote maturing year means OLD (05 years).

Q12. What VS denotes in brandy?
Ans. Its denote maturing year means VERY SUPERIOR (10-12 years).

Q12. What VSO denotes in brandy?
Ans. Its denote maturing year means VERY SUPERIOR OLD (15-20 years).

Q13. What VOP denotes in brandy?
Ans. Its denote maturing year means VERY OLD PALE (15-20 years).

Q14. What VSOP denotes in brandy?
Ans. Its denote maturing year means VERY SUPERIOR OLD PALE (Above 45 years).

Q15. What VSP denotes in brandy?

Ans. Its denote maturing year means VERY SUPERIOR PALE (15-20 years).

Q16. What XO denotes in brandy?

Ans. Its denote maturing year means EXTRA OLD (Above 45 years).

Q17. What is Napoleon brandy?

Ans. Napolean brandy meant signify superb and extravagant. These brandies of vintages 1810 to 1820 were referred to Napoleon brandy.

Q18. What is Armagnac?

Ans. Its is other kind of fine France brandy.

Q19. Mention ten names of cognac?

Ans Martell, Hennessy, Remy martin, Courvoisier, Hine, Otard, Monnet, Girad, Rouyer, Croizet.

Q20. What are the three regions of Armagnac?

Ans. There are three regions.

- Bas-armagnac
- Tenareze
- Haut- Armagnac.

VODKA

Q1. What originally was the base ingredient in the manufacture of vodka?

Ans. Originally it was potatoes, through it is now more likely be grain or molasses.

Q2. Vodka + Ginger Ale =?

Ans. A "Moscow Mule" cocktail.

Q3. Name some famous brands of vodka?

Ans. Smirnoff, Cossack, Romanott, Strolichnaya, Wyborowa, Finland, bolskaya, Volga, abosolut vodka, bolchoi, limonnaya, pieprzowka, Stolichnaya.

Q4. What is vodka?

Ans. Vodka is fine quality distilled beverage, neutral sprit with a unique characteristic of being colourless, tasteless and odorless.

Q5. Vodka distilled in___?
Ans. It is distilled in a continuous still proofed at 190°c.

Q6. Name some India brands of vodka?
Ans. Red czar, High society, Haywards, Volga, Redribbon, Doors.

Q7. Vodka is national drink of___?
Ans. Russia.

Q8. Russian vodka can be sold at an alcohol strength?
Ans. It can be sold at an alcoholic strength of up to 69 per cent as its not governed by British laws.

TEQUILLA

Q1. Tequila is the national drink of___?
Ans. Mexico.

Q2. What is tequila?
Ans. A Mexican spirit distilled from the fermented juice of the agave plant. Its traditionally drunk after a lick of salt and squeeze of lime and lemon.

Q3. What is base of tequila?
Ans. Pulque.

Q4. Two most common brand of tequila?
Ans. Cuervo and Montezuma.

Q5. Alcoholic strength of tequila?
Ans. 38 per cent vol.

Q6. Tequila is matured in___?
Ans. Wooden cask.

Q7. Most expensive tequila in the world?
Ans. Tequila Connoisseur is most expensive tequila in the world (US$ 225000): passion Azteca, Plantinum liquor bottle by tequila ley 0.925.

Q8. Mention some name of tequila brand?
Ans. Acumbaro, Amate, Chinaco, Corralejo, Centinela, Chamucos, Fortaleza, Herradura.

WHISKY

Q1. What is scotch whisky?

Ans. Scotch Whisky is a distillate made in Scotland from the element of cereals. Water and yeast, all of which nature will in due course replace.

Q2. When consumers ask for a scotch. What exactly do then mean?

Ans. They usually mean a blended Scotch Whisky, that is blend of as many as to individual Scotch Malt and Scotch Grain Whiskies. The wide range of single whiskies available in Scotland ensure the continued high quality and consistency of brands of blended Scotch whisky and year in year out, enables blenders to ensure that all their brands maintain their individual characteristics. Blends whiskies accounts for 98 per cent of all Scotch whisky sold in world markets.

Q3. What is a single whisky?

Ans. It is the product of a single distillery. Most distilleries produce scotch whisky primarily for the purpose of blending, but many retain some of their production for sale as single whiskies. A single Malt whisky is the product of one Malt whiskey distillery and a single grain whisky is the product of the Grain whisky distillery.

Q4. What is a Blended Scotch Whisky?

Ans. A Blended Scotch Whiskey is a blend of a number of distillates each of which separately is entitled to the description "Scotch Whiskey."

The period for which any blended Scotch whisky is regarded as having been matured is that of the most recently distilled of the spirits contained in the blend.

Q5. What is the difference between Scotchs? Irish, Ray and Bourbon Whiskies?

Ans. Scotch Whiskey means whiskey distilled and matured in Scotland and Irish. Whiskey means distilled and matured in Ireland. Whiskey is distilled in Scotland from malted barley in pot stills and from malted and UN malted barley or other cereals in patent stills. The well known brands of Scotch Whiskey are blends of a number of pot still and patent still whiskey. Trish whiskey distillers tend to favour three distillation rater than two as is general in Scotland in the case of Pot Still Whiskey and the range of cereals used is wider.

Q6. What is the origin of the name 'whisky'?

Ans. The term 'whisky' derives from the Gaelic 'using beatha' or usque baugh, meaning' 'water of life' Gaelic is that branch of Celtic spoken in the highland of Scotland.

Q7. What are the main kinds of Scotch Whisky?

Ans. There are two kinds of Scotch Whisky–Malt whisky and Grain whisky. The Malt whisky are divided in to four groups according to the geographical location of the distilleries in which they are made as follow:

1. Lowland Malt whiskey, made South of an imaginary line drawn from Dundee on the east to Greenock or the west.
2. Highland Malt whiskey, made north of that line and, within that area, speyside Malt whiskey from the Valley of the River Spey.
3. Islay Malt Whiskies from the island of Islay.
4. Campbeltown Malt Whiskies from Campbeltown in the Mull of Kintyre.

Each group has its own clearly defined characteristics. Ranging from the lighter Lowland Malt Whiskies to those distilled on Islay which are generally regards as the heaviest malt whiskies. Many blenders regards whiskies distilled in the seaside area as being quite distinctive from highland Malt whiskies.

Malt whiskies which differ considerable in flavour according to the distillery from which then come. Have a more pronounced bouquet and flavour than the Grain whiskies has not been so influenced by geographical factor and it may be distilled anywhere in Scotland.

Q8. What gives Scotch Whiskies, its distinctive flavour and bouquet?

Ans. The distilling process itself is one factor. Scotch Whiskey, after it has been dustilled, contains not only.

Q9. What gives scotch whisky its distinctive flavour and bouquet?

Ans. The distilling process itself is one factor. Scotch Whisky, after it has been distilled, contains not only ethyl alcohol and water but certain secondary constituents. The exact nature of these is not fully understood, but it is believed they include some of the essentials oils from the malted barley and other cereals and substances that derive from the peat.

The natural elements of water, peat and the Scottish climate all certainly have a profound effect on the flavour of scotch source of good, soft after is essential to a distillery. Peat, which is used in the kiln or oven in which the malt is dried, also has an influence that can be detected in the peaty or smoky flavour of many scotch whiskies . The Scottish climate is extremely important. Particularly when the whisky is maturing. At this stage the soft air permeates the casks and works on the whisky, eliminating harsher constituents at exactly the correct rate to produce a mellow whisky.

Q10. Why do whiskies produced in different distilleries vary in flavour?

Ans. This again is a question which it is very difficult answer with certainty. Most people would agree that the water used is the decisive factor. Adjoining distilleries which draw their water from different sources are known produce whiskies that are quite dissimilar in flavour. The size and shape of the stills are also important as are the skill and experience of the men who manage them.

Q11. What is blending? What is its object?

Ans. A number of distilleries sell part of the whisky the distill for consumption as single or unblended whiskies. By the greater part of them production however, is used to make the well known brands of blended whisky that are sold all over the world.

Blending is the art of containing whiskies from several different distilleries malt as well as grain. The combining of malt with grain is known as vatting. A blend will content of anything from 15 to 50 different single whiskies combined in the proportions of a formula that is the secret of the blending company concerned. Blending whisky is a considerable art acquired only after years of experience. Whiskies from different distilleries have a character of their own and, just a people of different temperaments are often incompatible, so some whiskies cannot be blended with certain others if a satisfactory result is to be achieved. The malts and grain in a blend must be chosen to complement and enhance their respective flavours. Thus blending is in no sense a dilution, but the combining of like with like, to produce whisky that brings out the best qualities of each of this constituents parts.

The objective of the blender is first to produce a whisky of a definite and recognizable character. It is of the greatest importance that his blend should never vary from this standard which his customers all over the world have come to expect. His second objective is, therefore, to achieve is consistency.

The blender must also decide when the different single whiskies are ready to be used in his blend. They are brought from the warehouse where they have been maturing to the blending establishment, where they are mixed together in a blending vat. They are usually returned to cask and left to marry for a period of months, before bottling. Some companies prefer to visit their malts and grains separately and solely bring the two together before bottling.

Q12. Where whisky is used in cooking?

Ans. Its is best used in fish and beef dishes and also used in rich dessert.

Q13. What is the percentage of malt and grain whisky in blended scotch whisky?

Ans. There is no fixed percentage and the proportion differ from one blender to the other. No brand owner is willing to reveal the proportion of the different whiskies used, but the bender determined the portion according to the character of the blend. The character is determined not only the proportions of malt and grain whisky which it contains, but also by factors such as age of the individual whisky and the manner in which they combine to bring out the finest qualities in each other.

Q14. What is luxe blended scotch whisky?

Ans. Its is a blend which contains a higher percentage of carefully selected older whisky, hence therefore more expensive whisky.

Q15. When there is an age label on the bottle of blended whisky does it refer to the average of the whisky of that blended?

Ans. No, the law requires that when the age is declared on a label, it must refer to the youngest whisky in the blended. For example if a blend described as begin 12 years old, the youngest whisky in that blend must have been matured for at least 12 years.

Q16. How soon after it is distilled is whisky usually sold?

Ans. The normal practice is for the blender to buy whisky as soon as it is distilled. It's then kept under bond in are hose at the distillery to mature until the blender requires its. By law whisky must mature for minimum of three years, although in practice minimum age is much greater. After blending scotch whisky is usually returned to cask and left further period of several months to allow the constituent whiskies to marry. Its then bottled for sale.

Q17. What are the best blends?

Ans. This is entirely the method of taste. All well-know brands on the market are blended by experts and consumer can be confident that in drinking their product they are drinking whisky consistently blended to bring out the best characteristics of malt and grain whiskies of which it is composed.

Q18. Why some scotch whisky has smoky flavour what cause behind this?

Ans. The smoky flavour of certain whiskies originates from the peat fire over which the green malt is dried prior to grinding and mashing.

Q19. Is it possible to tell the difference between one brand of scotch whisky and another by smell alone?

Ans. Yes, it is possible to differentiate between different well-know established brands of scotch whisky by smell alone if one is sufficiently expert and experienced. The blenders employed by the blending and bottling firms, who blend the different whiskies which go to make the customary brands, are guided by smell alone in producing a uniform product over the years. At the most they moisten their hands with the little of spirit. Usually it is enough to smell the whisky in a glass.

Q20. Does scotch whisky in a bottle lose its with age?

Ans. Once bottled, whisky doesn't lose its strength.

Q21. Does scotch whisky improve in a bottle which is kept sealed?

Ans. No, there is no change in whisky once it has bottled and securely sealed. As oxygen in the air cannot get the whisky the there is no further maturing.

Q22. At what temperature is whisky best served?

Ans. This is entirely a matter of personal choice and no rules. Such as chilling for certain wine. Can be laid down. In the United Kingdom it is usually served at room temperature; but in some overseas the convention has grown up of putting ice the glass.

Q23. What is the alcoholic strength of Scotch Whisky?

Ans. When distilled it is usually reduced for filling into casks at a strength of 68.5 per cent of alcohol by volume.

At bottling, the strength is normally 40 per cent vol. for home trade sale. And 43 per cent vol. For export sale but with occasional variations from those strengths.

Q24. What is a single whisky?

Ans. A single whiskey is the product of one particular distillery.

Q25. What is meant by Saccharify?

Ans. To saccharif means to convert to sugar. In whisky distilling refers to the process which take place during the malting and mash –tun stages by which enzymes in the, malt, referred to as diastase, turn the starch in the cereals into sugar ready for the fermenting action of the yeast.

Q26. What is diastase?

Ans. When conditions to temperature and moisture favour germination, the embryo and associated part of the barley grain secrete a mixture of enzymes commonly knows as diastase. These act to modify and make soluble the starch in the barley, thus preparing it for conversion at alater stage to maltose.

Q27. What is wort?

Ans. Its liquid drawn off the mash-ton in which the malted and unmalted cereals have been mashed with warm water. Wort contains all the sugars of the malt and certain secondary constituents after cooling, it is passed to the fermenting vats.

In malt distilleries the cereals are all malted in grain distilleries a proportion only is malted, the remainder begin unmalted. In some case, grain distilleries do not separate off wort, passing the complete mash to the fermentation vessels.

Q28. What is wash?

Ans. The wash technically becomes wash as soon as yeast is added to start fermentation. However the term is usually used to refer to the liquid at the end of fermentation. It is the wash which forms the raw material of the first distillation in the pot still process and of the only distillation in the patent still process.

Q29. What are the three other names of patent still?

Ans. Continuous still, Coffey's till and column still.

Q30. Why rectification is used in whisky?

Ans. Its mainly done to improve the spirit quality.

Q31. What is meant by proof spirit?

Ans. Proof spirit is a measure of the alcoholic content of beverage. The term originally arose from the old customs method of checking alcoholic content.

Q32. What is worm?

Ans. The worm itself is a coiled copper tube of decreasing diameter attached by the line arm to the head of the pot still and kept continuously cold by running water.

The worm is being replaced gradually by the more modern tabular condenser.

Q33. What are low wines?

Ans. This name given to the product of the first distillation in the pot still process of manufacture.

Q34. What is pot ale?

Ans. Pot ale, alternatively burnt ale is the liquor left in the wash still after the first distillation in the pot still process that is it is the residue of the wash after extraction by distillation of low wines.

Q35. Mention the four regions of scotch whisky?

Ans. Four regions scotch whisky are as follows:

- Low land whiskies
- Campbeltowns
- Islay
- Highlands malt.

Q36. Specialties of Low land whiskies?

Ans. Low land whiskies are the gentlest and sweetest style of scotch.

Q37. Specialties of Campbelt towns whiskies?

Ans. These whiskies are fresh and ozoney.

Q38. Specialties of Islay whiskies?

Ans. Islay produces an instantly recognizable pungent spirit, full of seaweed aromas, and particularly marked by the influence of the peat that fires the drying kilns for the grain.

Q39. Specialties of Highland whiskies?

Ans. Its has soft smokiness as compare to Islay.

Q40. What are Vatted malts?

Ans. Some malts that are blended produce of several single malts, in which they case they are knows as Vatted malts.

Q41. Which scotch whiskies are highly prized?

Ans. The most highly prized scotch whiskies are the single malts. These are whiskies that are produce entirely from malted barley, double distilled.

Q42. What are grain whiskies?

Ans. Whiskies made from corn or unmalted barley are knows as grain whiskies.

Q43. Traditionally method of distilled scotch whiskies is know as___?

Ans. Double distilled in the traditional copper pot stil.

Q44. Whiskies from the state of kentucky are entitled to be called as___?

Ans. Bourbons.

Q45. Kentucky straight bourbon whiskies are mixture of___?

Ans. Its made up of 51 per cent of corn with malted barley and is aged for minimum two years in charred new barrels.

Q46. In scotch whiskies which wood oak is used?

Ans. In this American wood oak is used to imparting great richness to the whiskies.

Q47. Difference between bourbon and Scotch oak barrel?

Ans. In both case American oak is used but difference is in bourbon barrel are heavily charred or toasted, on the insides to a depth of about.

Q48. Standard alcoholic strength of Scotch whiskies?

Ans Its is usually bottled 40 per cent ABV or slightly above.

Q49. Standard alcoholic strength of Bourbon whiskies?

Ans. Its is usually bottled 43-45 per cent ABV.

Q50. Standard alcoholic strength of Tennessee whiskies?

Ans. Its is usually bottled 45 per cent ABV.

Q51. Standard alcoholic strength of Ireland whiskies?

Ans. Its is usually bottled 40 per cent ABV.

Q52. Standard alcoholic strength of Canadian whiskies?

Ans. Its is usually bottled 40 per cent ABV.

Q53. Standard alcoholic strength of Japan whiskies?

Ans. Its is usually bottled 43 per cent ABV.

Q54. Reasons for the greater accessibility of Irish whiskies?

Ans. Its lies in its production process. No peat is used in the kilns, so that there is none of the smoky pungency that is present in some what in scotch whiskies.

Q55. Traditional method of distilled Irish whiskies?

Ans. Its is subjected to a triple distillation by the copper pot still method.

Q56. Traditional method of distilled Canadian whiskies?

Ans. Distillation is by the process, in a gigantic column still.

Q57. Traditional method of distilled Japan whiskies?

Ans. Distillation by pot still method.

Q58. What blend of different grains used in Canadian whiskey?

Ans. The greater proportion of each brand based on an original mash that combines rye, corn and malted barley.

Q59. What are foreshots?

Ans. Foreshots is the term applied to the first fraction of the distillate received during the distillation of the low wines in the spirit still used in the pot still process of manufacture. They form the first raw runnings of this second distillation and their collection is terminated by the judgment of the still man. The following fraction of the distillate is the potable spirit. The foreshots are returned to the still, together with the feints.

Q60. What are feints?

Ans. Feints is the name given to the third section of the distillate received from the second distillation in the pot still process. They form the undesirable last running's of the distillation. As noted above, they are returned with the foreshots to the spirit still when it is charged with low wines.

The term is also applied to the first the last running's from the patent still, in which process they are returned to the wash for re-distillation.

The feints are foreshots from the last distillation of the season are kept for adding to the first low wines of the succeeding season.

Q61. What are spent less?

Ans. Spent lees are the residue in the spirit still after the distillation of the foreshots, potable spirits and feints. They usually treated and run to waste.

Q62. What is draff?

Ans. Draff is the spent grain left in the mash-tun after the liquor, wort, has been drawn off. It represents as a rule about 25 per cent of the malt and unmalted cereals, if any, put into the mash-tun. Draff enjoys a large market in cattle food.

Q63: What are the principal by-products of scotch whisky?

Ans. The liquids and solids remaining after distillation are not wasted, nor are they allowed to pollute rivers or coastlines. In recent years the scotch whisky. Industry has invested heavily in developing methods of treating the residue of distillation so that it now makes an important contribution to the animal food stuffs industry.

Most distilleries now possess by-products plants or, in the case of smaller distilleries in remote areas, send their waste materials to the area plants which process it into dark grains. These are extremely rich in protein and are sold in pelletized form to farmers who use them to enrich cattle food.

Grain whisky distilleries usually recover the carbon dioxide produced during the fermentation stage. This has several applicate to industry and in the production of soft drinks.

Q64. Name some deluxe scotch whisky?

Ans. Johnny Walker Deluxe (Blue label), Royal Salute, King of Kings.

Q65. Name some premium scotch whiskies?

Ans. Johnny Walker Black Label, Black Dog, Johnny Walker Swing, Chivas Regal.

Q66. Name some regular scotch whiskies?

Ans. Johnny Walker Red label, Vat 69, Cutty Sark, Teachers, Black and White, 100 Pipers, Dimple Haig and Haig, Ballantine, Grant's, Dewar.

Q67. Name some malt whiskies?

Ans. Glenlivet, Cardhu, Glennfidich, Glenmorgan, Mortlach, Laphroaig, Little Mill, Glenfarclas.

Q68. Explain Vatted malt?

Ans. A vatted malt is produced by marrying together malt whiskies from several distilleries.

Q69. What is cask strength whisky?

Ans. This is whisky sold at the strength taken from the cask. Cask strength is normally 60 per cent AV .

Q70. What is grist?
Ans. The dried malt is ground finely and is then know as grist.

Q71. What is spent-lees?
Ans. Waste material produce during distillation.

Q72. What is Draff?
Ans. The solids which remains at the base of the mash rare removed and used for cattle feed.

Q73. What is the difference in the basic ingredients used for scotch and for Bourbons?
Ans. Scotch uses Malted barley, bourbon uses corn.

Q74. Name some famous Bourbons?
Ans. Jim Bream, Old Parr, Old Granddad, Jack Daniels, Old Crow, Old Forsyer, Old Taylor, Kentucky, Old Heaven Hill, Early Times, Wild Turkey.

Q75. Name some famous Canadian whiskey?
Ans. Old Mr. Boston, Seagrams V.O., Canadian Club, Canadian River, Canadian Mist, Black Velvet, Hiram Walker.

Q76. Name some Iris Whisky?
Ans. Paddyes, Tullamore Dew, Old Bushmills Jhon Janeson.

Q77. What is light whiskies?
Ans. Light whiskies is product of various cereals grains distilled at 160-180 proof before been reduce and stored in used or Uncharred barrels.

Q78. Name some blended scotch whiskies?
Ans. Ballantine, J&b, Chives Regal, Cutty Sark, Old Smuggler, Passport, Vat 69, Teachers, White Horse.

Q79. Name some malt scotch?
Ans. Cardhu,Talisker, Balvenie, Glenlivet, Glenfiddich, Glendronach, Aultomore.

Q80. Name some famous Tennessee?
Ans. Jack Daniels, George Dickel.

Q81. Name some Canadian whiskies?

Ans. Canadian Club, Seagram's Crown Royal, Windros, G&W Special.

Q82. Name some American bourbon whisky?

Ans. Southern Comfort, Old Grand Dad, I.W. Harper, Old Crow, Old Turkey, Old Hickory, Jim Beam.

Q83. Mention name of some Indian deluxe whisky ?

Ans. Peter Scot, Single Malt, Royal Challenge, Vintage, McDowell's, Signature, McDowell's Premium, Colonel's Special.

Q84. Mention name of so:me Indian regular brands?

Ans. Director's Special, Aristocrat, Diplomat, White House, Mcdowell's No. 1, Solan No. 1, Bagpiper.

CHAPTER

9 Cocktails

Q1. What is a cocktail?
Ans. A mixed drink containing at least one alcoholic beverage with addition of juices, liqueurs or other flavouring agents.

Q2. List some type of cocktails?
Ans. Blended Drinks– Using in blender.

- Champagne cocktail – Using Champagne as the alcoholic base.
- Cobblers–Wine and sprit based–usually tall drinks.
- Collins–Tall, hot weather drinks.
- Coolers–Similar to Collins but with a fruit peel spiral– sprit or wine based.
- Fizzes–Drinks topped with sodas.
- Frappe's–Usually a liquer served on crushed ice.
- Highballs–A spirit with a mixer.
- Juleps–Containing mint with wine or whiskey.
- Pick-me- ups–To aid digestion.
- Pousse Café–Layered drinks of specific densities.

Q3. What is the difference between a Rob Ray and a Manhattan?
Ans. Rob Ray is Scotch and Vermouth is a Manhattan is a Bourbon and Vermouth.

Q4. Name ten whisky based cocktail?
Ans. Rusty Nail, Manhattan, Rob Roy Godfather, Old Fashioned, Mamic Tailor, Scotch Mist, Whisky Sour, Bobbie Burns, Morning Glory.

Q5. What is used to make a pink Lady blush?
Ans. Grenadine Syrup.

Q6. What is the flavour of grenadine syrup?
Ans. Pomegranate.

Q7. What is used to colour a Pink Gin?
Ans. Angustra bitters.

Q8. What is used to flavour tonic water?
Ans. Quinine.

Q9. Name Ten Gin based cocktail?
Ans. Martini, Singapore Sling, Pink Lady, White Lady, Blue Lady, Pink Gin Tom Collins, Orange Blossom, Gibson, Gimlet.

Q10. Which glass is used to serve a Brandy Alexander?
Ans. Champagne Saucer.

Q11. Sidecar uses which liqueur?
Ans. Cointreau.

Q12. Name ten brandy based cocktails?
Ans. Alexander, Sidecar, Between the Sheets, B&B, Stinger, Horses Neck, Harvard, Gotham, Cassisco, Piscola.

Q13. Which cocktail contains all three types of rum?
Ans. Zombie.

Q14. Which cocktail uses white rum, coconut milk and Pineapple juice?
Ans. Pine Colada.

Q15. Rum and cola is known as___?
Ans. Cube Libre.

Q16. Name Ten rum based cocktail?
Ans. Cuban Manhattan, Treacle, Redwood, Black Rose, Caipirinha, Beja Flor, Boston Cooler, Daiquiri, Mojito, Mai Tai.

Q17. A Black Russian contains___&___?
Ans. Vodka and Kahlua.

Q18. What is the difference between a screwdriver and a Harvey Wallbanger?
Ans. The Wallbanger contains Galliano.

Q19. Name ten vodka based cocktails?
Ans. Screwdriver, Harvey Wallbanger, Salty Dog, Moscow Mule,

Vodkatini, Black Russian, Blood Mary Vodka Mist, Godmother, Blue Waters, Martini.

Q20. Name ten tequila based cocktails.
Ans. Tequila Sunrise, Margarita, Brava Bull, Mocking Bird. El Diablo, Brave Bull, Cactus Banger, Chimayo, Tequini.

Q21. Name 10 champagne based cocktails.
Ans. Bucks Fizz, Black Velvet, Rolls Royce, Jackie, Kir Royal, Alfonso, Bellini, Mimosa, Royal Highland, Hemingway, Ambosia.

Q22. What is Kir?
Ans. A combination of white wine and crème de cassis (Black currant flavoured liqueur) Kir Royale is whit champagne.

Q23. What is a grasshopper?
Ans. A cocktail of crème de menthe and white crème de cacao and cream.

Q24. What are Pimms?
Ans. Wine and fruit juice based coolers.

Q25. What is Gomme syrup?
Ans. A thick sugar syrup.

Q26. What are the three components of cocktails?
Ans. The three components of cocktail:
- The base
- The modifier
- The flavourings and colouring agents.

Q27. What are the three conditions of successful cocktail?
Ans.
- The taste
- The appearance
- The name.

Q28. What are the different way of serving cocktails?
Ans. Float, frappe, frozen, on the rocks, straight up.

Q29. What is float?
Ans. The term refers to when alcohol is poured over the mixing spoon so that its float on the top of other ingredients.

Q30. What are the essential equipments for cocktails?

Ans. Sifter, Pourer, Shot Glass, Measures, Paring Knife, Salt Saucer, Bar Strainer, Cocktails Sticks, Straws, Mixing Glass, Cocktail Shaker, Blender, Straws.

Q31. Standard garnish of dry martini?

Ans. Olive or twist of lemon in the drink.

Q32. Standard garnish of Grasshopper?

Ans. Cherry on rim glass.

Q33. Standard garnish of daiquiri?

Ans. Cherry in the drink.

Q34. Standard garnish of bloody marry?

Ans. Stick of celery on the drinks and lemon wheel.

Q35. Standard garnish of Gibson?

Ans. Cocktail onion.

Q36. Standard garnish of kir?

Ans. Its has no garnish.

Q37. Standard garnish of Manhattan?

Ans. Cherry in the drink.

Q38. Standard garnish of Pina colada?

Ans. Wedge of pine apple and cherry on rim.

Q39. Standard garnish of Screwdriver?

Ans. Orange wheel on rim of glass and two black straws.

Q40. Standard garnish of Margarita?

Ans. Salt frosted glass, wheel of lemon in the drink.

CHAPTER

10 Liqueurs

Q1. What is liqueur?
Ans. Any spirit mixer with flavourings and containing at least 2.5 per cent sugar by volume may be called a liqueur.

Q2: When is a liqueur called a Crème?
Ans. When it contains 2.5–10 per cent sweetener.

Q3. When did liqueurs gain popularity?
Ans. During the 1930's on America due to prohibition, strong alcoholic brews being made clandestinely. Liqueurs were used to tone down the fiery nature of such spirits.

Q4. Name some flavouring ingredients used to flavour liqueurs?
Ans. Leaves, blossoms, flowers, seeds, beans, nuts, kernels, berries, herbs, roots, spices, citrus fruit, other fruits.

Q5. Give the flavour, colour, Abv, country of origin and one cocktail of following Liqueurs.
Ans.

Name	*Flavourings*	*Colour*	*ABV*	*Country of Orign*	*Cocktail*
Advocaat	Oranges, lemon Cherries,vanilla	Yellow as tinned custard	Around 17%	Dutch	Snowball
Amaretto	Almonds, apricots	Golden amber	Around 28%	Italy	God-mother
Anis	Anise berries	White (like water)	Around 25%	France	
Apricot brandy	apricot	Golden	Around 43%	Hungary, France	Angle face

Contd...

Name	*Flavourings*	*Colour*	*ABV*	*Country of Orign*	*Cocktail*
Baileys Irish cream	Chocolate, coffee	Light brown	Around 17%	Iceland	
Crème de banana	Banana	Light yellow	Around 25-30 %	France	Oraca-bessa
Curacao	Bitter Orange	Golden	Around 27-40%	Holland	Oasis
Irish mist	Honey & spices	Golden	40%	Iceland	
Kahlua	Coffee	Darkbrown	26.5%	Mexico	Black Russian
Kummel	Caraway	White (like water)	Around 35-41%	Mexico	Tovarich
Mailbu	Coconut milk	White	24%	England	Pina colada
Tia maria	Coffee & spices	Brown	26.5%	Jamica	Sunburn
Gold wasser	Aniseed, caraway, citrus fruits	White (water)	40%	German	Golden slipper
Peach brandy	Peach	White (water)	30-36%	France	Wally
Drambuie	Honey and herbs	Golden	40%	Scotland	Rusty nail
Gallino	Anise, Vanilla	Golden Yellow	35%	Italy	Milano
Maraschino	Marasca cherries	White (water)	50%	Italian	Tropical cocktail

Q6. Mention the method of producing liqueurs?

Ans. There are two methods:

A: Heat or infusion method.

B: Cold or maceration method.

Q7. What is Orgeat syrup?

Ans. Simply sweetened almond syrup with a little orange flower water.

CHAPTER

11 Cigars

Q1. When first cigars is made?

Ans. First made in Spain in Italy 18 century. Using Cuban tobacco.

Q2. Mention the structure of cigars?

Ans. Its has three parts:

- Filler
- Binder
- Wrapper.

Q3. Different types of cigars?

Ans. Cuban cigars, Partagas cigar, Aston cigar, Acid cigar, Cohiba cigar, Macanudo cigar, Pardon cigar, Montecristo cigar and Arturo fuente cigar.

Q4. What are the common names for cigars names?

Ans.

Name	*Length*	*Ring Gauge*
Corona	5½ to 6	42 to 45
Panatela	5½ to 6½	34 to 38
Lonsdale	6 to 6½	42 to 44
Churchill	6 ½ to 7	46 to 48
Robusto	4½ to 5	48 to 50
Toro	6 to 6½	48 to 50
President	7 to 8½	52 to 60
Torpedo (cone shaped head)	5½ to 6½	46 to 52

Q5. What is ring gauge?

Ans. Which determines the thickness of cigar knows as ring gauge.

Q6. Storage temperature of cigars?

Ans. 15°-18°c between 55 to 60 per cent of humidity is the storing temperature of cigars.

Q7. Most expensive cigar in the world?

Ans. BEHIKE cigars cost each cigar $420.

CHAPTER

12 Food Accompliments

Dish	*Cover*	*Accompliments*	*Remarks*
1	*2*	*3*	*4*
Meat Roast Beef (Boeuf roti)	Joint knife & Fork Hot joint plate	French and English mustard Horse-radish pudding Roast gravy	
Roast Lamb (Agneau roti)	As above	Mint sauce Roast gravy	It is traditional in certain areas of the country to offer either mint sauce or red currant jelly with roast lamb. On occasion both may be offered
Roast Mutton	As above	Red currant jelly (saddle or leg) Onion sauce (shoulder) Roast gravy	
Roast Pork (Porc roti)	As above	Sage and onion stuffing Apple sauce Roast gravy	
Paultry Chicken (Poulet roti)	Joint knife and fork Hot joint plate	Bread sauce, Roast gravy, Parsley and thyme stuffing	
Duck (Caneton roti)	As above	Sage and onion stuffing Apple sauce, Water cress, Roast gravy	
Goose (Oie roti)	As above	Sage and onion stuffing Apple sauce, Roast gravy	

Contd...

1	*2*	*3*	*4*
Turkey (Dindonneau)	As above	Cranberry sauce, Bread sauce Chestnut stuffing, Chipolatas, Game chips, Watercress, Roast gravy	
Grapefruit cocktail	Coupe Doily on sideplate grapefruit spoon or teaspoon	Castor sugar	Other fruit cocktails served as a grapefruit cocktail e.g., Florida cocktail
ATC Juices de tomate	5 oz globet/ small tumbler or club shaped glass. Dailly on sideplate Teaspoon	Warcester sauce	Worcester sauce: bottle shaken, lid removed. Pace on doily on sideplate head of cover. Serve tomato juice chilled and decorate edge of glass with twist of lemon
Oysters	Soup plate or welled silver dish filled with crushed ice and placed on underplate Oyster fork Finger bowl filled with lukewarm water and slice of lemon Doily on sideplate at the top left hand corner of the cover Spare serviette	Cayenne pepper peppermill Chilli vinegar Tabasco sauce (Oyster cruet set) Half a lemon Brown bread and butter	Oyster are normally offered 6 per portion. If another 6 are required then a fresh service would be laid, Oysters are served in the deep half of the shell on the crushed ice surrounding the half a lemon
SNAILS (Les escargots)	Snail tongs: left of cover Snail fork: right of cover Snail disk: Which is round and has 6-12 indentations to hold the snail shells doily on under plate	Brown bread and butter	Snails shell are placed in the snail dish with their openings uppermost to stop garlic bitter running out

Contd...

1	*2*	*3*	*4*
SMOKED SALMON (Saumon fume)	Fish knife and fork Cold fish plate	Cayenne pepper peppermill segment of lemon Brown bread and butter	If not pre-portioned in leder than the side of smoked salmon would be carved on the buffet
CAVIARE	Caviare or fish knife on right hand side of the cover cold fish plate	Hot breakfast toast Butter Segments of lemon Fnnely chopped shallots Sieved had boiled yolk and white of egg	Size of portion here will be approximately 30 gms or 1 oz
CHILLED MELON (Melon frappe)	Sweet spoon and fork Cold fish plate Teaspoon if Charentaise malon is offered	Ground ginger Castor sugar	Variety of melon normally offered would be honey, Cantaloups.Ogen, Charentaise
Fresh Prawns (Les crevettes roses)	Wine globlet on doily on an under plate Fish knife & fork cold fish plate finger bowl as for gulls eggs spare serviette	Brown bread and butter sauce mayonnaise	
ASPARAGUS Asperges au beurre ondue	Asparagus rack grid serviette As paragus tongs right of cover Hot/ cold joint plate joint fork Finger bowl as for gulls eggs and a spare serviette	If served hot hollandaise sauce or beurre fondue If served cold: sauce vinaigratte	The joint fork is placed upside on the right of the cover so that joint plate when placed on the fork is tilted from right to left. The asparagus when being served should have the tips on the plate, the lower part, so that when the accompanying sauce is served it settles over the tips of asparagus. Asparagus my be served either as

Contd...

1	2	3	4
			an hors-d-oeuvre substitute or as a separate vegetable course
Artichoke	Joint fork on right of cover Fingerbowl Doily on an under plate spare napkin Hot/cold fish plate as appropriates	If served hot: Holland sauce or beurre fondue If served Cold: Sauce vinaigrette	Globe artichoke may be served either hot or cold as an hors-d'oeuvre substitute or asa separate vegetable course.
Pate de foie gras	Side knife Sweet fork Cold fish plate	Hot breakfast toast with crusts removed cut into triangles and served in a napkin on a side plate	True plate is made from goose liver. Often seen on the menu as pate' maison made according to the recipe of the 'house'
SHELL FISH COCKTAIL (Cocktail de crevettes)	Teaspoon Oyster fork Shelfish cocktail holder Doily on a side plate	Brown bread and butter	The table ware required may be placed either on the right and left of the cover or on the side plate on either side of the shellfish cocktail holder
AVOCADO (Avocado vinaigrette/ aux crevettes)	Cold Fish plate Teaspoon	Brown bread and butter	On occasions ax special avocado dish is used replacing the cold fish plate
SOUPS MINTESTRONI	Soup spoon Soup plate Under plate	Grated Parmesan cheese Grilled flutes	Clear soup heavily garnished with assoorate vegetables and spaghetti
ONION SOUP (Soup a l' oignon)	Soup spoon Soup plate Under plate	Grated Parmesan cheese Grilled flutes	French onion soup
CONSOMME	Sweet spoon Consommé cup and saucer Fish plate	Depending on garnished	

Contd...

1	2	3	4
CONSOMME EN GELEE	As for consommé		Jelled cleat soup
BOUILLABAISSE	Soup plate Under plate Fish knife/fork Sweet spoon	Thin slice of French bread dipper in oil and grilled	'Bouillabaisse' a Mediterranean fish stew
POACHED SALMON (Saumon poche) (served hot)	Fish knife and fork Hot fish plate	Hollandaise Sauce Mousseline	
(Served Cold)	Fish knife and fork Cold fish plate		
MUSSELS (Moules mariniere)	Soup plate Under plate Fish knife/fork Sweet spoon	Brown bread and butter Cayenne pepper	A soup plate is used here owing to the large amount of sauce offered
COLD LOBSTER (Homard)	Fish knife and fork Lobster pick soare plate for the sell finger bowl cont-aining luke warm water and a slice of lemon Spare serviette	Sauce mayonnaise	The lobster pick would be used to help extract the flesh from the claw of the lobster
FISH (Fried)	Fish knife and fork Hot fish plate	Segmants of lemon or slice of lemon with skin removed Sauce: Tartare Remoulade Gribiche	The three sauce mentioned are all cold sauce with a mayonnaise base
FISH (Grilled)	As above	Lemon as above Cold sauce as above Hat sauce: Bearnaise Tyrolienne	
Fish (poached)	As above	Lemon as above Cold sauce as above Hollandaisa sauce Mousselian sauce Beurre fondue	

Contd...

1	*2*	*3*	*4*
BORTSCH	Soup plate Under plate Sweet spoon	1. Sour cream 2. Beetroot juice 3. Bouchees filled with a duck paste served in the order listed	Brotsh is a duch flavoured consommé. Garnished with duck diced beef & turned vegetables. Although a consommé type soup a soup plate is used as part of the cover because of the large amount of garnished and accompaniments offered
TURTEL (Torue vraieaux	Consomme cup Consomme saucer Fish plate Sweet spoon	Brown bread and butter Segments of lemon cheese straws Mersure of sherry	The segment of lemon may be offered in a lemon press. The sherry would either be added in the kitchen Immediately before serving or from the gueridon at the table by heating the sherry in a ladle ever a lamp
FARINACEOUS DISHES SPAGHETTI	Joint fork Sweet spoon Hoy Soup plate on an under plate	Grated Parmesan	The joint fork is placed on the right hand side of the cover and the dessart spoon on the left
FISH DISHES Grilled Herring (Hareng grille')	Fish knife and fork Hot fish plate	Mustard sauce	
Chowder	Hot soup bowl on an under plate with a napkin	Crushed water biscuits. Sherry peppers & rum	Soup spoon (r)
Souffle	Hot sweet plate (dessert plate)	Sauce anglaise or brandy butter or brandy cream	Dessert fork (L) Dessert spoon (R)

CHAPTER

13

Matching Food with Wine

WINE WITH APPETIZERS

Appetizers	*Dessert and Fortified Wine*	*Red Wine*	*White Wine*	*Sparkling Wine*	*Rose Wine*
Antipasti	Marsala	Barbera Bardolino Dolcetto Zinfandel	Muscadet Verdicchio		
Baked ricotta on toast			Chardonnay		
Blinis				Sparkling Shiraz	
Canapes	Sherry oloroso			Champagne, Champagne – blanc-de-noirs, Spanish cava, Italian-prosecco,	
Chinese dumplings				Champagne blanc-de-noirs	
Consommés	Sherry manzanilla				
Fish pate			Sauvignon Blanc: pouilly – fume/sancerre	Spanish cava	
Garlic bread		Valdepenas			
Liver pate			Pinot gris/ pinot grigio		
Olives	Sherry fino Sherry–manzanilla Sherry–amontillado	Zinfandel	Retsina Verdelho		

Contd...

Appetizers	*Dessert and Fortified Wine*	*Red Wine*	*White Wine*	*Sparkling Wine*	*Rose Wine*
Rich pates			Chateauneuf-du-pape, Coteaux-du-lyon	Sparkling shiraz	Dry & still
Salted nuts	Marsala Sherry–Manzanilla, Sherry amontillado		Montilla verdelho		
Smoked salmon		Pinot noir,	Sauvignon Blanc: pouilly–fume/ sancerre		
Spanish tapas	Sherry amontillado, Sherry fino, Sherry oloroso,			Spanish cava	
Stuffed mushroom		Valpolicella, Pinot: german spatsbur-gunder			

WINE WITH BEEF

Beef	*Dessert and Fortified Wine*	*Red Wine*	*White Wine*	*Sparkling Wine*	*Rose Wine*
Barbecued beef ribs		Shiraz/syrah, Malbec, Beaujolias, Zinfandel			Off-dry & white zinfan-del
Beef stroganoff		Barbera, Cote-du–rhone			
Beef wellington		Barolo, Rioja, Bordeaux, Malbec, Hermitage, Shiraz/syrah, Barbaresco, Beaujolais-Moulin–A-vent,			

Contd...

Beef	*Dessert and Fortified Wine*	*Red Wine*	*White Wine*	*Sparkling Wine*	*Rose Wine*
Casserole & stews		Barolo, Rioja, Bordeaux, Malbec, Hermitage, Shiraz/syrah, Barbaresco, Beaujolais-Moulin–A-vent, Amarone, Cornas, Copertinto, Chateauneuf-pape,Shiraz/syrah			
Cheese burger		Cabernet-sauvignon, Merlot, Rioja, Zinfandel			
Chateaubriand		Cabernet–sauvignon, Crozes-hermitage			
Corned beef	Sherry palo cortado	Bordeaux, Cabernet Sauvignon	Pinot–blanc, Sauvignon–blanc		
Rare steak		Hermitage, Malbec, Crozes-hermitage			
Kebabs		Valdepenas			
Tenderloin		Chianti, Malbec			
Steak		Petit syrah, Syrah, Tempranillo, Gigondas, Chianti–classico, Pinot noir, Barolo, Rioja, Bordeaux, Malbec, Hermitage, Shiraz/syrah, Barbaresco, Beaujolais–Moulin–A-vent,			

Contd...

Beef	*Dessert and Fortified Wine*	*Red Wine*	*White Wine*	*Sparkling Wine*	*Rose Wine*
Shepherd's pie		Bordeaux, Zinfandel	Chardonnay, sauvignon		
Roast beef		Barolo, Barbaresco, Burgundy, Malbec, Merlot, Rioza, Syrah, Shiraz/syrah, Dolcetto, Burgundy, Bordeaux–saint-emilion.			
Meat balls		Malbec, Nemea, Merlot, Crozes-heimitage.			

WINE WITH BREADS

Breads	*Dessert and Fortified Wine*	*Red Wine*	*White Wine*	*Sparkling Wine*	*Rose Wine*
Brioche bread	Semillon Botrytised/ sauternes		Muscadet	Champagne	
Butter milk cheese bread			Chablis		
French baguette	Monbazillac, Semillon botrytised/ sauternes	Merlot, Pinot noir,	Burgundy, Chardonnay, Muscadet, Riesling, Silvaner, Fume blanc.		
Multi grain		Merlot, Pinot noir, Sancerre, Beaujolais (gamay)	Muscadet, Silvaner, Chablis		
Italian bread			Pinot gris/ pinot grigio, Soave, Sauvignon-blanc,		
Potato bread			Chardonnay		
Challah (egg bread)			Chardonnay, Riesling.		

CHEESE WITH WINE

Cheese	Dessert and Fortified Wine	Red Wine	White Wine	Sparkling Wine	Rose Wine
Parmesan		Amarone, Petit syrah, Syrah, Tempranillo, Gigondas, Chianti–classico, Pinot noir, Barolo, Rioja, Bordeaux, Malbec, Hermitage, Shiraz/syrah, Barbaresco, Beaujolais–Moulin–A-vent,			Dry & still
Blue cheese	Barsac, Port; vintage, Sherry oloroso, Tokaji, Sherry palo-cortado,	Cabernet sauvignon	Passito		
Brie	Riesling late harvest	Beaujolias chiroubles, Burgundy chassagne-montrachet	Boreaux: Semillion/ sauvignon blanc. Chardonnay, Pinot blanc, Sauvignon blanc: pouilly-fume.		
Cheddar	Port; vintage	Barolo, Rioja, Bordeaux, Malbec, Hermitage, Shiraz/syrah, Barbaresco, Beaujolais-Moulin–A-vent, Amarone, Cornas, Copertinto, Chateauneuf-pape, Shiraz/syrah			

Contd...

Cheese	*Dessert and Fortified Wine*	*Red Wine*	*White Wine*	*Sparkling Wine*	*Rose Wine*
Camembert		Bordeaux pomerol, Bordeaux saint–emilion	Pinot blanc, Pinot gris, Chenin blanc off–dry.		Dry & still
Cheese founde	Riesling late harvest		Jurancon, Silvaner, Riesling–spatiese Jurancon		
Emmenthal			Chardonnay		
Goat	Sherry-oloroso	Cabernet–franc, Chinon, Merlot, sancerre	Sauvignon-blanc, soave	Champagne, Sparkling shiraz	
Swiss		Chianti Rioja, Dolcetto	Sauvignon blanc, Chardonnay, Gewürz-traminer		

WINE WITH CHICKEN

Chicken	*Dessert and Fortified Wine*	*Red Wine*	*White Wine*	*Sparkling Wine*	*Rose Wine*
Grilled chicken			Chardonnay, Chateauneuf-du-pape, Semillion		
Herb Roast chicken			Trebbiano		
Roasted chicken		Bardolino, Bergerac, Pinot Noir, Bordeaux-medoc	Burgundy, Semillon, Burgundy-macon, Chateauneuf-du–pape		
Fried chicken		Barbera, Pinot noir,	Sauvignon blanc,	Champagne	Dry & Still

Contd...

Chicken	*Dessert and Fortified Wine*	*Red Wine*	*White Wine*	*Sparkling Wine*	*Rose Wine*
		Rioja, Dolcetto, Valpoliocella	Chardonnay, Gewürztraminer Pinot blanc, Riesling		
Chicken pie		Bordeaux saint-emilion	Sauvignon blanc, Chateauneuf-du-pape		
Chicken stir fry		Merlot, Rioja	Gewürztraminer semillion		
Chicken with creamy sauce			Burgundy, Semillon, Burgundy-macon, Chateauneuf-du–pape. Pinot blanc, Pinot gris	Champagne	
Chicken with lemon sauce			Riesling, Semillon, chablis		
Chicken cold cuts		Zinfandel			
Barbequed chicken			Chenin blanc		Off dry & white zin-fandel

WINE WITH LAMB

Lambs	*Dessert and Fortified Wine*	*Red Wine*	*White Wine*	*Sparkling Wine*	*Rose Wine*
Braised lamb shanks		Malbec, Crozes-hermitage, shiraz			
Herb roasted lamb		Malbec, Crozes-hermitage, Shiraz, Valdepenas, Bordeaux–margaux			

Contd...

Lambs	*Dessert and Fortified Wine*	*Red Wine*	*White Wine*	*Sparkling Wine*	*Rose Wine*
Irish stews		Malbec, Madiran, Bordeaux, Cabernet sauvignon	Sauvignon blanc, Gruner–veltliner		
Lamb chops (grilled)		Amarone, Rioja, Merlot, Malbec, Madiran, Bordeaux, Cabernet Sauvignon			
Lamb kebabs		Pinot noir, Zinfandel, Shiraz, Valdepenas			
Shepherd's pie		Bordeaux, Zinfandel, Cabernet-Sauvignon	Chardonnay, Sauvignon blanc, Gruner–veltliner		
Roast lamb		Barolo, Cahors, Chianti, Tempranillo, Rioja, Merlot, Malbec, Madiran, Bordeaux, Cabernet Sauvignon			
Lamb ragout with roasted sweet		Cabernet sauvignon			
Lamb with garlic & rose mary		Dao-Portugal, Bordeaux Pauillac			

WINE WITH SEAFOODS AND SHELL FISH

Sea Food & Shell Fish	*Dessert and Fortified Wine*	*Red Wine*	*White Wine*	*Sparkling Wine*	*Rose Wine*
Fish & chips		Rose	Semillon, Bergerac, Verdicchio		
Grilled salmon			Chardonnay, Sauvignon blanc, Gewürztraminer, Viognier		
Grilled sardines	Sherry fino				
Grilled turbot			Chateauneuf–du–pape Burgundy chassagne-montrachet		
Lobster			Condrieu, Viognier, Semillon, Chardonnay, Sauvignon blanc, Gewürztraminer, Viognier, Burgundy–chevalier-montrachet	Champagne Champagne blanc-de-noirs	
Scallops			Burgundy–chevalier-montrachet. Chardonnay, Burgundy–corton-charlegmagne	Champagne	
Fried shrimp, clams, oyster			Chardonnay, Pinot-gris	Champagne	
Mussels			Aligote, Chenin blanc, Muscadet, Semillon, Chenin blanc Aligote		
Oyster			Chenin blanc Muscadet Pinot blanc Sauvignon blanc	Champagne Champagne–brut Sparkling-wine	

WINE WITH PASTA DISHES

Pasta	*Dessert and Fortified Wine*	*Red Wine*	*White Wine*	*Sparkling Wine*	*Rose Wine*
Cannelloni		Barbaresco, Bardolino, Chianti,			
Pasta bolognese		Sangiovese			
Macaroni & cheese		Merlot			
Pasta in carbonara		Cotes–du–rhone, Dolcetto, Merlot, Rioja, Syrah.	Orvieto, Trebbiano.		
Pasta in pesto			Sauvignon -blanc		
Pasta in tomato sauce		Amarone, Chianti, Zinfandel, Primivito			
Penne arrabbiata		Mrontepulciano D' abruzzo			
Vegetable lasagne		Chianti, Rioja	Chardonnay, Sauvignon–blanc, Chateauneuf-Du—pape		
Pasta in vodka sauce			**Gewürztraminer** Chardonnay, Sauvignon–blanc, Chateauneuf-Du—pape		
Pasta in primavera sauce			**Gewürztraminer** Chardonnay, Sauvignon–blanc, Chateauneuf-Du—pape		
Pasta in oil based sauce		Dolcetto, Chianti, Rioja	**Gewürztraminer** Chardonnay, Sauvignon–blanc, Chateauneuf-Du—pape		
Pasta in alfredo sauce		Dolcetto, Chianti, Rioja	**Gewürztraminer** Chardonnay, Sauvignon–blanc		

WINE WITH PORK DISHES

Pork	*Dessert and Fortified Wine*	*Red Wine*	*White Wine*	*Sparkling Wine*	*Rose Wine*
Bacon		Pinot noir Shiraz/syrah, Tempranillo			
Ham		Pinot noir, Beaujolais-Moulin–A-vent, Burgundy-pommard	Chardonnay, Sauvignon-Blanc	Shiraz	
Parma ham			Burgundy, Cote-Chalonnaise	Lambrusco secco	
Charcuterie		Pinot noir, Beaujolais, Chinon, Fleurie.	Gewürztraminer Muscadet, Vouvray.		Dry & still
Pork chops		Pinot noir, Syrah, Morellino–Di-scansano			
Pork chops (grilled)		Chianti, Rioja, Zinfandel, Pinot Noir	Viognier		
Salami		Barbera, Taurasi, Valpolicella	Lambrusco secco		
Roast pork		Bordeaux-medoc, Merlot, Pinot noir Syrah Ribera–del-duero. Rioja Rully	Chateauneuf-Du—pape Riesling-Spatlese		Dry & still
Sausages		Flurie, Malbec, Kekfrankos, Fleurie, Saint-joseph, Valpolicella, Beaujolais, Corbieres, Pinot noir			
Prosciutto Tenderloin	Sherry fino	Chianti, Malbec			

WINE WITH VEGETABLES DISHES

Vegetables & Salads	*Dessert and Fortified Wine*	*Red Wine*	*White Wine*	*Sparkling Wine*	*Rose Wine*
Asparagus in hollandaise		Burgundy-meursault			
Caprese salad		Pinot noir	Semillon, Sauvignon-blanc		
Fried mushroom		Pinot noir			
Grilled eggplant Moùssaka		Tempranillo Cote–du–rhone, Nemea, Gigondas			
Ratatouille		Barbera, Barbaresco, Barolo, Cahors, Chianti, Tempranillo, Rioja, Merlot, Malbec, Madiran, Bordeaux, Cabernet-sauvignon, Rose,			
Baked vegetables		Fitou			
Minestrone soup			Soave Sauvignon-blanc		
Carrot soup			Viognier, Riesling-spatlese		
Corn on the cob			Chardonnay, Collio		
Salad Nicoise					Dry & still
French fries	Riesling late harvest		Sauvignon-blanc		
Gazpacho	Sherry fino		Soave		
Tomato & mozzarella salad			Pinot gris/ pinot grigio		

Contd...

Vegetables & Salads	*Dessert and Fortified Wine*	*Red Wine*	*White Wine*	*Sparkling Wine*	*Rose Wine*
Casseroles & stews		Cornas, Amarone, Hermitage Copertinto Barbera, Barbaresco, Barolo, Cahors, Chianti, Tempranillo, Rioja, Merlot, Malbec, Madiran, Bordeaux, Cabernet-sauvignon, Rose			

WINE WITH INDIAN FOOD

Indian Dishes	*Dessert and Fortified Wine*	*Red Wine*	*White Wine*	*Sparkling Wine*	*Rose Wine*
Chicken korma			Viognier		
Chicken tikka		Cotes-du-ventoux	Viognier	Champagne	
Curries–spices			Riesling Off dry, Viognier	Sparkling wine	Dry & still
Rogan josh		Cornas, Amarone, Hermitage Copertinto Barbera, Barbaresco, Barolo, Cahors, Chianti, Tempranillo, Rioja, Merlot, Malbec, Madiran, Bordeaux, Cabernet-sauvignon, Rose, syrah			
Prawn curry			Rieslings		

CHAPTER

14 House Keeping

Q1. What is housekeeping?

Ans. The housekeeping department in a hotel is responsible for cleanliness, maintenance and aesthetic upkeep of the hotel.

Q2. What are the major functions of housekeeping?

Ans.
- Cleaning
- Maintenance
- Aesthetic upkeep
- Upkeep of the property.

Q3. Housekeeping interacts with whom people including external and internal?

Ans. Guests, group leader, suppliers, airlines crews, corporate executive, delegates, front office bellboy, cashier, valvet, engineer, laundry manager, security officer, room service order taker.

Q4. On which basic we categories the hotel?

Ans. On location, number of rooms, owner ship, pricing plan, type of clientele, length of guest stay, facilities offered.

Q5. Who we categories hotels by location?

Ans. On following basic we categories hotels by location
- Down town
- Suburban
- Resorts
- Airport
- Motel.

Q6. Who we categories hotels by number of rooms?

Ans Its categories by their sizes.

- 25 rooms and less room SMALL
- 26-100 room MEDIUM
- 101-300 room LARGE
- 300-1000 room VERY LARGE
- Above -1000 rooms MEGA.

Q7. How you classified hotels by pricing plan?

Ans.
- European plan– Room charges only
- American plan–Rooms + all meals
- Modify American plan–Room+ Breakfast+ Lunch or Dinner
- Continental plan–Room + Continental breakfast
- Bed and breakfast plan–Room+ English breakfasts.

Q8. How you categories hotels by clientele?

Ans. Categories are as follows:
- Business hotels
- Group hotels
- Family hotels
- Convention hotels.

Q9. How you categories hotels by length of stay?

Ans. Categories are as follows:
- Transient hotels
- Residential hotels
- Semi residential hotels.

Q10. What is perspective plan?

Ans. A plan for 5 to 10 years called perspective plan.

Q11. What is annual plan?

Ans. Short term plan for a year is called annual plan.

Q12. What is long term plan?

Ans. A plan for 3-5 years is called long term plan.

Q13. On which basic we classified hotels?

Ans. On following basic such as:
- By location
- Size of property
- Length of stay
- Level of services

- Themes
- Target market.

Q14. What is Amenity?

Ans. Items placed in guests rooms for convenience and comfort of guests, at no extra costs.

Q15. Explain term back of the house?

Ans. The functional areas of the hotel in which employees have little or no guest contact such as engineering, maintenance and so on.

Q16. Explain term back to back?

Ans. When hotel is fooled occupied on that date means heavy check out and check in activities on the same day of few hours gap, so that as soon as a room is made up and new guests check in that position is called back to back.

Q17. Explain the term check in?

Ans. When guest arrived at the hotel and registration of the guest is done and he comes that term as know as check in.

Q18. Explain the terms check out?

Ans. When guests departure from the hotel is called check out. Its is an American term adopted by India hotels.

Q19. Explain the term CMMS?

Ans. Its is installed by the hotel to make sure that maintenance activities take place before the point of breakdown is reached is knows as computerized maintenance management system.

Q20. Light emitted is measure by?

Ans. Lumens.

Q21. Minimum lighting requirement for restaurant?

Ans. 7 lumens /929cm_2

Q22. Minimum lighting requirement for bathroom?

Ans. 10 lumens /929cm_2

Q23. Minimum lighting requirement for stairs?

Ans. 10 lumens /929cm_2

Q24. Minimum lighting requirement for general office?

Ans. 15-20 lumens /929cm_2.

Q 25. Minimum lighting requirement for casual reading/in room guest table?

Ans. 15 lumens /929cm_2

Q 26. What is deep cleaning?

Ans. Specialized cleaning undertakes in guest rooms or public areas or back area often conducted according to a special schedule or on weekly basic depends upon the organization.

Q27. What are adjacent rooms?

Ans. Two rooms besides each other across the corridors are know adjacent rooms.

Q28. What are adjoining rooms?

Ans. Two rooms which are either on same side or beside each other and /or have an interconnecting door.

Q29. Explain term cabana?

Ans. A room with a sofa cum bed ideally situated beside the swimming pools knows as cabana.

Q30 Explain term double room?

Ans. A room with king sized double bed is called double room.

Q31. Explain term connecting room?

Ans. Two rooms with an interconnecting door, specially for family are also knows adjoining/connecting room.

Q32. Explain term DND?

Ans. Means "do not disturb" it's a card is hung outside the rooms to inform hotel staff. A guest occupant doesn't wish to be disturbed.

Q33. Explain double locked?

Ans. An occupied room in which dead bolt has been turned to prohibit entry from the corridor.

Q34. Explain term crib?

Ans. Cot for babies. (Its provided to a guests on his/her request).

Q35. Explain break knob cards?
Ans. This is a card the hung on the knob of the door to preorder breakfast at night so that orders reaches on time.

Q36. Explain term single room?
Ans. A room with single bed.

Q37. Explain the term studio?
Ans. A room with sofa cum bed.

Q38. Explain term triplet?
Ans. A double room with a extra roll away cot.

Q39. Explain term twin room?
Ans. A room with two single bed.

Q40. Explain term Quad?
Ans. A room assigned to 4 people sitted with twin beds and two roll away beds.

Q41. Explain term queen?
Ans. A room with queen sized bed for single and double occupancy.

Q42. Explain term junior suite?
Ans. A room with a seating parlour and a bed.

Q43. Explain the term double suite?
Ans. Two rooms one serving as a living cum dining area and other with a double bed.

Q44. Explain the term president suite?
Ans Four rooms, one serving as dining rooms, one drawing room, two double bed room. (mainly for high profile people such as president of country or princess of country or high profiled guests with there family).

Q45. Explain the term chalets?
Ans. Independent home that are on lease mainly found in Switzerland called chalets.

Q46. Explain the term OOO?
Ans. Its a term means "out of order" its show the status of a guests room that is not in position to sale/or not rentable because it may be repaired.

Q47. What is occupancy reports?

Ans. A report which is prepared by the front office staff which list the rooms occupied that nights and indicate guests who are expected to check out on date.

Q48. What is control desk?

Ans. The heart of the housekeeping where all communication is pass/center of communications.

Q49. Explain the term lost and found room?

Ans. The section where misplaced items of guests /belongings are kept that is called lost and found room.

Q50. Explain the term facility planner?

Ans. A person who design floor layouts of service areas are knows as facility planner.

Q51. Explain the term linen room?

Ans. Its is placed where all house linen are in circulation are stored and from were linen are issued.

Q52. Explain the term uniform room?

Ans. The room where all staff uniform are in circulation are stored and issued.

Q53. Explain the term budget?

Ans. A formal financial statement of anticipated revenues and expenses for future period.

Q54. What is room discrepancy?

Ans. An occupancy discrepancy between floor supervisors and the front office room rack.

Q55. Explain the term scanty baggage?

Ans. A person with light baggage who can be potential skipper.

Q56. Explain term skipper?

Ans. A guest departs with out paying his/her bills.

Q57. What are guest amenities for rooms?

Ans. Followings are as follows:

- Bed linen
- Mini fridge

- Safety deposit locker
- Shoe shine
- Television
- Iron
- Coffee maker
- Sewing kit
- Tent card
- Knob cards and so on.....

Q58. What are the guest amenities for bathroom?

Ans. Followings are as follows:

- Hair dryer
- Soaps
- Shampoos
- Shoe mitts
- Sanitary disposals
- Bathroom linen and so on ......

Q59. What is master key?

Ans. That accesses all doors are called master key.

Q60. Explain term upholstery?

Ans. Textiles, padding, springs and other materials used for decorating furniture and rendering it more comfortable.

Q61. Explain term WWP?

Ans. Waste water preventer to hold the right amount of water required to flush toilet.

Q62. Explain term WC?

Ans. Sanitary fittings consisting of the toilet bowl and the cistern.

Q63. Explain term contingency plan?

Ans. Planning done for uncertain events for ex. Marriage party in open lawn but unfortunately rains come in that situation what we do to shift that programmed in other safe place is called contingency plan.

Q64. What is floor pantry?

Ans. A service room provided in each floor of the wing for room boys to store cleaning equipments, linen, guest supplies and maid cart.

Q65. What is graveyard shift?
Ans. Its is a Night shift.

Q66. What is hand caddy?
Ans. A portable container for storing and transporting cleaning supplies, carried on a room maid cart.

Q67. What is shoe mitts?
Ans. Flannel cloth for cleaning shoes.

Q68. What is vanity unity/vanity area?
Ans. A unit comprising a wash basin, mirror, surrounded by flat area where soap, dental kits, shaving kits are kept.

Q69. What is bedding?
Ans. A terms for all collective articles on a bed but normally refers to launderables.

Q70. What is Faucets?
Ans. Means Taps.

Q71. What is sani-bin?
Ans. Plastic container or some other metal container with lids, kept in toilets for the collection of soiled sanitary towels.

Q72. What is swab cloth?
Ans. It's a soft absorbent cleaning cloth used for wet cleaning work such as for washbasin and so on.

Q73. Explain term tooth glass?
Ans. It's a glass placed on vanity unit/area as a guest supply and basically used for gargling or to hold a guest toothbrush.

Q74. What are the different categories of brooms?
Ans. Basically there are 3 categories of brooms:
- Soft bristled brooms
- Hard/coarse bristled brooms
- Wall brooms.

Q75. What are the different categories of mops?
Ans. There are two categories of mops:
- Dry mops
- Wet /damp mops.

Q76. Explain term lint?
Ans. Short fibers that may be loosened and shed from the fabric called lint.

Q77. What is shams?
Ans. American term for pillow cases.

Q78. Explain the term king size bed?
Ans. King sized bed is the largest bed available with a dimension of 6ft by 6ft.

Q79. Explain term Lanai?
Ans. A room overlooked a landscape area, water body or garden is called lanai room.

Q80. What is Sico bed/Murphy bed?
Ans. It's a bed that fold up into the walls and look like a bookshelf or cupboard when folded away, its named by a leading manufacturing company of this bed.

Q81. Explain the term queen size bed?
Ans. It's a large bed with dimension of 5ft 6inch × 6ft 6inch.

Q82. Explain term Dutch wife/sewing kits?
Ans. Basic sewing supplies provided in rooms.

Q83. What WHB?
Ans. Terms refer to wash basins.

Q84. What is zed bed?
Ans. A bed which is fold away mainly with slatted wood frame that fold into double hunged shape.

Q85. Explain term luggage rack?
Ans. Its a furniture items provide in a guest room for placing the guest luggage.

Q86. What type of linen available in housekeeping department?
Ans. There are four type of linen available in housekeeping department.

- Bedroom linen
- Bathroom linen

- Restaurant linen
- Banquet linen.

Q87. Size of bath rug?
Ans. 24 inches × 42 inches.

Q88. Size of bath towel
Ans. 25 inches × 45 inches.

Q89. Size of Hand towel?
Ans. 6 inches × 7½ inches.

Q90. Size of face towel?
Ans. 9½ inches × 10½ inches.

Q91. Size of pillow slip?
Ans. 24 inches × 32 inches.

Q92. Size of pool towels?
Ans. 36 inches × 80 inches.

Q93. Size of blanket?
Ans. 72 inches × 108 inches.

Q94 Size of bed spreads?
Ans. 72 inches × 108 inches.

Q95. Size of staff towel?
Ans. 36 inches × 62 inches.

Q96. Size mattress protector ?
Ans. 64 inches × 96 inches for single bed.

Q97. Size of bed sheet?
Ans. 72 inches × 108 inches.

Q98. Explain term soap suds?
Ans. Provide in guest bath rooms for guest to wash there own cloths.

Q99. Explain term Valet?
Ans. A person from a laundry. Who collect laundry from guest room and return to guest after cleaning/ironing.

Q100. Explain term pent house?
Ans. A room that opens onto the roof and may accompany by a swimming pool, tennis court and other facilities.

Q101. Explain the term quad room?
Ans. A room mainly assigned to a four pax which may have two or more beds.

Q102. What are the standard size of single beds are?
Ans. 100×200cm (3ft 3$^3/_8$ inches × 6ft 6$^3/_4$ inches)
85×190cm (2ft 9½ inches × 6ft 3 inches)

Q103. What are the standard size of double beds?
Ans. 150×200cm (4ft 11 inches × 6ft 6$^3/_4$ inches), 135×190cm (4ft 5 inches × 6ft 3 inches)

Q104. How much shrinkage you considered for bed linen?
Ans. In ten wash as much as 5 per cent.

Q105. Minimum hanging space in single wardrobes?
Ans. 60cm minimum.

Q106. Minimum hanging space in double wardrobes?
Ans. 90cm minimum.

Q107. What is colour of wheel in housekeeping?
Ans. It's a wheel divided colour into 3 main section:
- Primary colour
- Secondary colour
- Tertiary colour.

Q108. What are primary colours?
Ans. Red, yellow and blue are primary colours.

Q109. What are secondary colours?
Ans. Orange green and violet are secondary colours.

Q110. What are tertiary colour?
Ans. Russet, burnt orange and coral are tertiary colours.

Q111. What are the recommended standard of warmth?
Ans. For lounges: 20°-21°c
For bedrooms: 13°-16°c
For general offices: 20°c.

Q112. Explain term refurbish?

Ans. Gave a new look to a room by redecorating, the renewing of soft furnishing, new electronic gadgets and possibly the carpet and touching up the furniture.

Q113. Define stain?

Ans. Stain is a spot or mark discoloration left on fabric due to contact with or absorption of foreign substance.

Q114. What is the classification of stain?

Ans. Classifications of stains are as follows:

- Animal stains
- Vegetable stains
- Grease stains
- Dye stains
- Mineral stains
- Scorch stains.

Q115. What are the main stain removal agent?

Ans. There are five main stain removal agents:

- Organic solvents
- Acids
- Alkalis
- Bleaches
- Enzymes.

Q116. Define stock taking?

Ans. Stock taking is the physical verification by counting of stock of all items for the accuracy of recoding entries in books so that average or shortage can be found out by variance in physical balance.

Q117. Which type of cleaning agent is used for bathroom?

Ans. Acid, glass cleanser, liquid detergent, cream cleanser, sanitizer.

Q118. Which type of cleaning agent is used for floor?

Ans. Liquid detergent, sanitizer, solvent base detergent, mild alkali detergent, non split polish.

Q119. Which type of cleaning agent for furniture?

Ans. Wax polish, spray wax polish, silicon based spray polish.

Q120. What characterizes of sanitizer?
Ans. A detergent that is mix with a bacterial agent and can destroyed harmful bacteria.

Q121. What is evening service?
Ans. Evening service is also know as turn down service. The basic purpose of this service is making night bed for the guest to sleep and freshen up the room from day uses.

Q122. Which is most common cleaning agents company?
Ans. Johnson Diversy.

Q123. What is R1 cleaning agents by Johnson Diversy?
Ans. R1 is multipurpose cleaner especially for bathroom. Its colour is light orange.

Q124. What is R2 cleaning agents by Johnson Diversy?
Ans. R2 is hard surface cleaner and its colour is Blue.

Q125. What is R3 cleaning agents by Johnson Diversy?
Ans. R3 is glass cleaner and its colour is Light sky blue.

Q126. What is R4 cleaning agents by Johnson Diversy?
Ans. R4 is furniture maintainer and its colour is milky.

Q127. What is R5 cleaning agents by Johnson Diversy?
Ans. R5 is air freshners.

Q128. What is R6 cleaning agents by Johnson Diversy?
Ans. R6 is toilet bowl cleaner and its colour is dark blue.

Q129. What is R7 cleaning agents by Johnson Diversy?
Ans. R7 is hard surface floor cleaner and its colour is translucent Benge.

Q130. What is TR 101 cleaning agents by Johnson Diversy?
Ans. TR101 is carpet shampoo and its colour is Translucent Orange.

Q131. Traditional / natural cleaning agents?
Ans. For marble polish with milk, copper can be clean by lemon and salt, brass can be clean by tamarind.

Q132. Define wicking?

Ans. A process in which wetness or strains are drawn up from the packing through the face or backing or usually for carpet.

Q133. What is upholstery?

Ans. Textile used for furniture décor.

Q134. What is tapestry?

Ans. Tapestry is a form of textile art. It is woven by hand on a vertical loom. It is weft-faced weaving, in which all the warp threads are hidden in the completed work, unlike cloth weaving where both the warp and the weft threads may be visible.

Q135. Define stain.

Ans. A spot or discoloration left on fabric from contact, with and absorption of foreign substance.

Q136. What is floor par?

Ans. Linen required to outfit the room serviced from particular floor.

Q137. What is antichlor?

Ans. It is use to remove excess chlorine from fabric after bleaching.

Q138. What is burnishing?

Ans. High speed polishing to give wet look to the floor.

Q139. What is thread count?

Ans. Number of wrap and weft yarns per square inch.

Q140. What is 'warp'?

Ans. Lengthwise arrangement of fibers on loom.

Q141. What is horticulture?

Ans. Science of growing plants.

Q142. What is second service?

Ans. Service provided by the housekeeping on special request of the guest.

Q143. What is Due-out?

Ans. Room status indicating that guest is due to depart that day at regular check-out time.

Q144. What is F.F.E.?

Ans. Furniture, Fixture and Equipment.

Q145. What is Operating Budget?

Ans. Financial outline of all expenditure for goods and services that will be used within one year.

Q146. Define job specification?

Ans. An explanation of the minimum requirement that must be met by a job applicant.

Q147. What is second service?

Ans. Service provided by the housekeeping on special request of the guest.

Q148. What is Yarn?

Ans. Strands of fiber laid or twisted by spinning.

Q149. What is Transient hotel?

Ans. Lodging that caters to short duration travellers.

Q150. What is Floor seal?

Ans. Semi permanent finish applied to flooring to render it impermeable.

Q151. Which chemical is used in dry cleaning?

Ans. Per chloro ethylene.

Q152. Two examples of oxidizing agent

Ans. Sodium Hypochlorite
Sodium Perborate.

Q153. To remove ball pen ink which of the chemical is used?

Ans. Surgical spirit.

Q154. What is muslin?

Ans. A fabric that had been carded rather than fine comb, usually referred to fabric used for sheet.

Q155. Define Renovation?

Ans. Process of renewing, updating and modifying space to meet the needs of changing market.

Q156. What is restoration?

Ans. Restoring a property to its exact original design during authentic materials.

Q157. What is valance?

Ans. Decorative heading of window made of frilled or pleated material.

Q158. Define Par Level?

Ans. Standard No. of each inventoried item that must be on hand to support daily routine housekeeping operation.

Q159. Define Damask?

Ans. Glossy Fabric with intricate jacquard, woven design made from cotton, silk or blends. It is preferred for table linen.

Q160. Define sorting?

Ans. Process of separating soiled linen into different categories.

Q161. What is weaving?

Ans. Process of interlacing yarns or fibers to make fabrics.

Q162. Define Inventory?

Ans. Stock of purchased operating supplies, equipment and other items held for future use in House keeping operation.

Q163. Define Stock taking?

Ans. Physical verification of inventory items by counting up stocks of all items at periodic intervals.

Q164. What is SOP?

Ans. Document of standing nature that specifies a certain method of operating procedure for the accomplishment of a task.

Q165. Define Log Book.

Ans. Register having instructions and message for staff on the next shift is written down by the employees on the previous shift.

Q166. Define Dirty Dozen?

Ans. Hard to reach area and are hidden from the guests eye.

Q167. What is buffing?

Ans. Polishing the floor with a low speed polishing machine.

Q168. What is duvet?
Ans. Quilt filled with feather or synthetic fibers.

Q169. What is Linen Chute?
Ans. Passage in the form of a tunnel foe sending soiled linen down from the floor pantries to central laundry.

Q170. What is tarnish?
Ans. Discoloration caused by a chemical reaction between a metal surface and substances found in water, air and food.

Q171. Define case goods?
Ans. Furniture made of wood with a top and sides.

Q172. What is ticking?
Ans. Strong, sturdy cloth used to cover mattresses.

Q173. Marble/granite chips with polyester resin make___?
Ans. Agglomerate flooring.

Q174. Ticking is used to cover___?
Ans. Carpet.

Q175. Shellac is made up of ___?
Ans. Alcohol + refined lac.

CHAPTER

15 Front Office

Q1. What is front office?

Ans. Most prominent part of the organization where guest first interact with the organization people. IT'S called the face of the organization Or department that reserves register and assigns and act as a continuous source of information.

Q2. In hotels industry when manual elevator are first comes?

Ans. Its first come in American hotel industry in 1859.

Q3. In hotels industry when electronic elevator are first comes?

Ans. Electric elevator first come in America in 1950.

Q4. After invented colour television when its come to hotels industry?

Ans. Its come in 1970.

Q5. When in room telephone comes in hotel industry?

Ans. In room telephone come in 1907.

Q6. Where first centralized reservation come first?

Ans. In 1964 Holiday inn America.

Q7. What is amendment chart?

Ans. A chart in which changes occur from the original chart.

Q8. What is bell desk?

Ans. A desk in the hotel lobby where bell boy are positioned and may be contacted at the time of guest arrival.

Q10. What is advance reservation chart/bed allocation chart?

Ans. A chart is made for the advance reservation of allocation of rooms to reservation.

Q11. On which basic we categories the hotel?

Ans. On location, number of rooms, owner ship, pricing plan, type of clientele, length of guest stay, facilities offered.

Q12. Who we categories hotels by location?

Ans. On following basic we categories hotels by location

- Down town
- Suburban
- Resorts
- Airport
- Motel.

Q13. Who we categories hotels by number of rooms?

Ans. Its categories by their sizes:

- 25 rooms and less room SMALL
- 26-100 room MEDIUM
- 101-300 room LARGE
- 300-1000 room VERY LARGE
- Above-1000 rooms MEGA.

Q14. How you classified hotels by pricing plan?

Ans. Followings plans are as follows:

- European plan– Room charges only
- American plan–Rooms + all meals
- Modify American plan–Room+ Breakfast+Lunch or Dinner
- Continental plan– Room + Continental breakfast
- Bed and breakfast plan–Room+ English breakfasts.

Q15. How you categories hotels by clientele?

Ans. Categories are as follows:

- Business hotels
- Group hotels
- Family hotels
- Convention hotels.

Q16. How you categories hotels by length of stay?

Ans. Categories are as follows:

- Transient hotels
- Residential hotels
- Semi residential hotels.

Q17. On which basic we classified hotels?

Ans. On following basic such as:

- By location
- Size of property
- Length of stay
- Level of services
- Themes
- Target market.

Q18. What is Amenity?

Ans. Items placed in guests rooms for convenience and comfort of guests, at no extra costs.

Q19. Explain term back of the house?

Ans. The functional areas of the hotel in which employees have little or no guest contact such as engineering, maintenance and so on.

Q20. Explain term back to back?

Ans. When hotel is fooled occupied on that date means heavy check out and check in activities on the same day of few hours gap, so that as soon as a room is made up and new guests check in that position is called back to back.

Q21. Explain the term check in?

Ans. When guest arrived at the hotel and registration of the guest is done and he comes that term as know as check in.

Q22. Explain the terms check out?

Ans. When guests departure from the hotel is called check out. Its is an American term adopted by India hotels.

Q23. Explain terms Bag delivery?

Ans. Delivering of luggage of a group member to a individual group members room after the group check into the room.

Q24. Explain term bed occupancy?

Ans. A list prepared by the housekeeper indicating which rooms are occupied and by how many paxs.

Q25. Explain term cancellation?

Ans. When a room reservation is withdrawn by the guest.

Q26. Explain term black-listed guest?
Ans. A record authorized by the management of the names, address, of all person that are not welcome in the hotels. A list of unwanted guests. Some times FHRAI is usually informed about these guest.

Q27. Explain the term block booking?
Ans. The term used for a reservation made for several people at the same time for the same period so rooms are blocked that booking is mainly done by firms, travel agency and so on.

Q28. Explain the term bumped reservation?
Ans. Is a reservation when guest holding a confirmed reservation, refusal of accommodation but putting some guest in some other hotel.

Q29. Explain term booked room?
Ans. A specific room that is reserved by the guest, also called blocking.

Q30. Abbreviation of WTO?
Ans. World Tourism Organization.

Q31. Abbreviation of C.I.P.?
Ans. Commercially Important Person

Q32. Abbreviation of ABTA?
Ans. Association of British Travel Agents.

Q33. Abbreviation of T.A.A.I.?
Ans. Travel Agents Association of India.

Q34. Abbreviation of HAI?
Ans. Hotel Association of India.

Q35. Abbreviation of I.A.T.O.?
Ans. Indian Association of Tour Operator.

Q36. Abbreviation of I.A.A.I.?
Ans. International Airport Authority of India.

Q37. Abbreviation of I.H.A.?
Ans. International Hotel Association.

Q38. Abbreviation of IH & RA?
Ans. International Hotel and Restaurant Associates.

Q39. Abbreviation of F.H.R.A.I.?
Ans. Federation of Hotel and Restaurant Association of India.

Q40. Abbreviation of H & RA.?
Ans. Hotel and Restaurant Association.

Q41. Abbreviation of P.A.T.A.?
Ans. Pacific Asia Travel Associates.

Q42. Abbreviation of P.P.P.N.?
Ans. Per Person Per Night.

Q43. Abbreviation of P.R.P.N.?
Ans. Per Room Per Night.

Q44. Explain term Pax?
Ans. Means number of persons.

Q45. What are adjacent rooms?
Ans. Two rooms besides each other across the corridors are know adjacent rooms.

Q46. What are adjoining rooms?
Ans. Two rooms which are either on same side or beside each other and /or have an interconnecting door.

Q47. Explain term cabana?
Ans. A room with a sofa cum bed ideally situated beside the swimming pools knows as cabana.

Q48. Explain term double room?
Ans. A room with king sized double bed is called double room.

Q49. Explain term connecting room?
Ans. Two rooms with an interconnecting door, specially for family are also knows adjoining/connecting room.

Q50. Explain term crib?
Ans. Cot for babies. (Its provided to a guests on his/her request).

Q51. Explain term single room?
Ans. A room with single bed.

Q52. Explain the term studio?
Ans. A room with sofa cum bed.

Q53. Explain term triplet?
Ans. A double room with a extra roll away cot.

Q54. Explain term twin room?
Ans. A room with two single bed.

Q55. Explain term Quad?
Ans. A room assigned to 4 people sitted with twin beds and two roll away beds.

Q56. Explain term queen?
Ans. A room with queen sized bed for single and double occupancy.

Q58. Explain term junior suite?
Ans. A room with a seating parlour and a bed.

Q59. Explain the term double suite?
Ans. Two rooms one serving as a living cum dining area and other with a double bed.

Q60. Explain the term president suite?
Ans. Four rooms, one serving as dining rooms, one drawing room, two double bed room. (mainly for high profile people such as president of country or princess of country or high profiled guests with there family).

Q61. Explain the term chalets?
Ans. Independent home that are on lease mainly found in Switzerland called chalets.

Q63. Explain the term OOO?
Ans. Its a term means "out of order" its show the status of a guests room that is not in position to sale/or not rentable because it may be repaired.

Q64. What is occupancy reports?
Ans. A report which is prepared by the front office staff which list

the rooms occupied that nights and indicate guests who are expected to check out on date.

Q66. What is occupancy mix?

Ans. Its also refers to profile of occupancy which means percentage breakup of sold rooms on single, double and annual occupancy.

Q67. What is guest cycle?

Ans. A division of flow of business through that identify the financial exchange and physical contact between the guests and hotel employees.The cycle includes:

- Pre arrival
- Arrival
- Occupancy
- Departure.

Q68. Explain term guest folio?

Ans. A form (paper or electronic) used to chart all account transaction of the guests those are in house guest.

Q69. Explain term house limit?

Ans. A credit limit that established by the hotel.

Q70. Explain term late charge?

Ans. A charges which are not reached before guest check out and guests left the hotel and closed his /her account that charges called late charges.

Q71. Explain term registration card?

Ans. A printed form of registration record.

Q72. Explain term registration form?

Ans. This form is fill up by the guest at the hotel when he/she arrived. It contain complete information about themselves, some of which is required by law. This information may be kept for 12 months.

Q73. Explain term reservation?

Ans. A department or a counter which received documents and reservation request.

Q74. Explain term resident guest?
Ans. One who is staying in the hotel.

Q75. Explain term sleeper?
Ans. Room available for sale but not sold.

Q76. Explain term No-show?
Ans. A guest who made a room reservation but is not arrived and he/she not cancelled that reservation.

Q77. Explain term guaranteed reservation?
Ans. A reservation in which guest gave guarantee of payment if guest arrived or not. Even if it is not used, Until the reservation is properly cancelled.

Q78. Explain term room rate/rack rate?
Ans. A price the hotels charges for overnight accommodation.

Q79. Explain the term Up selling?
Ans. It's a sale technique whereby a guest is offered more expensive room than what guests reserved and then persuade to rent that room on the basic of features.

Q80. Explain the term Walk-in?
Ans. A guest who arrives at the hotel without a reservation.

Q81. Explain terms walking?
Ans. Turning away a guest who has reservation because of lack of rooms.

Q82. Explain terms over selling?
Ans. A situation when more rooms, than actually what is available are sold out by the hotel.

Q83. What is room discrepancy?
Ans. An occupancy discrepancy between floor supervisors and the front office room rack.

Q84. Explain the term scanty baggage?
Ans. A person with light baggage who can be potential skipper.

Q85. Explain term skipper?
Ans. A guest departs with out paying his/her bills.

Q86. What is master key?
Ans. That accesses all doors are called master key.

Q87. Explain term pent house?
Ans. A room that opens onto the roof and may accompany by a swimming pool, tennis court and other facilities.

Q88. Explain the term quad room?
Ans. A room mainly assigned to a four pax which may have two or more beds.

Q89. Explain the term Float?
Ans. An amount of money entrusted to the member of the staff for the purpose of making small payments.

Q90. Explain the term house count?
Ans. Number of guest staying in the hotel.

Q91. Explain term Wake up-call?
Ans. A line given to the front office telephone to call a guest for wake up. (its done against guest request).

Q92. Explain term sold out?
Ans. More than occupancy or rooms not available.

Q93. Explain term occupancy?
Ans. Number of rooms sold to the total.

Q94. Explain term express check out?
Ans. A pre departure activity that involves the production and early morning distribution of guest folios for guest expected to check out that morning.

Q95. Explain term Under stay?
Ans. A guest who check out before his or her stated departure date.

Q96. Abbreviation of F.I.T.?
Ans. Means Free Individual Traveller.

Q97. Abbreviation of F.F.I.T.?
Ans. Means Foreign Free Independent Traveller.

Q98. Explain term left luggage?

Ans. Guest baggage kept in custody of the hotel after the guest check out which will be inter locked by him.

Q99. Explain term supper?

Ans. A term referring to a late night meal.

Q100. Explain terms Displacement?

Ans. When hotel accept group business and turns away transient guest, that situation is called displacement.

Q101. How you calculate occupancy percentage?

Ans.

$$\frac{\text{Number of room sold}}{\text{Number of saleable room.}} \times 100$$

Q102. How you calculate double occupancy percentage?

Ans.

$$\frac{\text{House count — rooms occupied}}{\text{Numbers of rooms available.}} \times 100$$

Q103. How you calculate house count?

Ans. House count of previous day brought forward+ today arrivals-today departure.

Q104. How you calculate average daily rate?

Ans.

$$\frac{\text{Rooms revenue}}{\text{Number of room sold.}}$$

Q105. How you calculate revenue per available room?

Ans.

$$\frac{\text{Actual Room revenue}}{\text{Number of available rooms.}}$$

Q106. How you calculate average rate per guest?

Ans.

$$\frac{\text{Room's revenue}}{\text{Number of guests (house count).}}$$

Q107. How you calculate locals occupancy?

Ans. $\dfrac{\text{Local in the house}}{\text{House count.}}$

Q108. How you calculate foreign occupancy?

Ans. 100--local occupancy.

Q109. How you calculate average room rate?

Ans. $\dfrac{\text{Total room revenue}}{\text{Number of room sold.}}$

Q110. How you calculate room occupancy?

Ans. $\dfrac{\text{Rooms occupied}}{\text{Total room available.}} \times 100$

Q111. How you calculate bed occupancy?

Ans. $\dfrac{\text{Bed occupied}}{\text{Total beds available.}} \times 100$

Q112. How you calculate double occupancy?

Ans. $\dfrac{\text{Double let to two person}}{\text{Total doubles.}} \times 100$

Q113. How you calculate forecasted room revenue?

Ans. Rooms available × occupancy percentage × average daily rate.

Q114. How you calculate percentage of NO-shows?

Ans. $\dfrac{\text{Number of room no-show}}{\text{Number of room reservation.}} \times 100$

Q115. How you calculate percentage of walk-ins?

Ans. $\dfrac{\text{Number of room walk-in}}{\text{Total number of room arrivals.}} \times 100$

Q116. How you calculate percentage over stay?

Ans. $$\frac{\text{Number of over stay rooms}}{\text{Number of expected check out}} \times 100$$

Number of expected check out = (actual checkout on the books—under stay+ overstay).

Q117. How you calculate percentage under stay?

Ans. $$\frac{\text{Number of under stay rooms}}{\text{Number of expected check out.}} \times 100$$

Q118. When first commercial hotel come in world?

Ans. The first commercial building for the hotel purpose called "The city hotel" was constructed in New York, U.S.A.

Q119. When first class hotel was constructed?

Ans. The "Tremount house" first class hotel was constructed in Boston,U.S.A.

Q120. Explain term Concierges?

Ans. Person who assist the guest by making restaurant reservation, arranging for transportation, and sporting or other special events.

Q121. Explain term credit card?

Ans. A credit card is a financial instrument, which can be used more than once to borrow money or buy products and services on credit. Banks retail stores and other businesses generally issues these.

Q122. Name the type of card?

Ans. Master cards, VISA card, Affinity cards, Standard cards, Classic Card, Gold card/Executive cards, Platinum card, Titanium card, Secured card, Smart card, Change card, Rebate card, Travel card, Debit card.

Q123. Abbreviation of AH & LA?

Ans. American Hotel and Lodging Association.

Q124. Abbreviation of DFIT?

Ans. Domestic Free Individual Traveller.

Q125. Abbreviation of GIT?
Ans. Group Inclusive Traveller.

Q126. Abbreviation of FRRO?
Ans. Foreigner's Regional Registration Office.

Q127. What is golden tourist triangle in India?
Ans. Delhi, Agra and Jaipur is called golden tourist triangle.

Q128. Explain term Minus?
Ans. When guests expected exceed rooms available.

Q129. Explain term turn room?
Ans. Rooms with two single bed.

Q130. Explain term sold out?
Ans. Rooms not available.

Q131. Explain term Hurdle rate?
Ans. These rate are in the context of revenue management, the lowest expectable room rate for a given period.

Q132. Explain the term Night auditor?
Ans. An employee who check the accuracy of front office accounting records and complying a daily summary of hotel financial data, as the part of the night audit, that person who do these financial things in hotel are called night auditor.

Q133. What are the Five A's of a destination?
Ans.
- Accessibility
- Accommodation
- Attraction
- Activities
- Amenities.

Q134. What is in-bound tour operator?
Ans. Handling tours coming into the country.

Q135. What is out bound tour operator?
Ans. Operating tours to other countries.

Q136. What is domestic tour operator?
Ans. Handling tours for people of the same country in which travel take place.

Q137. Abbreviation For GMT?

Ans. Green Witch Mean Time.

Q138. Slogan of the followings Air ways?

Ans.
- Indian Airlines–New horizon enduring Vault
- Kingfisher–Fly the good times
- Air India–Fly well
- Air Deccan–Simplify
- Air Sahara–Emotionally tour
- Go air lines–Fly smart
- Spice jet airline–Flying for every one.

Q139. Mention types of passport?

Ans. Basically three types of passport:
- Normal passport
- Diplomatic passport
- Seaman's book.

Q140. Explain term VISA?

Ans. Visitor Intended To stay Abroad.

Q141. Mention Types of VISA?

Ans.
- Visitor visa /Tourist visa
- Business visa
- Medical visa
- Student visa
- Transit visa
- Transit with out visa.

Q142. What Y class means in Airbus?

Ans. Its means Economy class. In this only 20kg. baggage weight is allowed to passenger.

Q143. What Z class means in Airbus?

Ans. Its means Business class. In this only 30kg. baggage weight is allowed to passenger.

Q144. What F class means in Airbus?

Ans. Its means First class. In this only 40kg. baggage weight is allowed to passenger.

Q145. Mention Indian Domestic Airlines with their name and code?

Ans.

Airline Name	*Code*
Indian Airline	IC
Jet airways	9w
Sahara India	S2
Gujarat air ways	G8
U.P. air ways	UZ
East west air line	4S
Archana Airways	F5

Q146. Mention the Credit card company names?

Ans.

Card Names	*Codes*
American express	AE
Barclay card	BC
Dinners club	DC
En Route	ER
Master Card	MC
Access	AC
Euro Card	EC
JCB International	JC
Visa Card	VS

Q147. What is zero costing?

Ans. At the time of departure to bring balance to zero debits and credits off setting one another.

Q148. What is crib Rate?

Ans. Special rate given to children is called crib rate.

Q149. Three methods establishing room rate?

Ans. Market condition approach. Rule of thumb approach. Hobart formula.

CHAPTER

16

World Ranking of Hotels (2007)

TOP 100 HOTELS OVERALL

RANKING–2007

		Name	*Score*
1.	3	Oberoi Udaivilas, Udaipur, India	94.36
2.	1	Singita Sabi Sand, Kruger National Park, South Africa	94.30
3.	9	The Oriental, Bangkok	94.23
4.	48	Four Seasons Hotel Istanbul at Sultanahmet	93.55
5.	n/a	Milestone Hotel, London	93.06
6.	n/a	Relais Il Falconiere, Cortona, Italy	92.97
7.	97	Sabi Sabi Private Game Reserve, Sabi Sands, South Africa	92.81
8.	n/a	Mandarin Oriental, Munich	92.73
9.	12	Four Seasons Resort Hualalai, Hawaii	92.65
10.	54	Oberoi Amarvilas, Agra, India	92.56
11.	6	Oberoi Rajvilas, Jaipur, India	92.50
12.	4	The Peninsula, Bangkok	92.41
13.	18	Château Les Crayères, Reims, France	92.39
14.	n/a	Jumby Bay, a Rosewood Resort, Antigua	92.24

15.	14	Four Seasons Hotel Gresham Palace, Budapest	92.15
16.	24	Mombo Camp, Moremi Game Reserve, Botswana	92.08
17.	n/a	Four Seasons Hotel Cairo at Nile Plaza	92.00
18.	11	Four Seasons Resort, Chiang Mai, Thailand	91.90
19.	52	Cape Grace, Cape Town	91.52
20.	32	MalaMala Game Reserve, Mpumalanga, South Africa	91.38
21.	27	Ladera, St. Lucia	91.34
22.	28	La Casa Que Canta, Zihuatanejo, Mexico	91.28
23.	35	Kichwa Tembo, Masai Mara, Kenya	91.25
24.	n/a	Le Sirenuse, Positano, Italy	91.18
25.	n/a	Ngorongoro Crater Lodge, Tanzania	91.11
26.	n/a	Woodlands Resort & Inn, Summerville, South Carolina	91.09
27.	43	Four Seasons Hotel, Prague	91.07
28.	69	Four Seasons Hotel George V, Paris	91.05
29.	n/a	Four Seasons Hotel, Amman, Jordan	90.95
30.	n/a	41, London	90.68
31.	n/a	Post Hotel & Spa, Lake Louise, Alberta	90.61
32.	n/a	Ritz-Carlton, Millenia, Singapore	90.59
33.	n/a	The Strand, Yangon, Myanmar	90.56
34.	n/a	Sweetwaters Tented Camp, Sweetwaters Game Reserve, Kenya	90.50
35.	n/a	Blantyre, Lenox, Massachusetts	90.43

36.	20	The Peninsula, Hong Kong	90.37
37.	19	Halekulani, Honolulu	90.29
38.	n/a	Londolozi Private Game Reserve, Sabi Sands, South Africa	90.19
39.	60	Raffles Hotel, Singapore	90.15
40.	n/a	Four Seasons Hotel Cairo at the First Residence, Cairo	90.14
41.	78	Four Seasons Hotel, Buenos Aires	90.12
42.	n/a	Sanctuary at Kiawah Island Golf Resort, South Carolina	90.07
43.	n/a	Tortilis Camp, Amboseli National Park, Kenya	90.00
44.	57	The Peninsula, Beverly Hills	89.99
45.	n/a	Four Seasons Hotel, Bangkok	89.93
46.	39	Kirawira Luxury Tented Camp, Serengeti National Park, Tanzania	89.92
47.	n/a	Fairmont Mara Safari Club, Masai Mara, Kenya	89.87
48.	n/a	Jamaica Inn, Ocho Rios, Jamaica	89.78
49.	91	Four Seasons Resort Maui at Wailea	89.72
50.	n/a	Esperanza, Los Cabos, Mexico	89.68
51.	n/a	Il Pellicano, Porto Ercole, Italy	89.64
52.	n/a	Planters Inn, Charleston, South Carolina	89.64
53.	n/a	Inn at Spanish Bay, Pebble Beach, California	89.63
54.	37	Four Seasons Resort, Jackson Hole, Wyoming	89.50
55.	n/a	Jao Camp, Moremi Game Reserve, Botswana	89.47
56.	n/a	Hôtel d'Europe, Avignon, France	89.42

57.	38	Huka Lodge, Taupo, New Zealand	89.38
58.	n/a	Château de la Chèvre d'Or, Èze Village, France	89.35
59.	44	Four Seasons Resort Lanai, The Lodge at Koele	89.29
60.	n/a	Table Bay Hotel, Cape Town	89.23
61.	n/a	Hôtel Hermitage, Monte Carlo	89.14
62.	n/a	Madrona Manor, Healdsburg, California	89.09
63.	n/a	La Bastide de Moustiers, Moustiers-Ste.-Marie, France	89.04
64.	n/a	Domaine des Hauts de Loire, Onzain, France	89.00
65.	n/a	Le Quartier Français, Franschhoek, South Africa	89.00
66.	n/a	Hôtel du Cap Eden-Roc, Antibes, France	88.89
67.	25	Ritz-Carlton, Santiago, Chile	88.86
68.	n/a	Malliouhana Hotel & Spa, Anguilla	88.86
69.	n/a	Four Seasons Resort Lanai at Manele Bay **Formerly Manele Bay Hotel, Lanai*	88.86
70.	5	Four Seasons Resort Bali at Jimbaran Bay	88.83
71.	n/a	Il San Pietro, Positano, Italy	88.82
72.	n/a	Hotel Saint-Barth Isle de France, St. Bart's	88.81
73.	n/a	Eden Rock, St. Bart's	88.70
74.	n/a	The Westcliff, Johannesburg	88.68
75.	82	Blackberry Farm, Walland, Tennessee	88.62
76.	n/a	Fullerton Hotel, Singapore	88.61
77.	n/a	Ritz-Carlton, Istanbul	88.60

78.	n/a	Shangri-La's Far Eastern Plaza Hotel, Taipei	88.59
79.	n/a	Beau-Rivage Palace, Lausanne, Switzerland	88.57
80.	n/a	Willows Lodge, Woodinville, Washington	88.57
81.	10	Taj Lake Palace, Udaipur, India	88.55
82.	n/a	Horned Dorset Primavera, Rincón, Puerto Rico	88.54
83.	n/a	Auberge Saint-Antoine, Quebec City	88.52
84.	34	Four Seasons Hotel, Hong Kong	88.50
85.	59	The Peninsula, Chicago	88.38
86.	n/a	Bernardus Lodge, Carmel Valley, California	88.37
87.	100	One & Only Palmilla, Los Cabos, Mexico	88.32
88.	n/a	Shangri-La Hotel, Bangkok	88.28
89.	29	Hotel Villa Cipriani, Asolo, Italy	88.27
90.	51	Four Seasons Hotel, Singapore	88.24
91.	n/a	Hotel Hassler, Rome	88.18
92.	n/a	Gleneagles Hotel, Auchterarder, Scotland	88.18
93.	n/a	Katikies Hotel, Santorini, Greece	88.17
94.	n/a	Ritz-Carlton, Berlin	88.17
95.	n/a	Four Seasons Resort, Nevis	88.10
96.	n/a	Four Seasons Hotel, Shanghai	88.08
97.	63	Four Seasons Hotel, Chicago	88.03
98.	n/a	Mount Nelson Hotel, Cape Town	87.94
99.	n/a	Gravetye Manor Hotel, West Sussex, England	87.92

* "N/A" means that the property was not among the top-ranked in this category last year.

Throughout the World's Best Awards, scores are rounded to the nearest hundredth of a point; in the event of an exact tie, properties, companies, or destinations share the same ranking.

CHAPTER

17

Biggest Hotels of the World (2007)

Name of the Hotel	*Location*	*Numbers of Rooms*
Venetian/Palazzo "MEGACENTER"	Las Vegas	7128
Genting Highlands (First World Hotel)	Malaysia	6118
MGM Grand	Las Vegas	5044
Luxor	Las Vegas	4408
Mandalay Bay / THEHotel	Las Vegas	4332
Ambassador City Jomtien	Thailand	4210
Excalibur	Las Vegas	4008
Bellagio	Las Vegas	3993
Circus Circus	Las Vegas	3774
Flamingo	Las Vegas	3565
Hilton Hawaiian Village	Honolulu	3386
Caesars Palace	Las Vegas	3348
Mirage	Las Vegas	3044
Monte Carlo	Las Vegas	3002
Venetian (Macau)	Macau-China	3000

Contd...

Name of the Hotel	*Location*	*Numbers of Rooms*
Las Vegas Hilton	Las Vegas	2956
Paris	Las Vegas	2916
Treasure Island	Las Vegas	2885
Gaylord Opryland Resort	Nashville	2881
Disney's Pop Century Resort	Orlando	2880
Bally's	Las Vegas	2814
Wynn Las Vegas / Encore	Las Vegas	2716
Imperial Palace	Las Vegas	2635
Harrah's	Las Vegas	2576
Planet Hollywood (Aladdin)	Las Vegas	2567

Timeshares and condo-hotel rooms not included in the count.

CHAPTER

18

Airlines Codes and Country International Airlines

International Airlines	*Two Letter Codes*
Mile Air	Q5
AB Airlines	7L
ABSA Cargo—Aerolinhas Breseleiras SA	M3
AccessAir	ZA
ACES Colombia	VX
Action Airlines	XQ
Acvilla Air —Aor Romanian Carrier	WZ
Ade Air Albania	ZY
Adria Airways	JP
Advance Leasing	4G
Aer Arann	RE
Aer Lingus	EI
Aero Asia International	E4
Aero Continente	N6
Aero Contractors Company of Nigeria - ACN	NU
Aero Lloyd	YP
Aero Santa	UJ

Aero Services Executive W4

Aero Zambia Z9

Aerocalifornia JR

Aerocaribe QA

Aerocondor P2

Aeroexo—Aero Ejectivo SX

Aeroflot Russian International Airlines SU

Aerolineas Argentinas AR

Aerolineas Internacionales N2

Aerolineas Santo Domingo EX

Aerolineas Sosa P4

AeroLyon 4Q

Aeromar BQ

Aeromar Airlines VW

Aeromexico AM

Aeromexpress QO

Aeroperlas (Apair - Aerolineas Pacificio Atlantico) WL

Aeroperu PL

Aeropostal VH

Aerorepublica Colombia P5

Aeroservice BF

Aerosucre 6N

Aerosur 5L

Aerosweet Airlines	VV
Affertair	ZL
Africa West	3L
African International Airways	OY
Aiborne of Sweden	ZF
Aipac Airlines	LQ
Air 2000	DP
Air Afrique	RK
Air Alaska Cargo	8S
Air Alfa	H7
Air Algerie	AH
Air Alliance	3J
Air Anatolia	TD
Air Aruba	FQ
Air Asia	AK
Air Atlanta—Atlanta Icelandic Air Transport	CC
Air Atlantic	9A
Air Atlantic Dominicana	LU
Air Atlantic Spain	QD
Air Austral	UU
Air Baltic	BT
Air BC	ZX
Air Belgium International	AJ

Air Berlin	AB
Air Bosna	JA
Air Botnia	KF
Air Botswana	BP
Air Burkina	2J
Air Caledonie	TY
Air Caledonie International	SB
Air Canada	AC
Air Caraibes	WS
Air Cargo Express	3K
Air Carribean	C2
Air Carribean—CLTM Airlines	XC
Air Chathams	CV
Air China	CA
Air City	4F
Air Comet	2Z
Air Contracors	AG
Air Creebec	YN
Air d'Ayiti	2N
Air Direct	C7
Air Djibouti - Red Sea Airlines	DY
Air Dolomiti	EN
Air East Africa	K5

Air Europa	UX
Air Europe Italy	PE
Air Facilities	FZ
Air Fiji (Fiji Air Services)	PC
Air Florida Express	FD
Air Foyle	GS
Air France	AF
Air Gabon	GN
Air Georgia	DA
Air Glaciers	GB
Air Greece	JG
Air Guadeloupe	TX
Air Holland	GG
Air Hong Kong	LD
Air Iceland—Flugfelag Islands	NY
Air India	AI
Air Inuit	3H
Air Ivoire	VU
Air Jamaica	JM
Air Jet	BC
Air Kazakstan	9Y
Air Kenya Aviation	QP
Air Koryo	JS

Air Labrador—Labrador Airways	WJ
Air Lanka	UL
Air Liberte	IJ
Air Link	DR
Air Lithuania—Aviakompanija Lietuva	TT
Air Littoral	FU
Air Macau	NX
Air Madagascar	MD
Air Malawi	QM
Air Maldives	L6
Air Mali	L9
Air Malta	KM
Air Mandalay	6T
Air Marshall Islands	CW
Air Mauritanie	MR
Air Mauritius	MK
Air Moldova	9U
Air Moldova International	3R
Air Montreal	F8
Air Namibia	SW
Air Nauru	ON
Air Negril	5T
Air New Zealand	NZ

Air New Zealand Link / Mount Cook Airlines	NM
Air Nippon	EL
Air Niugini	PX
Air North Charter	4N
Air North Regional	TL
Air Nostrum	YW
Air Nova	QK
Air One	9Q
Air One	AP
Air Ontario	GX
Air Orient	UT
Air Ostrava	8K
Air Pacific	FJ
Air Philippines	2P
Air Plus	OB
Air Provence International	DG
Air Roratonga	GZ
Air Routing International	ZJ
Air Saint Barthelemy (Barths Aviation)	OJ
Air Saint Martin	S6
Air Saint Pierre	PJ
Air Saint Thomas	ZP
Air Seychelles	HM
Air Sicilia	BM

Air Sinai	4D
Air Slovakia	GM
Air Sofia	CT
Air Stord	GO
Air Sultan	0O
Air Sunshine	YI
Air Tahiti	VT
Air Tahiti NUI	TN
Air Tanzania	TC
Air Team	8W
Air Toulouse International	SH
Air Transat	TS
Air Transport International—ATI	8C
Air Trindi	8T
Air Ukraine—Avialinii Ukrainy	6U
Air Urga	3N
Air Vallee	DO
Air Vanuatu	NF
Air Vegas	6V
Air Virginia	DO
Air Wings	XR
Air Zambezi	ZT
Air Zena	A9

Air Zimbabwe	UM
Airborne Express—ABX Air	GB
Aires—Aerovias de Integracion Regional	4C
Airlines of Carriacou	C4
Airlines of South Australia	RT
Airlink	ND
Airmax Airlines	ID
Airtours International Airways	VZ
Airtran Airways	FL
AJT Air International	E9
Aklak	6L
Alaska Airlines	AS
Alaska Central Express—ACE	KO
Alaska Seaplane Service	UI
Albanian Airlines MAK	LV
Alidaunia	D4
Alitalia	AZ
Alitalia Express	XM
Alitalia Team	RD
All Nippon Airways	NH
Allegro Air	LL
Alliance Air	CD
Alliance Airlines	3A

ALM Antillean Airlines	LM
Aloha Airlines	AQ
Aloha Island Air	WP
Alpi Eagles	E8
Alpine Air	5A
Alyemen—Airlines of Yemen	DY
AMC Aviation	9V
America West Airlines	HP
American Airlines	AA
Ameri Jet International	M6
Amiri Flight (Abu Dhabi)	MO
Angel Airlines	8G
Angkor Airlines	TI
Ansett Australia	AN
Ansett New Zealand	ZQ
AOM French Airlines	IW
APA International	7P
Ararat Avia	4A
Arax Airways	Y5
Archana Airways	F5
Arctic Circle Air Service	5F
Arctic Transportation Services	7S
Ariana Afghan Airlines	FG

Aries del Sur	D4
Arkia Israeli Airlines	IZ
Armenian Airlines	R3
ARPA—Aerolineas Paraguayas	A8
Arrow Air	JW
ASA / Delta Connection—Atlantic Southeast Airlines	EV
ASERCA—Aeroservicios Carabobo	R7
Asian Express Airlines	HJ
Asiana Airlines	OZ
Aspen Mountain Air	AD
Aspiring Air	OI
Astanair Kazakstan	A7
ATA—American Trans Air	TZ
ATA Aerocondor	2B
Athabaska Airways	9T
Atlant Soyuz Airlines	3G
Atlantic Airways	RC
Atlantic Coast Airlines	DH
Atlas Air	5Y
ATRAN—Aviatrans Cargo Airlines	V8
Augsburg Airways	IQ
Aurigny Air Services	GR
Aus Air	NO

Austin Express	7V
Austral Lineas Aereas	AU
Australian Air Express	XM
Austrian Airlines	OS
Avant Airlines—Linheas Aereas Chilenas	OT
Avcom—Aviation Commercial	J6
Avensa	VE
Avia Express	RX
Aviaco	AO
Aviacsa	6A
Avialeasing	AD
Avianca	AV
Aviaprima—Sochi Airlines	J5
Aviateca	GU
Avioimpex Makedonija Airways	M4
AVIOR—Aviones de Oriente	3B
Aviosarda Airlines	DF
Azerbaijan Airlines—AZAL Avia	J2
Azzurra Air	ZS
B Airways	BF
Bahamasair	UP
Baikal Airlines	X3
Baker Aviation	8Q

Balair/CTA Leisure	BB
Balkan Bulgarian Airlines	LZ
Bangkok Airways	PG
Bankair	B4
BASE Airlines	5E
Bashkirian Airlines—Bashkirskjie Avialinii	V9
BAX Global	8W
Baxter Aviation	6B
Bearskin Airlines	JV
Belair Ile de France	BL
Belavia	B2
Bellair	7G
Bellview Airlines	B3
Bemidji Airlines	CH
Bering Air	8E
Berjaya Air	J8
Besit Servizi Aerei	B1
Bhoja Airlines	B4
Big Sky Airlines	GQ
Biman Bangladesh Airlines	BG
Binter Canarias	NT
Binter Mediterraneo	AX
Bleu Panorama Airlines	BP

Bouraq Indonesia Airlines BO

Braathens BU

Braathens Malmo Aviation 6E

Britair DB

Britannia Airways BY

Britannia Airways Deutschland BN

British Airways BA

British International Helicopters BS

British Mediterranean Airways KJ

British Midland Airways BD

British Regional Airlines TH

British World Airlines VF

Brittania Airways Sweden 6B

Buffalo Airways J4

Business Express Airlines—BEX HQ

BWIA International Airways BW

CAL—Cargo Airlines 5C

Calm Air MO

Camai Air R9

Cameroon Airlines UY

Canada 3000 2T

Canadian Airlies International CP

Canarias Regional Air FW

Cape Air	9K
Cape Smythe Air Service	6C
Cape York Air	NS
Capital Cargo International Airlines	PT
Cardinal Airlines	NN
Cargolux Airlines International	CV
Carib Aviation	K7
Carribean Air Transport—CLTM Airlines	XC
Casino Express	XP
Cathay Pacific Airways	CX
Cayman Airways	KX
Cebu Pacific Air	5J
Central Mountain Air	9M
Centralafrican Airlines	GC
Chalair	M6
Chalk's International Airline	OP
Challenge Air Cargo	WE
Champion Air	MG
Changan Airlines	2Z
Channel Express	LS
Chelal—Chelyabinsk Air Enterprise	H6
Chicago Express Airwasy (ATA Connection)	C8
China Airlines	CI

China Eastern Airlines	MU
China National Aviation Corporation—CNAC	F6
China Northern Airlines	CJ
China Northwest Airlines	WH
China Southern Airlines	CZ
China Southwest Airlines	SZ
China Xinjiang Airlines	XO
China Yunnan Airlines	3Q
Chitaavia	X7
Cimber Air	QI
Circle Air Freight	FO
Cirrus Airlines	C9
City Bird Airlines	H2
Cityflyer	FD
Cityjet	WX
CLA Air Transport	C9
Coast Air	BX
Coastal Air Transport	DQ
Colgan Air	9L
Color Air	CA
Columbia Pacific Airlines	7C
Comair	MN
Comair/Delta Connection	OH

Compagnie Africaine d'Aviation	E9
Compagnie Corse Mediterranee	XK
Condor	DE
Congo Airlines—CAL	EO
Constellation International Airlines	CQ
Contact Air	V8
Continental Airlines	CO
Continental Airways	PC
Continental Micronesia	CS
COPA Panama	CM
Corporate Airlines	3C
Corsair	SS
Cosmos Air	ZE
Country Connection Airlines	XL
Coyne Airways	7C
Crimea Air	OR
Croatia Airlines	OU
Cronus Airlines	X5
Crossair	LX
Crossair Europe	QE
CSA Czech Airlines—Ceske Aerolinie	OK
Cubana	CU
Custom Air Transport	DG

Cyprus Airways	CY
Daallo Airlines	D3
Damania Airways	D2
Danish Air Transport	DX
DAS—Dirgantara Air Service	AW
DAS Air Cargo	SE
Debonair Airways	2G
Delta Airlines	DL
Denim Air	3D
Deutsche BA	DI
Deutsche Rettungsflugwacht	DV
DHL Aero Expreso	DS
DHL Airways	ER
DHL de Guatemala	Z8
DHL International EC	ES
Diamond International Airlines	9X
Diamond Sakha Airlines	D8
Dinar Lineas Aereas	D7
Dnieproavia Aviation Company	Z6
Dominair—Aerolineas Dominicanas	YU
Domodedovo Airlines	E3
Donavia	D9
Donbass Eastern Ukranian Airlines	7D

Dragonair (Hong Kong Dragon Airlines)	KA
Dutchbird	5D
Eagle Airlines	ZN
Eagle Aviation	Y4
Eagle Canyon Airlines	FE
East Line Airlines	P7
Eastland Air—Moores Air Charter	DK
Eastwind Airlines	W9
Eastwind Airlines—The Bee Line	9W
EasyJet Airlines	U2
Easyjet Switzerland	BH
Ecuatoriana	EU
Edelweiss Air	ED
Egypt Air	MS
El Al Israel Airlines	LY
ELK Airways Estonian Aviation—Eesti Lennukompanii	S8
Emerald Airways	G3
Emery Worldwide Airlines	EB
Emirates	EK
Empire Airlines	EM
Enkor	5Z
Equaflight Service	8H
ERA Aviation	7H

Estonian Air	OV
Ethiopian Airlines	ET
Euralair International	RN
Eureca	F4
Eurocypria Airlines	UI
Eurofly	GJ
Europe Elite	Y6
European Air Transport—EAT	QY
European Regions Airlines—ERA	EA
Euroscot Express Airways	MY
Eurowings	EW
EVA Air	BR
Evergreen International Airlines	EZ
Execaire Aviation	MB
Executive Express	5W
Executive Jet Aviation	1L
Expedition Airways	FO
Expo Airlines	8D
Express One International	EO
Falcon Air	IH
Falcon Air Express	F2
Falcon Express Air Cargo	FC
Far Eastern Air Transport	EF

Fast Air	UD
Faucett	CF
Federico II Airways	2D
FedEx—Federall Express	FM
FedEx—Federall Express	FX
Fika Salaama Airlines	HG
Fine Airlines	FB
Finnair	AY
First Air	7F
Fischer Air	8F
Flandre Air	IX
Flight West Airlines	YC
Florida West Airlines	RF
Fly FTI	FT
Flying Colours Airlines	MT
Flying Enterprise	F3
Forward Air Int'l Airlines	BN
Four Star Air Cargo	HK
Frontier Airlines	F9
Frontier Commuter—ITR Airlines	F9
Frontier Flying Service	2F
FS Air Service	Y7
Fujian Airlines	IV

Futura International	FH
Garuda Indonesia	GA
GB Airways	GT
Gemini Air Cargo	GR
Gemini Airlines	GR
Georgian Airlines	3P
Germania	ST
Gestair Executive Jet	GP
Ghana Airways	GH
Gill Airways	9C
GMG Airlines	Z5
GO Fly	OG
Go One Airways	GK
Golden Air	DC
Golden West Airlines	GW
Gomelavia	YD
Government of Brunei—His Majesty The Sultan's Flight	UR
GP Express Airlines	8G
Grant Aviation	GS
Great Barrier Airlines	GB
Greenlandair—Gronlandsfly	GL
Guard Air	FB
Gujarat Airways	G8

Gulf Air	GF
Gulfstream International Airlines	3M
Guyana Airways	GY
Hageland Aviation Services	H6
Hahn Air Businesslines	HR
Hainan Airlines	H4
Haines Airways	7A
Haiti Air International	9F
Haiti International Airlines	HG
Hapag Lloyd	HF
Harbor Airlines	HB
Harbour Air	H3
Harlequin Air	JH
Hawaiian Airlines	HA
Hazelton Airlines	ZL
Heavylift Cargo Airlines	NP
Helenair	2Y
Helgoland Airlines	LE
Heli Air Monaco	YO
Heli Inter	EC
Heli Trans	5H
Helicopterservice Euro Air	YQ
Helijet Airways	JB

Helikopter Service	L5
Helisul	H9
Helisul Taxi Aereo	H9
Helisureste	UV
Hemus Air	DU
Hex'Air	UD
Highland Air	HS
Highland Airways	8R
Hinduja Cargo Services—Lufthansa Cargo India	LF
Hokkaido International Airlines—Air Do	HD
Horizon Air/Alaska Airlines Commuter	QX
Horizon Airlines	YK
Iberia	IB
Iberostar Airlines	TY
Iberworld Airlines	TY
ICAR Airlines	C3
Icaro	1I
Icelandair	FI
Iliamna Air taxi	LS
Improtex—Imair	IK
Impulse Airlines	VQ
Indian Airlines	IC
Inercontinental Colombia	RS

Intensive Air	IM
Inter Air Lines	D6
Interbrasil Star	Q9
International Business Air	U5
Iran Air (Iran National Airlines)	IR
Iraqi Airways	IA
Island Air	G5
Island Air	IS
Island Airlines	DG
Islands Nationair	CN
Islandsflug—Icebird Airline	HH
Isles of Scilly Skybus	5Y
Israir	6H
Istanbul Airlines	IL
ITA Itapemirim Transportes Aereos	5W
Italair	B8
JAL Express	JC
Japan Air Charter	JZ
Japan Air Commuter	3X
Japan Air Lines	JL
Japan Air System	JD
Japan Asia Airways	EG
Japan Transocean Air	NU

JAT Yugoslav Airlines	JU
Jersey European Airways	JY
Jet Airways	9W
Jet Aviation Business Jets	PP
Kaliningrad Avia Entreprise	K8
Kampuchea Airlines	KT
Karat—Aviacompany Karat	2U
Kavminvodyavia	KV
KD Air	XC
Kendell Airlines (Australia)	KD
Kenmore Air	M5
Kenn Borek Air	4K
Kenya Airways	KQ
Keystone Air Services	BZ
Khabarovsk Aviation	H8
Khors Air	X9
Kibris Turkish Airlines—KTHY (Cyprus Turkish Airlines)	YK
King Island Airlines	KG
Kitty Hawk Air Cargo	KR
Kitty Hawk International	KR
Kiwi International Airlines	KP
KLM Cityhopper	WA
KLM Exel	XT

KLM Royal Dutch Airlines	KL
KLM UK	UK
Kogalymavia	7K
Korean Air	KE
Kras Air—Krasnoyarskavia	7B
Kronflyg	K4
Kuban Airlines	GW
Kuwait Airways	KU
Kyrgystan Airlines	K2
La Ronge Aviation Services—Air Sask Aviation	7W
LAB—Lloyd Aereo Boliviano	LB
LAB Flying Service—Alaska Airlines Commuter	JF
LACSA—Lineasaereas Costarricenses SA	LR
LADECO—Linea Aerea Del Cobre	UC
LADECO Cargo	UC
LAI—Linea Aerea IAACA	KG
Laker Airways	6F
Laker Airways (Bahamas)	7Z
LAM—Linheas Aereas de Mocambique	TM
LAN Chile	LA
Lao Aviation	QV
Laoag International	L7
LAPA—Lineas Aereas Privadas Argentinas	MJ

Laparkan Airlines	L8
Larry's Flying Service	J6
Las Vegas Airlines	6G
LASER—Lineas Aereas de Servicio Ejecutivo Regional	KZ
LASTP	KY
Latpass Airlines	QJ
Lauda Air	NG
Lauda Air Italy	L4
Lebanese Air Transport	LQ
LGW—Luftfahrt Gesellschaft Walter	HE
LIAt—The Carribean Airline	LI
Libyan Arab Airlines	LN
Link Airways of Australia	XU
Lithuanian Airlines	TE
LOT Polish Airlines	LO
Lotus Air	T2
Loveair	4J
LTE International Airways	XO
LTU International Airways	LT
Lufthansa	LH
Lufthansa Cargo Airlines	LH
Lufthansa Cityline	CL
Luxair	LG

Lynden Air Cargo	L2
Macair Airlines	CC
Macedonian Airlines	SX
Macedonian Airlines—Makedonski Aviotransport	IN
Maersk Air	DM
Maersk Air (UK)	VB
MAF Australia—Missionary Aviation Fellowship	FS
Mafira Air	3A
Magadan Airlines	H5
Mahfooz Aviation	M2
Malev—Hungarian Airlines	MA
Malta Air Charter	R5
Mandarin Airlines	AE
Manx Airlines	JE
Mario's Air	M2
Maroomba Airlines	KN
Martinair	MP
MAS—Malaysian Airlines System	MH
Mas Air Cargo	MY
Maya Island Air	MW
Mayan World Airlines	EY
MBA Air	CG
MDA Airlines	KR

MEA—Middle East Airlines	ME
Med Airlines	M8
Mediterranean Air Service	MG
Mercury Air Cargo	BX
Meridiana	IG
Merpati Nusantara Airlines	MZ
Mesa Airlines	YV
Metavia Airlines	OW
Mexicana	MX
Mexicargo	GJ
Miami Air International	GL
MIAT Mongolian Airlines	OM
Midway Airlines	JI
Midwest Express Airlines	YX
Millair	2Q
Minerva Airlines	Q2
Miravia	N3
MK Airlines	7G
MN Aviation	W4
MNG Airlines Cargo	MB
Modiluft	M9
Moldavian Airlines	2M
Monarch Airlines	ZB

Montenegro Airlines	1I
Muk Air	ZR
Mustique Airways (Air Saint Vincent)	Q4
Naske Air	HC
National Airlines	N4
National Airways Corporation—NAC	YJ
National Jet Systems	NC
Nations Air	N5
Nationwide Airlines	CE
Nature Island Express	XV
Necon Air	3Z
NEPC Airlines	D5
New England Airlines	EJ
New York Helicopter	HD
NICA—Nicaraguenses de Aviacion	6Y
Nice Helicopteres	JX
Nigeria Airways	WT
Nippon Cargo Airlines	KZ
Nordeste—Linhas Aereas regionais	JH
Normandie Aviation	ID
North American Airlines	XG
North Coast Aviation	N9
North Vancouver Airliners	VL

North Wright Airways	HW
Northeast Airlines	NE
Northern Air Cargo—NAC	NC
Northern Thunderbird Air	4R
Northwest Airlines	NW
Northwest Airlink/Express Airlines	9E
Northwest Airlink/Mesaba Airlines	XJ
Northwestern Air	J3
Nouvelair Tunesie	BJ
Novair—Nova Airlines	1I
Novosibirsk Airlines	L8
NWT Air—Northwest Territorial Airways	NV
O'Connor Airlines—Mount Gambier Airline	UQ
Odessa Airlines	5K
Olson Air Service	4B
OLT—Ostfriesische Lufttransport	OL
Olympic Airways	OA
Oman Aviation	WY
Oman Royal Flight	RS
Onur Air	8Q
Ord air Charter	RF
Orenburg Avia	R2
Orient Thai Airlines	OX

Origin Pacific Airways	QO
Pacific Airlines	BL
Pacific Airways Corporation—Pacificair	GX
Pacific Coastal Airways	8P
Pacific Island Aviation	9J
Palestinian Airlines	PF
Panagra Airways	7E
Panair	PV
Pantanal—Linhas Aereas Sul Matogrossenses	P8
Papillon Grand Canyon Helicopters	HI
Par Avion	FP
Passaredo Transportes Aereos	Y8
Pel Air	QH
Pelangi Airways	9P
Pem Air	PD
Pena Transportes Aereos—PENTA	5P
Penair—Peninsula Airways	KS
Philippines—Philippine Air Lines	PR
PIA—Pakistan International Airlines	PK
PINAIR Panamian International	2Q
PLUNA	PU
Polar Air Cargo	PO
Polynesian Airline of Samoa	PH

Portugalia	NI
Precision Air Services	PW
Premiar	DK
Premier Trans Air	P3
President Airlines	TO
Pro Air	P9
Pro Mech Air	Z3
Proteus Air System	YS
Provincial Airlines	AG
Pulkovo Avia	Z8
Qantas	QF
Qatar Airways	QR
Queen Air	7Q
Qwestair	QD
RAS Fluggesellschaft	RW
Redwing Airways	RX
Reeve Aleutian Airways—RAA	RV
Region Air	7S
Regional Air	QT
Regional Airlines	FN
Regional Airlines	VM
Regional Lineas Aereas	XG
Regionnair	RH

Reguljair	R8
Reno Air	QQ
Rheintalflug	WE
Riga Airlines—RiAir	GV
Rio Sul	SL
ROAN Air	Q3
Romavia	WQ
Roots Air	6J
Rover Airways International	5R
Royal Air Cambodge	VJ
Royal Air Maroc	AT
Royal Airlines	QN
Royal Brunei Airlines	BI
Royal Jordanian	RJ
Royal Nepal Airlines	RA
Royal Tongan Airlines (Friendly Island Airways)	WR
Rusavia Int'l Aviatransport	2Q
Ryan International Airlines	1I
Ryanair	FR
SA Airlink—Midlands Aviation	4Z
SA Alliance	Y2
Sabena	SN
Sabre Airways	TJ

SAETA—Sociedad Ecuatoriana de Aereos	EH
Safair	FA
Sahara Airlines	S2
Saint Barth Commuter	PV
Sakha Avia	K7
Sakhalinskie Aviatrassy—SAT	HZ
SAM—Sociedad Aeronautica de Medellin	MM
Samara Airlines	E5
Samoa Air	SE
SAN—Servicios Aereos Nationales	WB
San Air Company	S3
SANSA—Servicios Aereos Nacionales SA	RZ
Santa Barbara Airlines	BJ
SAS—Scandinavian Airlines System	SK
SATA Air Acores	SP
SATA International	S4
Saudi Arabian Airlines	SV
Sayakhat	W7
Scenic Air	3L
Scenic Airlines	YR
Schreiner Airways	AW
Seaborne Aviation	BB
Sempati Air Transport	SG

Servivensa—Empresa Servicios Avensa SA	VC
Shaheen Air International	NL
Shanghai Airlines	FM
Shanxi Airlines	8C
Shenzen Airlines	4G
Shepparton Airlines	OB
Shorouk Air	7Q
Shunshine Express Airlines	CQ
Shuswap Flight Centre	3S
Shuttle America	S5
Sibaviatrans	5M
Siberia Airlines	S7
Sichuan Airlines	3U
Sierra National Airlines	LJ
Sierra Pacific Airlines	SI
Silkair	MI
Singapore Airlines	SQ
SK Air	S9
Skargardsflyg	5Q
Skippers Aviation	SY
Sky Cabs	2E
Sky Trek International Airlines	1I
Skyking	RU

Skymark Airlines	BC
Skytrans	NP
Skyward Aviation	K9
Skyway Airlines / Midwest Express Connection	AL
Skyways	JZ
Skywest Airlines	OO
Skywest Airlines	YT
Slovak Airlines—Slovenske Aerolinie	6Q
Sobelair	Q7
Solomon Airlines	IE
South African Airways—SAA	SA
South African Express Airways	YB
South Central Air	XE
Southern Winds	A4
Southwest Airlines	WN
Spanair	JK
Special Cargo Airlines	C7
Spirit Airlines	NK
STAF—Servicios de Transportes Aereos Fueguino	FS
Star Airlines	2R
Starwelt Airways	2N
State Transport Company of Russia	R4
Suckling Airways	CB

Sudan Airways	SD
Sun Air	BV
Sun Air of Scandinavia	EZ
Sun Country Airlines	SY
Sun Express	XQ
Sunflower Airlines	PI
Sunjet International Airlines	JX
Sunrise Airlines	OQ
Sunworld International Airways	SM
Superior Aviation	AB
Surinam Airways / SLM	PY
Svea Flyg	SI
Swazi Airlink	ZC
Swedeways Air Lines	HJ
Swiss Wings	RQ
Swissair	SR
Syrianair—Syrian Arab Airlines	RB
TAAG—Linhas Aereas de Angola—Angola Airlines	DT
TACA International Airlines	TA
TACV—Cabo Verde Airlines	VR
TAESA—Transportes Aereos Ejecutivos SA	GD
TAG Aviation	FP
TAM—Transportes Aereos Meridionais	JJ

TAM —Transportes Aereos Regionais	KK
TAM—Travaux Aeriens de Madagascar	OF
TAME—Transportes Aereos Militares Ecuatoriana	EQ
TAMPA Colombia	QT
TAN—Transportes Aereos Neuquen	T8
Tanana Air Services	4E
TAP Air Portugal	TP
Taquan Air Service	K3
TAROM—Transporturile Aerienne Romane	RQ
Tasawi Air Service	9X
Tashkent Aircraft Production Corporation	PQ
Tatra Air	QS
TAVAJ—Transportes Aereos Regulares	4U
Tavrey Aircompany	T6
Teddy Air	ZJ
Tempelhoff Express Airlines—TEX	FC
Tesis	UZ
Thai Air Cargo	2Y
Thai Airways International	TG
TMA—Trans Mediterranean Airlines	TL
Tolair Services	TI
Tower Air	FF
Trade Winds Airlines	WI

Trans Air	P6
Trans America Peru	ES
Trans Asian Airlines	T7
Trans European Airlines	UE
Trans International Express	5B
Trans States Airlines	9N
Trans Travel Airlines—TTA	6N
Trans World Airlines—TWA	TW
Transaero Airlines	UN
Transasia Airways	GE
Transavia Airlines	HV
TransAvia Export	AL
Transbrasil	TR
Transcaraibes Air International	DZ
Transeast Airlines	T4
Transmeridian Airlines	T9
Transmile Air Services	TH
Transstate Airlines	BH
Travelair	U3
Tropic Air	PM
Tunisair	TU
Tunisinter	UG
Turanair	3T

Turkish Airlines	TK
Turkmenistan Airlines—Turkmenhavayollari	T5
Turks and Caicos Airways	QW
Turtle Airways	KT
Tyrolean Airways	VO
Tyumen Airlines	7M
TyumenAviaTrans	P2
U Land Airlines	WI
Uganda Airlines	QU
Ukraine International Airlines	PS
UNA—Southern Independent Air Company	F2
UNI Air	B7
United Airlines	UA
United Express / Great Lakes Airlines	ZK
United Express/Air Wisconsin	ZW
United Express/Atlantic Coast Airlines	DH
United Express/Trans States Airlines	9N
United Express/United Feeder Services	U2
Universal Airways	UV
UPS—United Parcel Service	5X
Ural Airlines—Uralskie Avialinii	U6
US Airways	US
US Airways Express	US

US Airways Express/Air Midwest	ZV
US Airways Express/Allegheny Commuter Airlines	US
US Airways Express/Chautauqua Airlines	US
US Airways Express/Piedmont Airlines	US
US Airways Shuttle	TB
USA Jet Airlines	U7
Uzbekistan Airways	HY
V-Air—Varmlandsflyg	T9
Vanguard Airlines	NJ
Varig	RG
VASP	VP
VIA—Air VIA Bulgarian Airways	VL
Vieques Air Link	VI
Vietnam Airlines	VN
Vip Air	9V
Virgin Atlantic	VS
Virgin Express	TV
Viva Air	FV
Vladivostok Air	XF
VLM—Vlaamse Luchtvaart Maatschappij	VG
Vnukovo Airlines	V5
Volare Air Transport	OP
Volare Airlines	8D

Volare Ukraine	F7
Volga Airlines	G6
Volga Dnepr Airlines	VI
Voronezh Avia	ZT
Voyageur Airways	4V
Wairapa Airlines—Pacific Midland Airlines	2W
Warbelow's Air Ventures	4W
Wasaya Airways	WG
Welcome Air	2W
West Coast Air	8O
West Isle Air	7Y
Westair	OE
Western Air Freight	WZ
Western Airlines	EM
Westjet Airlines	M3
Whyalla Airlines	WW
Wideroe—Wideroe's Flyveselskap	WF
Winair—Windward Island Airways International	WM
Wings of Alaska	K5
Winnport Air Cargo	KN
World Airways	WO
Wright Air Service	8V
Xiamen Airlines	MF

Yanda Airlines	ST
Yangon Airways	HK
Yemenia—Yemen Airways	IY
Yute Air Alaska	4Y
Zimbabwe Express Airlines	Z7
Zimex Aviation	C4

CHAPTER

19

Country Codes with there Capital, Language and Currency

Country	*Capital*	*Official Name*	*Location*	*Chief Language*	*Currency*
Afghanistan	Kabul	Islamic Emirate of Afghanistan	Asia	Pushtu Dari	Afghani
Albania	Tirana	Republic of Albania	Europe	Albanian	Lek
Algeria	Algiers	Democratic People's Republic of Algeria	Africa	Arabic, French	Dinar
Andorra	Andorre La Vieille	Principality of Andorra	Europe	Catalan	French Franc, Spanish Peseta
Angola	Luanda	People's Republic of Angola	Africa	Portuguese	re-adjusted Kwanza
Antigua Barbuda	St. John's	Antigua and Barbuda	Caribbean Sea	English	East Caribbean Dollar US
Argentina	Buenos Aires	Argentine Republic	South America	Spanish	Peso
Armenia	Yerevan	Republic of Armenia	Asia	Armenian	the Dram
Australia	Canberra	Common-wealth of Australia	Australia	English	Australian Dollar
Ashmore & Cartier Islands	Kingston (Adminis-trative Centre)	(Territories under Australia in the Indian Ocean)	Indian Ocean	English	Australian Dollar

Christmas Island	Kingston (Adminis-trative Centre)	(Territories under Australia in Indian Ocean	Indian Ocean	English	Australian Dollar
Cocos (Keeling) Islands	Kingston (Adminis-trative Centre)	(Territories under Australia in the Indian Ocean)	Indian Ocean	English	Australian Dollar
Herd & Mcdonald Islands	Kingston (Adminis-trative Centre)	(Territories under Australia in the Indian Ocean)	Indian Ocean	English	Australian Dollar
Norfolk Islands	Kingston (Adminis-trative Centre)	(Territories under Australia in the Indian Ocean)	Indian Ocean	English	Australian Dollar
Coral Sea Islands	Kingston (Adminis-trative Centre)	(Territories under Australia in the Indian Ocean)	Pacific Ocean	English	Australian Dollar
Australian Antarctic Territory	Kingston (Adminis-trative Centre)	(Territories under Australia in the Indian Ocean)	Antarctica	English	Australian Dollar
Austria	Vienna	Republic of Austria	Europe	German	Euro Schilling
Azerbaijan	Baku	Azerbaijan Republic	Asia	Azeri	Manat
The Baha-mas	Nassau	Common-wealth of the Bahamas	Atlantic Ocean	English	Bahamian Dollar
Bahrain	Manama	State of Bahrain	Asia	Arabic, English	Dinar, Bahraini
Bangladesh	Dhaka	People's Republic of Bangladesh	Asia	Bangla	Taka
Barbados	Bridgetown	Barbados	Atlantic Ocean	English	Barbados Dollar
Belarus Byelorussia	Minsk	Republic of Belarus	Europe	Belorussian	Ruble

Belgium	Brussels	Kingdom of Belgium	Europe	Flemish (Dutch), French, German	Euro
Belize	Belmopan	Belize	Central America	English	Belize Dollar
Benin	Porto-Novo	Republic of Benin	Africa	French	Franc
Bhutan	Thimphu	Kingdom of Bhutan	Asia	Dzongkha	Ngultrum
Bolivia	La Paz; Sucre	Republic of Bolivia	South America	Aymara Spanish, Quechua	The Boliviano
Bosnia-Herze-govina	Sarajevo	Republic of Bosnia-Herzegovina	Europe	Serbo-Croatian	Conv.Mark
Botswana	Gaborone	Republic of Botswana	Africa	English	Pula
Brazil	Brazilia	Federative Republic of Brazil	South America	Portuguese	Real
Brunei	Bander Seri Bagawan	State of Brunei Darussalam	Asia	Malay, Chinese	Brunei Dollar
Bulgaria	Sofia	Republic of Bulgaria	Europe	Bulgarian	Lev
Burkina Faso	Ouaga-dougou	Burkina Faso	Africa	French	Franc
Burundi	Bujumbura	Republic of Burundi	Africa	Kirundi, French	Burundi Franc
Cambodia	Phnom-Penh	Kingdom of Cambodia	Asia	Khmer	Rial
Cameroon	Yaounde	Republic of Cameroon	Africa	French, English	Franc CFA
Canada	Ottawa	Canada	North America	French, English	Canadian Dollar
Cape Verde	Praia	Republlic of Cape Verde	Africa	Crioulo	Escudo
Central African Republic	Bangui	Central African Republic	Africa	French	Franc

Chad	N'Djamena	Republic of Chad	Africa	Arabic, French	Franc
Chile	Santiago	Republic of Chile	South America	Spanish	Peso
China	Beijing	People's Republic of China	Asia	Chinese (Mandarin)	Yuan
Hong Kong	Victoria	Chinese Territory in China Sea	Asia	English, Chinese	Hong Kong Dollar
Colombia	Bogota	Republic of Colombia	South America	Spanish	Peso
The Comoros	Moroni	Federal Islamic Republic of the Comoros	Africa	Comoran	Comoran Franc
Congo Formerly Zaire	Kinshasa	Democratic Republic of the Congo	Africa	French	Congolese Franc
Costa Rica	San Jose	Republic of Costa Rica	Central America	Spanish	Colon
Cote d'Ivoire (Ivory coast)	Abidjan	Republic of Cote d'Ivoire	Africa	French	Franc
Croatia	Zagreb	Republic of Croatia	Europe	Croatian	Kuna
Cuba	Havana	Republic of Cuba	Caribbean Sea	Spanish	Peso
Cyprus	Nicosia	Republic of Cyprus	Mediterr-anean Sea	Greek, Turkish	Cyprus Pound
Turkish Cyprus	Nicosia North	Turkish Republic of Northern Cyprus	Mediterr-anean Sea	Turkish	Turkish Lira
Czech Republic	Prague.	Ceska Republica	Europe	Czech	Koruna
Denmark	Copen-hagen	Kingdom of Denmark	Europe	Danish	Krone
Faeroe Islands	Rorshavn	Territories under Denmark	Atlantic Ocean in between Atlantic and Arctic Oceans	Danish	Krone

Greenland	Nuuk	Territories under Denmark	Atlantic Ocean in between Atlantic and Arctic Oceans	Danish and Greenlandic	Krone
Djibouti	Djibouti	Republic of Djibouti	Africa	Arabic	Djibouti Franc
Dominica	Roseau	Common-wealth of Dominica	Caribbean Sea	French patois, Eng.	East Carib-bean Dollar
Dominican Republic	Santo Domingo	Dominican Republic	Caribbean Sea	Spanish	Peso Oro
Ecuador	Quito	Republic of Ecuador	South America	Spanish	Sucre
Egypt	Cairo	Arab Republic of Egypt	Africa	Arabic	Egyptian Pound
El Salvador	San Salvador	Republic of El Salvador	Central America	Spanish	Colon
Equatorial Guinea	Malabo	Republic of Equatorial Guinea	Africa	Spanish	Franc
Eritrea	Asmara	State of Eritrea	Africa	Tigrigna	Nakfa
Estonia	Tallinn	Republic of Estonia	Europe	Estonian	Kroon
Ethiopia	Addis Ababa	Federal Democratic Republic of Ethiopia	Africa	Amharic	Birr
Fiji	Suva	Republic of Fiji	South Pacific Ocean	English	Fijian Dollar
Finland	Helsinki	Republic of Finland	Europe	Finnish, Swedish	Markka
France	Paris	French Republic	Europe	French	Euro
French Guayana	Caine	French Republic	South America	French	Euro
Pappeet	Pappeet	French Republic	Pacific Ocean	French	Euro
French Southern and Arabic Lands		French Republic	Antarctic Indian Ocean	French	Euro

Guadeloupe	Basse-Terre	French Republic	Caribbean Sea	French	Euro
Martinique	Fort-de-France	French Republic	Caribbean Sea	French	Euro
Mayotte	Dzaoudzic	French Republic	Indian Ocean (Mozambic Channel)	French	Euro
New Caledonia	Naumia	French Republic	Pacific Ocean	French	Euro
Reunion	Saint Dennis	French Republic	Indian Ocean	French	Euro
Saint Pierre & Miquelon	Saint-Pierre	French Republic	Atlantic Ocean	French	Euro
Wallis Futuna Islands	Matta-Uttu	French Republic	Pacific Ocean	French	Euro
Gabon	Libreville	Gabonese Republic	Africa	French	Franc
The Gambia	Banjul	Republic of the Gambia	Africa	English	Dalasi
Georgia	Tbilisi	Republic of Georgia	Asia	Georgian	The Lari
Germany	Berlin	Federal Republic of Germany	Europe	German	Euro
Ghana	Accra	Republic of Ghana	Africa	English	New Cedi
Greece	Athens	Hellenic Republic	Europe	Greek	Drachma
Grenada	St.Georges	State of Grenada	Caribbean Sea	English	East Carib-bean, Dollar
Guatemala	Guatemala City	Republic of Guatemala	Central America	Spanish	Quetzal
Guinea	Conakry	Republic of Guinea	Africa	French	Franc
Guinea-Bissau	Bissau	Republic of Guinea - Bissau	Africa	Portuguese	CFA Franc
Guyana	George-town	Co-operative Republic of Guyana	South America	English	Guyana Dollar
Haiti	Port-au-Prince	Republic of Haiti	Caribbean Sea	French	Gourde

Honduras	Tegucigalpa	Republic of Honduras	Central America	Spanish	Lempira
Hungary	Budapest	Republic of Hungary	Europe	Hungarian	Forint
Iceland	Reykjavik	Republic of Iceland	Europe	Icelandic	Krona
India	New Delhi	Republic of India-Bharat	Asia	Hindi	Rupee
Indonesia	Jakarta	Republic of Indonesia	Asia	Bahasa Indonesia	Rupiah
Iran	Tehran	Islamic Republic of Iran	Asia	Farsi	Rial
Iraq	Baghdad	Republic of Iraq	Asia	Arabic	Dinar
Ireland	Dublin	Republic of Ireland	Europe	Irish Gaelic, English	Irish-Pound
Isreal	Jerusalem	State of Isreal	Asia	Hebrew and Arabic	Shekel
Italy	Rome	Italian Republic	Europe	Italian	Lira Euro
Jamaica	Kingston	Jamaica	Caribbean Ocean	English	Jamaican Dollar
Japan	Tokyo	Nippon	Asia	Japanese	Yen
Jordan	Amman	The Hashe-mite Kingdom of Jorden	Asia	Arabic	Jordanian Dinar
Kazakhstan	Astana	Republic of Kazakhstan	Asia	Kazakh	Tenge
Kenya	Nairobi	Republic of Kenya	Africa	Kiswahili, English	Kenyan Shilling
Kiribati	Tarawa	Republic of Kiribati	Pacific Ocean	English Gilbertese	Australian Dollar
North Korea	Pyongyang	Democratic People's Republic of Korea	Asia	Korean	Won
South Korea	Seoul	Republic of Korea	Asia	Korean	Won
Kuwait	Kuwait City	State of Kuwait	Asia	Arabic	Kuwait Dinar

Kyrgyztan	Bishkek	The Kyrgyz Republic	Asia	Kirghiz	The Som
Laos	Vientiane	Lao People's Democratic Republic	Asia	Lao	Kip
Latvia	Riga	The Republic of Latvia	Europe	Latvian	Lat
Lesotho	Maseru	Kingdom of Lesotho	Africa	Sesotho	Loti
Liberia	Monrovia	Republic of Liberia	Africa	English	Liberian Dollar
Libya	Tripoli	Socialist People's Libyan Arab Republic	Africa	Arabic	Libyan Dinar
Liechtenstein	Vaduz	Principality of Liechten-stein	Europe	German	Swiss Franc
Lithuania	Vilnius	Republic of Lithuania	Europe	Lithuanian	Litas
Luxembourg	Luxemburg	Grand Duchy of Luxembourg	Europe	Luxem-burgish, French, English	Euro
Macedonia	Skopie	Republic of Macedonia	Europe	Macedonian	Dinar
Madagascar	Antan-anarivo	Democratic Republic of Madagascar	Indian Ocean	Malagasy, French	Malagasy Franc
Malawi	Lilongwe	Republic of Malawi	Africa	English, Chichewa	Kwacha
Malaysia	Kuala Lumpur	Malaysia	Asia	Malay	Ringgit
Maldives	Male	Republic of Maldives	Indian Ocean	Divehi	Maldivian Rufiya
Mali	Bamako	Republic of Mali	Africa	French	CFA Franc
Malta	Valletta	Republic of Malta	Mediter-ranean	Maltese, English	Maltese Lira
Marshall Islands	Majuro	Republic of the Marshall Islands	Pacific Ocean	Marshallese	U.S. Dollar

Mauritania	Nouakchott	Islamic Republic of Mauritania	Africa	Arabic	Ouguiya
Mauritius	Port Louis	Republic of Mauritius	Indian Ocean	English, Creole	Rupee
Mexico	Mexico City	United Mexican States	North America	Spanish	New Peso
Micronesia	Palikir	Federated States of Micronesia	Pacific Ocean	English	U.S. Dollar
Moldova	Chisinau	Republic of Moldova	Europe	Romanian	Leu
Monaco	Monaco	Principality of Monaco	Europe	French	Franc
Mongolia	Ultan Bator	Mongolian People's Republic	Asia	Mongolian	Tugrik
Morocco	Rabat	Kingdom of Morocco	Africa	Arabic	Dirham
Mozambique	Maputo	People's Republic of Mozambique	Africa	Portuguese	Metical
Myanmar	Yangon	Union of Myanmar	Asia	Burmese	Kyat
Namibia	Windhoek	Republic of Namibia	Africa	English	Rand
Nauru	Yaren	Republic of Nauru	Pacific Ocean	Nauruan, English	Australian Dollar
Nepal	Kathmandu	Kingdom of Nepal	Asia	Nepali	Nepali Rupee
The Netherlands	Amsterdam	Kingdom of The Netherlands	Europe	Dutch	Euro
Aruba	Orangestad	(Territories under the Netherlands)	Caribbean Sea	Spanish, Dutch, English	Euro
Antilles Netherlands	Willemstad	(Territories under the Netherlands)	Caribbean Sea	Spanish, Dutch, English	Euro
New Zeeland	Wellington	New Zeeland	Pacific Ocean	English and Maori	New Zeeland Dollar

Nicaragua	Managua	Republic of Nicaragua	Central America	Spanish	Gold Cordoba
Niger	Niamey	Republic of Niger	Africa	French	CFA Franc
Nigeria	Abuja	Federal Republic of Nigeria	Africa	English	Naira
Norway	Oslo	Kingdom of Norway	Europe	Norwegian	Euro
Bueve Island	Oslo	Kingdom of Norway	Europe	Norwegian	Euro
Jan Malen	Oslo	Kingdom of Norway	Europe	Norwegian	Euro
Sawal Bard	Oslo	Kingdom of Norway	Arctic Ocean	Norwegian	Euro
Oman	Muscat	Sultanate of Oman	Asia	Arabic	Omni Rial
Pakistan	Islamabad	Islamic Republic of Pakistan	Asia	Urdu	Pakistani Rupee
Palavu	Koror	Republic of Palavu	Pacific Ocean	Palavuwan	U.S. Dollar
Palestine		(The formation is not yet completed. Its capital might be Jericho)	Asia	Arabic Hebrew	New Israeli Shekel, Jordanian Dinar
Panama	Panama City	Republic of Panama	Central America	Spanish	Balboa
Papua New Guinea	Port Moresiby	Independent State of Papua New Guinea	Pacific Ocean	English	Kina
Paraguay	Asuncion	Republic of Paraguay	South America	Spanish	Guarani
Peru	Lima	Republic of Peru	South America	Spanish Quechua	Nuevo Sol
The Philippines	Manila	Republic of Philippines	Pacific Ocean	Filipino; English	Peso
Poland	Warsaw	Republic of Poland	Europe	Polish	Euro

Portugal	Lisbon	Portuguese Republic	Europe	Portuguese	Euro
Macao	Macao	(Territory under Portugal)	Asia	Portuguese	Euro
Azores Islands	Ponda Delgad		Atlantic Ocean	Portuguese	Euro
Madeira Islands	Funchal		Atlantic Ocean	Portuguese	Euro
Qatar	Doha	State of Qatar	Asia	Arabic	Qatar Riyal
Romania	Bucharest	Romania	Europe	Romanian	Leu
Russia	Moscow	Russian Federation	Europe	Russian	Rouble
Rwanda	Kigali	Republic of Rwanda	Africa	Kinyarwanda, French	Rwanda Franc
Western Sahara	El-lyun	Saharawi Arab Democratic Republic	Africa	Arabic; Spanish	Peseta
Sahara Arab	El-lyun	Saharawi Arab Democratic Republic	Africa	Arabic; Spanish	Peseta
Democratic Republic	El-lyun	Saharawi Arab Democratic Republic	Africa	Arabic; Spanish	Peseta
St. Kitts and Nevis	Besseterre	Federation of St. Kitts and Nevis	Caribbean Sea	English	East Caribbean Dollar
St. Lucia	Castries	St. Lucia	Caribbean Sea	English	East Caribbean Dollar
St. Vincent and Grenadines	Kingstown	Federation of St. Vincent and the Grenadines	Caribbean Sea	English, French	East Caribbean Dollar
Samoa	Apia	Independent State of Samoa	Pacific Ocean	Samoan English	Tala
San Marino	San Marino	Most Serene Republic of San Marino	Europe	Italian	Euro

Sao Tome and Principle	Sao Tome	Democratic Republic of Sao Tome and Principle	Africa	Portuguese	Dobra
San Marino	San Marino	Most Serene Republic of San Marino	Europe	Italian	Euro
Sao Tome and Principle	Sao Tome	Democratic Republic of Sao Tome and Principle	Africa	Portuguese	Dobra
Saudi Arabia	Riyadh	Kingdom of Saudi Arabia	Asia	Arabic	Riyal
Senegal	Dakar	Republic of Senegal	Africa	French	CFA Franc
Seychelles	Victoria	Republic of Seychelles	Indian Ocean	French, English, Creole	Seychelles Rupee
Sierra Leone	Freetown	Republic of Sierra Leone	Africa	English	Leone
Singapore	Singapore	Republic of Singapore	Asia	Malay, Chinese, Tamil	Singapore Dollar
Slovakia	Bratislava	Republic of Slovakia	Europe	Slovak	Koruna
Slovenia	Ljubljana	Republic of Slovenia	Europe	Slovenian	Tolar
Solomon Islands	Honiara	Solomon Islands	Pacific Ocean	English	Solomon Islands Dollar

CHAPTER

20

Environment Management

Q1. What is EMS?

Ans. Environment management system refers to system for managing an organization environment programme in a formal, systematic and planned. Its help the organization structure, for developing and implementing the policies for the protection of environment.

Q2. Standard certificate for EMS?

Ans. ISO14001.

Q3. What is ISO?

Ans. The international standard for organization.

Q4. What are the 5 components of ISO 14001?

Ans. Environment policy, planning, implementation, monitoring and evaluation, review.

Q5. What is halons?

Ans. Substance that damage ozone layer. Montreal protocol prohibits manufacture of halons.

CHAPTER

21

Brain Storming Exercises

1. What does the term "HVAC" stand for?

2. The Calorific value of Charcoal is:
   (a) 20,000 kj/kg (b) 5,000 kj/kg
   (c) 30,000 kj/kg (c) 2,000 kj/kg

3. What is the abbreviation for "EPBX"?

4. Name the brine solution used in Absorption Refrigeration cycle of cooling.

5. What does the term 'Acoustics' stands for?

6. The currency of Morrocco is:
   (a) Dinar (b) Dirham
   (c) Riyal (d) Peso

7. The Nalagarh Fort Palace is located in:
   (a) Himachal Pradesh (b) Rajasthan
   (c) West Bengal (d) Uttaranchal

8. "Hydrogen peroxide" is a type of:
   (a) Sanitizer (b) Disinfectant
   (c) Germicide (d) Antiseptic

9. The incubation period of Clostridium Botulism is:
   (a) 18-36 hrs (b) 24 hrs
   (c) 6 hrs (d) 10-12 hrs

10. Tartrazine is a type of:
    (a) Anti-Caking agent (b) Acid Regulator
    (c) Food coloring agent (d) Emulsifier

11. Mercury can be ingested in the food through:
    (a) Pork (b) Fish
    (c) Citrus fruits (d) Sweet Potato

12. Arugula is a type of:
    (a) Green Leafy Vegetable (b) Citrus fruit
    (c) Cut of beef (d) Root vegetable

13. Following is the richest source of Vitamin C:
    (a) Drumstick (b) Spinach
    (c) Orange (d) Banana

14. Kwashiorkor is disease caused due the deficiency of:
    (a) Iron (b) Protein
    (c) Niacin (d) Iodine

15. Enlargement of Thyroid gland is a symptom of:
    (a) Pellagra (b) Goiter
    (c) Marasmus (d) Rickets

16. Deficiency of Thiamine results in:
    (a) Beriberi (b) Night Blindness
    (c) Obesity (d) Underweight

17. The term "Kosher" is related to the following religion:
    (a) Muslim (b) Parsi
    (c) Jew (d) Khoja

18. ___is India's largest Salt water lake.

19. The national fruit of India is___.

20. Name the world famous wax museum in London.

21. What does the abbreviation "SB" stands for?

22. What does the term "TA" stands for?

23. The Salarjung Museum is located in:
    (a) Ooty (b) Pune
    (c) Hyderabad (d) Bikaner

24. Coorg is famous for it's___plantation.

25. Famous Hindu Temple of Jagannath Puri is located in___.

26. The first property of "The Oberoi" was:
(a) The Cecil Shimla
(b) Amarvilas
(c) The Oberoi Mumbai
(d) Rajvilas

27. The Indian subcontinent if flanked by ___Sea on its East.

28. The Capital of Iraq is:
(a) Tehran
(b) Baghdad
(c) Jerusalem
(d) Cairo

29. Vitamin ___is responsible for blood clotting.

30. The famous Elephanta caves are located in ___.

31. The land of Golden Pagodas is
(a) Nepal *(b)* Myanmar
(c) Bhutan *(d)* Calicut

32. Bandipur National Park is located in
(a) Madhya Pradesh *(b)* Karnataka
(c) Andhra Pradesh *(d)* Maharashtra

33. The city of temples is:
(a) Kerala *(b)* Varanasi
(c) Haridwar *(d)* Rishikesh

34. The first Indian top get Noble prize was
(a) Lal Bahadur Shastri *(b)* Rabindranath Tagore
(c) Dr. Rajendra Prasad *(d)* Dr. Zakir Hussain

35. The famous Dilwara Temple is located in
(a) Mt. Abu *(b)* Junagadh
(c) Tanjore *(d)* Mysore

36. The capital of Mizoram is___.

37. The famous Trafalgar Square is located in___.

38. Following is a constituent of Panch Phoron:
    (*a*) Kalonji (*b*) Elaichi
    (*c*) Tejpatta (*d*) Dalchini

39. Modak is a dessert from:
    (*a*) Karnataka (*b*) Madhya Pradesh
    (*c*) Maharashtra (*d*) Andhra Pradesh

40. Karachi is located on the banks of the river
    (*a*) Yamuna (*b*) Jhelum
    (*c*) Indus (*d*) Ravi

41. The deficiency of Vitamin D causes:
    (*a*) Beri Beri (*b*) Marasmus
    (*c*) Rickets (*d*) Osteosarcorma

42. The Indian Breakfast Curry is:
    (*a*) Nihari (*b*) Dalia
    (*c*) Haleem (*d*) Sheer korma

43. The local language of Andhra Pradesh is:
    (*a*) Tamil (*b*) Tulu
    (*c*) Telgu (*d*) Malyalam

44. The Capital of Meghalaya is___.

45. Lepcha is the local language of:
    (*a*) Meghalaya (*b*) Sikkim
    (*c*) Mizoram (*d*) Nagaland

46. The word Nadroo means:
    (*a*) Eggplant (*b*) Lotus stem
    (*c*) Yam (*d*) Bottle Gourd

47. Fafda originates from:
    (*a*) Maharashtra (*b*) Gujarat
    (*c*) Rajasthan (*d*) Goa

48. What do you mean by garcon?
49. What do you mean by Nappe?
50. Which is the Liquid in which fish is poached?

ANSWERS

1. Heating Ventilation and Airconditioning
2. 30,000 kj/kg
3. Electronic private branch exchange system
4. Lithium Bromide solution
5. Bell type flushing cistern or Syphon flushing cistern
6. Dirham
7. Himachal Pradesh
8. Disinfectant
9. 18-36 hours
10. Food coloring agent
11. Fish
12. Green leafy vegetable
13. Drumstick
14. Protein
15. Goiter
16. Beriberi
17. Jews
18. Chilka
19. Mango
20. Madam Tussauds

21. Scanty Baggage
22. Travel Agent
23. Hyderabad
24. Coffee
25. Orissa
26. The Cecil Shimla
27. Bay of Bengal
28. Baghdad
29. Vitamin K
30. Maharashtra
31. Myanmar
32. Karnataka
33. Varanasi
34. Rabindranath Tagore
35. Mt. Abu
36. Aizwal
37. London
38. Kalonji
39. Maharashtra
40. Indus
41. Rickets
42. Nihari
43. Telgu

44. Shillong
45. Sikkim
46. Lotus stem
47. Gujarat
48. Waiter
49. Table Cloth
50. Courtbouillion

Exercise–1

Q1. Which of the following acts as a preservative in beer?
- *(a)* E.T.D.A. ☐
- *(b)* Gum Arabica ☐
- *(c)* Hydroxy Benzoate ☐
- *(d)* Ascorbic Acid ☐

Q2. Liquor licence L-3 in India is for:
- *(a)* Room Service in Hotel ☐
- *(b)* Duty free shops ☐
- *(c)* Service of Liquor in Bars in hotels ☐
- *(d)* Armed Forces and CSD ☐

Q3. Which of the following is a Bitter?
- *(a)* Galliano ☐
- *(b)* Noilly Prat ☐
- *(c)* Campari ☐
- *(d)* Drambuie ☐

Q4. Which of the following is not a herbal tea?
- *(a)* Camomile ☐
- *(b)* Senna ☐
- *(c)* Ceylon ☐
- *(d)* Basil and Green Mint ☐

Q5. Which of the following spirit is kept refrigerated?
- *(a)* Vodka ☐
- *(b)* Gin ☐

(c) Tequila ☐
(d) Rum ☐

Q6. The master key is most likely to be held by the:
(a) Room Maid ☐
(b) Floor Waiter ☐
(c) General Manager ☐
(d) Executive Housekeeper ☐

Q7. Which one of the following customer's request should be classed urgent at check-in
(a) Cold Drink ☐
(b) Extra writing paper ☐
(c) An extra pillow ☐
(d) Video ☐

Q8. Which one of the following is most likely to be classed as a VPO or disbursement?
(a) News Paper ☐
(b) Room Service ☐
(c) A restaurant meal ☐
(d) Room Charges ☐

Q9. Which reservation system uses arrows to record the date of arrivals to the day of departure?
(a) Density Chart ☐
(b) Conventional Charts ☐
(c) Bed room book ☐
(d) Whitney Rack ☐

Q10. The best sales opportunity for reception when a guest is leaving is to:
(a) Suggest use of the bar ☐
(b) Suggest a future reservation ☐
(c) Suggest a packed lunch ☐
(d) Offer free gives away ☐

Q11. A fire blanket is most frequently used to control fire on the:
(a) Linen Room ☐
(b) Kitchen ☐

(c) Bed rooms
(d) Dinning Rooms

Q12. Guest accounts on a tabular ledger are used:
(a) Daily
(b) Weekly
(c) At the close of guest stay
(d) When the guest leaves the hotel

Q13. Toxin is another name for
(a) Germicide
(b) Antiseptic
(c) Bactericide
(d) Poison

Q14. The main reason floor seals are applied is to:
(a) To improve the appearance of the floor
(b) To seal the tiles or blocks in place
(c) Give a longer lasting floor surface
(d) Prevent dirt or grease becoming embedded

Q15. A work schedule is used mainly to:
(a) Improve the efficiency of the work
(b) Help make up the wages sheets
(c) Give condition of employment
(d) Check that the work has been done

Q16. If it takes 12 seconds to damp dust a telephone and 40 seconds to empty a waste paper basket, the time required to dust 3 telephone and waste paper baskets is:
(a) 2 minutes 36 seconds
(b) 2 minutes 48 seconds
(c) 3 minutes 16 seconds
(d) 3 minutes 28 seconds

Q17. To minimize strain when lifting heavy equipments the knees should be:
(a) Bend and the feet apart
(b) Straight and feet apart
(c) Bend and the feet together
(d) Straight and the feet together

Q18. A painted wall should be washed:

(a) From Bottom to top ☐
(b) From top to bottom ☐
(c) In a circular movement ☐
(d) Side to side ☐

Q19. The most suitable floor covering for the bathroom area in a children's ward of a hospital is:

(a) Sheet Vinyl ☐
(b) Quarrt Tiles ☐
(c) Fitted carpet ☐
(d) Carpet Tiles ☐

Q20. What type of fire extinguisher should be used on an electric fire?

(a) Dry Powder ☐
(b) Fire Hose ☐
(c) Foam ☐
(d) Carbon dioxide ☐

Q21. How should the term steamed be described to a customer?

(a) Cooked in water, in an open pan on top of the cooker ☐
(b) Cooked over water, in a close pan, in the oven ☐
(c) Cooked over water, in a closed pan, on top of cooker ☐
(d) Cooked in water, in an open pan, in the oven ☐

Q22. Which one of the following menus would be suitable for a Muslim?

(a) Mackerel Pate, Stake and kidney pudding, Rum Baba ☐
(b) Parma Ham and melon, Spaghetti carbonara, Ice cream ☐
(c) Smoked trout, Roasted beef, Meringue Gateau ☐
(d) Garlic Mushrooms, Dover sole, and Pineapple Flambé ☐

Q23. What does the term VFR mean?

(a) Visiting friends and relatives ☐
(b) Very friendly relations ☐

(c) Very friendly reception ☐
(d) Visiting family and relatives ☐

Q24. Which ONE of these best describes the term "common interest"?
(a) Going on a walking holiday ☐
(b) Visiting friends and relatives ☐
(c) Meeting a business colleague ☐
(d) Attending a conference on tourism ☐

Q25. Which ONE of these is FALSE?
(a) Travel agencies are part of tourism industry ☐
(b) Tourism is a declining industry ☐
(c) Tourists need lots of help and reassurance ☐
(d) Government departments are in the public sector ☐

Q26. Which ONE is correct?
The danger zone is a range of temperatures between:
(a) -5°C and 63°C ☐
(b) 5°C and 37°C ☐
(c) 37°C and 63°C ☐
(d) 5°C and 63°C ☐

Q27. What does the term Béchamel sauce mean?
(a) Basic white sauce ☐
(b) Thickening agent ☐
(c) Rich brown stock ☐
(d) Sweet white sauce ☐

Q28. What is a salamander used for?
(a) Slicing ☐
(b) Grilling ☐
(c) Frying ☐
(d) Mixing ☐

Q29. Which one of these is a julienne?
(a) Very thin strips ☐
(b) Fine dice ☐
(c) Small cubes ☐
(d) Baton shape ☐

Q30. What is a palette knife used for?
- (a) Peeling vegetables
- (b) Filleting fish
- (c) Carving meat
- (d) Lifting food

Q31. A well planned store must be:
- (a) cool, well ventilated, well lit, clean
- (b) well stocked, spacious, dimly lit, easy to access
- (c) tidy, warm, well ventilated, clearly sign posted
- (d) damp, easy to access, secure, well equipped

Q32. The MAIN purpose of garnishing food is to:
- (a) ensure standards of hygiene are maintained
- (b) make the food appealing to the guest
- (c) decorate the food as much as possible
- (d) indicate the size of the portion

Q33. The classic garnish used for fried fish is:
- (a) raw vegetables
- (b) toasted nuts
- (c) fried croutons
- (d) lemon wedge

Q34. A consomme could be cloudy due to which ONE of these?
- (a) Clarifying with egg whites
- (b) Simmering slowly
- (c) Straining through muslin
- (d) Using greasy stock

Q35. Which ONE of the following foods would cocktail sauce be served with?
- (a) Seafood
- (b) Steak
- (c) Chipped potatoes
- (d) Cauliflower

Q36. Which cut of meat would be most suitable for braising?
- (a) Topside of beef
- (b) Leg of lamb
- (c) Shoulder of pork
- (d) Streaky bacon

Q37. What ONE of these is the garnish for grilled gammon?
- *(a)* Caper sauce ☐
- *(b)* Cooked onions ☐
- *(c)* Pineapple ☐
- *(d)* Orange ☐

Q38. What is the average cooking time for poultry per 500g (1lb)?
- *(a)* 10 to 15 minutes ☐
- *(b)* 20 to 25 minutes ☐
- *(c)* 25 to 30 minutes ☐
- *(d)* 30 to 35 minutes ☐

Q39. What does the term larding mean?
- *(a)* Soaking in a liquid overnight ☐
- *(b)* Shallow frying to develop colour ☐
- *(c)* Coating with cooking liquor during cooking ☐
- *(d)* Inserting strips of bacon or pork fat ☐

Q40. What are the accompaniments for roast lamb?
- *(a)* Roast gravy, mint sauce, watercress ☐
- *(b)* Roast gravy, Yorkshire pudding, horseradish sauce ☐
- *(c)* Thickened roast gravy, grilled bacon, watercress ☐
- *(d)* Thickened roast gravy, apple sauce, sage and onion stuffing ☐

Q41. What does the culinary term "bleu" mean?
- *(a)* Medium ☐
- *(b)* Rare ☐
- *(c)* Just done ☐
- *(d)* Well done ☐

Q42. Which ONE of these is a ROUND OILY fish?
- *(a)* Crayfish ☐
- *(b)* Tuna ☐
- *(c)* Plaice ☐
- *(d)* Skate ☐

Q43. How many fillets should be cut from a flat fish?
- *(a)* Eight ☐
- *(b)* Six ☐
- *(c)* Two ☐
- *(d)* Four ☐

Q44. Which piece of equipment should be used for deep-frying fish?
- *(a)* Small saucepan ☐
- *(b)* Automatic fryer ☐
- *(c)* Shallow frying pan ☐
- *(d)* Steamer ☐

Q45. Which type of rice should be used for pilaff?
- *(a)* Short grain ☐
- *(b)* Long grain ☐
- *(c)* Ground rice ☐
- *(d)* Brown rice ☐

Q46. Which ONE of these describes the shape of macaroni?
- *(a)* Short tubes ☐
- *(b)* Flat squares ☐
- *(c)* Large tubes ☐
- *(d)* Long spirals ☐

Q47. At what temperature should excess sandwich fillings be stored?
- *(a)* 5 to 10°C ☐
- *(b)* 37 to 63°C ☐
- *(c)* 5 to 63°C ☐
- *(d)* 0 to 5°C ☐

Q48. What is the filling for a Bookmaker sandwich?
- *(a)* Grilled steak ☐
- *(b)* Poached egg ☐
- *(c)* Roast chicken ☐
- *(d)* Sliced lamb ☐

Q49. What does the term "hors d'oeuvre' mean?
- *(a)* Preparation that takes place before service ☐
- *(b)* A small food item to stimulate the appetite ☐
- *(c)* To work hygienically in the kitchen ☐
- *(d)* A pre-dinner drink served with olives ☐

Q50. Which ONE of these plates should be used to serve a side salad?
- *(a)* Soup bowl ☐
- *(b)* Main course plate ☐
- *(c)* Crescent shaped plate ☐
- *(d)* Dessert plate ☐

Q51. At what temperature should yeast be stored?

(a) 37°C

(b) 0°C

(c) 5°C

(d) -18°C

Q52. What does the term "proving" mean?

(a) Remain the same size

(b) Half in size

(c) Triple in size

(d) Double in size

Q53. What is the substance called which gives dough its elasticity?

(a) Gluten

(b) Salt

(c) Sugar

(d) Yeast

Q54. Which ONE of these could choux pastry be used for?

(a) Cheese straws

(b) Bakewell tart

(c) Cream horns

(d) Chocolate eclairs

Q55. What does the term "baking blind" mean?

(a) Using dried beans to stop the pastry rising

(b) Cooking pastry at a low temperature

(c) Rubbing fat into flour to make a fine crumb

(d) Creaming castor sugar and fat together

Q56. How long should baked egg custard be cooked for at 160°C (320°F)

(a) 3 to 3½ hours

(b) 2 to 2½ hours

(c) 1 to 1½ hours

(d) 15 minutes to 1 hour

Q57. How long should tea be brewed for?

(a) 4 to 5 minutes

(b) 20 to 25 minutes

(c) 30 to 35 minutes

(d) 55 to 60 minutes

Q58. Why is it important to clean up spillages immediately?
- *(a)* To avoid shoes getting wet
- *(b)* To prevent wastage of chemicals
- *(c)* To prevent accidents and falls
- *(d)* To avoid walking around the spillage

Q59. What is the correct action to take before cleaning a piece of electrical equipment?
- *(a)* Clean around the machine
- *(b)* Warn other staff
- *(c)* Fill a sink with hot water
- *(d)* Switch off and isolate the machine

Q60. What is the correct action if you suffer from a minor burn?
- *(a)* Put it under clean cold running water
- *(b)* Apply a dressing or bandage
- *(c)* Put butter or cream on it
- *(d)* Put it under hot running water

Q61. When should you seek medical help for shock?
- *(a)* Breathing difficulty/vomiting
- *(b)* Eating and drinking too much
- *(c)* Hyperactivity and bleeding
- *(d)* Thirst and feeling faint

Q62. Why is it important to switch off equipment at the end of the service?
- *(a)* Make sure everything is tidy
- *(b)* In preparation for cleaning down
- *(c)* To save energy and prevent accidents
- *(d)* In preparation for the next service

Q63. A room on terrace is called:
- *(a)* Cabana
- *(b)* Parlor
- *(c)* Pent house
- *(d)* Hollywood

Q64. Hotels situated on highway are called:
- *(a)* Boatels
- *(b)* Motels
- *(c)* Roatels
- *(d)* Ecotels

Q65. A guest needing special attention is called:
(a) SPAAT
(b) VIP
(c) DG
(d) GIT

Q66. A mode of reservation is:
(a) Airline
(b) Internet
(c) Travel agent
(d) Telephone call

Q67. Plan in which room tariff includes all meals is called:
(a) American
(b) European
(c) Continental
(d) Modified American Plan

Q68. A date wise record of the events, Guest complaints, or requests is called:
(a) Ledger
(b) Information book
(c) Log book
(d) Diary

Q69. The first step in night audit routine is:
(a) Recapitulation reports
(b) Verification of all room rate
(c) Complete outstanding postings
(d) Reconciliation Statement

Q70. Guest who leaves the hotel without settling bill are called:
(a) Skipper
(b) Sleeper
(c) Sleep out
(d) No Show

Q71. Acknowledgement of good work done by an employee is:
(a) Negative praise
(b) Positive praise
(c) Neutral
(d) Neither

Q72. Base of Fromboise (Fruit brandy) is:

(a) Apricots
(b) Yellow Plums
(c) Strawberries
(d) Raspberries

Q73. Colour of Maraschino Liqueur is:

(a) Violet
(b) Cherry
(c) Red
(d) Clear

Q74. Which liquor is used in White lady cocktail with lime juice and cointreau?

(a) Vodka
(b) White Rum
(c) Gin
(d) Tequila

Q75. Wodka (Vodka) is the national drink of Russia and:

(a) Sweden
(b) Denmark
(c) Ireland
(d) Holland

Q76. Which Vodka has a blade of grass placed in every bottle?

(a) Starka
(b) Zubrowka
(c) Jarzebiak
(d) Vyborowa

Q77. Midori is:

(a) American Fruit Brandy
(b) Japanese bright green melon liqueur
(c) Red wine from Italy
(d) Sparkling wine from Germany

Q78. Which country is the birth place of Kahlua?

(a) France
(b) Italy
(c) Chile
(d) Mexico

Q79. Tonic water is flavoured with:
(*a*) Dry Ginger
(*b*) Bitter lemon
(*c*) Quinine
(*d*) Orange

Q80. Mineral water mixed with white wine is known as:
(*a*) Spritzer
(*b*) Perrier
(*c*) Appolinaris
(*d*) Bru

Exercise–2

Q1. Which brand of hop (used in beer) has maximum per cent of alpha acids?
(*a*) Crystal
(*b*) Nuggets
(*c*) Cascade
(*d*) Saaz

Q2. Which of the following is not a single malt whisky?
(*a*) Talisker
(*b*) Glenfiddich
(*c*) Macallan
(*d*) Black velvet

Q3. Most planted wine grape variety in the world:
(*a*) Cabernet Blanc
(*b*) Pinot Noir
(*c*) Merlot
(*d*) Cabernet Sauvignon

Q4. Crab will go well with:
(*a*) Sweet red wine
(*b*) Dry White wine
(*c*) Medium White wine
(*d*) Sparkling wine

Q5. Which of the following is a lemon flavoured syrup?
(*a*) Gomme
(*b*) Citronelle

(c) Cerise
(d) Orgeat

Q6. Napa valley is a region of which wine producing country?
(a) Chile
(b) France
(c) Spain
(d) US

Q7. If a customer requests a discount from you because they are staying a month, You should:
(a) Try to dissuade them
(b) Give them their keys tell them the management will contact them in due course
(c) Give them their keys tell them the request will be considered at the end of their stay
(d) Refer them immediately to a senior member of staff

Q8. The main purpose for taking a credit card imprint when a guest checks into a hotel is so that:
(a) The Guest can spend freely without worry
(b) The hotel can charge the guest account should the guest depart without checking out
(c) Foreign guest can avoid the inconvenience of changing currency
(d) Extras can be added to the guest account with minimum delay

Q9. The purpose of an adjustment on a tabular ledger is to show:
(a) A debit
(b) A credit
(c) An asset
(d) A liability

Q10. Which one of the following is most likely to lead to staff dissatisfaction?
(a) A busy work day
(b) Limited facility
(c) Requirement to use sophisticated computer programmes
(d) Poor Leadership

Q11. The receptionist receives a telephone call from a female who claims to be the wife of the VIP in room 206. The caller wishes to speak to the VIP. What action should the receptionist take?

(a) Put the call through immediately ☐
(b) Ask the caller to ring back later ☐
(c) Contact the VIP before transferring the call ☐
(d) Deny that VIP is staying at the hotel ☐

Q12. The best way of ensuring a sale to a chance customer is to

(a) Tell them their is only 1 room left ☐
(b) Show them the hotels promotional leaf lets ☐
(c) Tell them they must make up their mind immediately ☐
(d) Show them the room and services ☐

Q13. The correct cleaning chemical to use to strip emulsion wax polish from a floor surface is:

(a) Alkaline detergent ☐
(b) Methylated spirit ☐
(c) Neutral Detergent ☐
(d) White spirit ☐

Q14. When cleaning large floor areas, the most efficient way of organizing staff is into a:

(a) Team ☐
(b) Unit ☐
(c) Block ☐
(d) Group ☐

Q15. An advised note indicates that goods:

(a) Have been ordered ☐
(b) Have been delivered as stated ☐
(c) Have been invoiced ☐
(d) Will be dispatched at a certain time ☐

Q16. To provide maximum floor space in bed rooms, the furniture should be:

(a) Free standing ☐
(b) Build in ☐
(c) On castors ☐
(d) Cantilever ☐

Q17. Abrasive dirt is best described as particles which:
- *(a)* Are air born
- *(b)* Are greasy
- *(c)* Cut fibers
- *(d)* Cause staining

Q18. A water based fool polished is recommended for:
- *(a)* Unsealed wood, Vinyl and Terrazzo
- *(b)* Unsealed wood, cork and rubber
- *(c)* Thermo plastic, cork and terrazzo
- *(d)* Thermoplastic vinyl and rubber

Q19. The term low dusting refers to the control of dust from:
- *(a)* Skirting boards and surroundings only
- *(b)* Ceilings, pipes and ledges
- *(c)* Tables and chairs only
- *(d)* Surface with in arms length

Q20. The most suitable fabric for bed linen for use in an establishment with an on premises laundry is made from
- *(a)* Pure cotton
- *(b)* Polyester and cotton
- *(c)* Pure linen
- *(d)* Linen and cotton

Q21. The minimum working temperature for washing crockery to prevent food poisoning is
- *(a)* 65ºC
- *(b)* 80ºC
- *(c)* 95ºC
- *(d)* 100ºC

Q22. Which is the most important of the following keys?
- *(a)* Master
- *(b)* Office
- *(c)* Grand Master
- *(d)* Floor

Q23. The main Purpose of a control system is to:
- *(a)* Ensure that everything issued is accounted and charged for

(*b*) To provide a guide to the most popular items ☐
(*c*) To provide a form of collecting money from customers ☐
(*d*) Track discrepancy in stock ☐

Q24. Which ONE of these describes in-bound tourists?
(*a*) International tourists arriving in another country ☐
(*b*) Domestic tourists arriving at their destination ☐
(*c*) International tourists departing from another country ☐
(*d*) Domestic tourists departing for another country ☐

Q25. Which ONE of the following is the correct procedure for hand washing?
(*a*) Hot water, disinfectant soap, clean nailbrush, rinse hands, dry with clean paper towel ☐
(*b*) Cold water, disinfectant soap, rinse hands, dry with hand towel ☐
(*c*) Hot water, disinfectant soap, used nailbrush, rinse hands, dry with clean paper towel ☐
(*d*) Warm water, disinfectant soap, clean nailbrush, air dry ☐

Q26. Which ONE of these is a high risk food?
(*a*) Bread roll ☐
(*b*) Mayonnaise ☐
(*c*) Tin of tuna fish ☐
(*d*) Uncooked rice ☐

Q27. How often should a deep fat fryer be cleaned?
(*a*) Daily ☐
(*b*) Monthly ☐
(*c*) Yearly ☐
(*d*) Weekly ☐

Q28. What does the term "to season" mean?
(*a*) Add salt and pepper to food ☐
(*b*) Mix egg whites with food ☐
(*c*) Pass food through a sieve ☐
(*d*) Add aromatic herbs to stock ☐

Q29. What is dill seed?

- *(a)* Spice
- *(b)* Jelly
- *(c)* Flour
- *(d)* Stock

Q30. What does the term "soaking" mean?

- *(a)* Disinfect food items ready for preparation
- *(b)* Reconstitute food using clean cold water
- *(c)* Rinse food in clean, warm water
- *(d)* Blanch food prior to cooking

Q31. To run a kitchen effectively a chef must manage:

- *(a)* customers, prices, facilities, restaurant
- *(b)* the weather, profits, equipment, guests
- *(c)* ccupancy, tours, marketing, raw materials
- *(d)* facilities, equipment, staff, raw materials

Q32. What is an ultra violet insecticide used for?

- *(a)* Trap rats and mice
- *(b)* Kill beetles and weevils
- *(c)* Poison insects and flies
- *(d)* Kill flies and blue-bottles

Q33. Which ONE of the following foods could be whisked?

- *(a)* Pastry
- *(b)* Meringue
- *(c)* Bouquet garni
- *(d)* Parsley

Q34. Which ONE of these is a blond sauce?

- *(a)* Mushroom
- *(b)* Tartare
- *(c)* Mustard
- *(d)* Chasseur

Q35. How is French dressing made

- *(a)* Mayonnaise and tomato ketchup
- *(b)* Vinaigrette and mustard
- *(c)* Mayonnaise and natural yoghurt
- *(d)* Vinaigrette and garlic

Q36. Meat should be stored in the refrigerator at:
(a) 1°C to 5°C
(b) 5°C to 63°C
(c) 5°C to 10°C
(d) -18°C to -10°C

Q37. Which liver is considered the best quality?
(a) Calves
(b) Lamb
(c) Sheep
(d) Pig

Q38. Which nutrients are found in lamb's kidney?
(a) Vitamin A and potassium
(b) Vitamin D and sodium
(c) Vitamin A and iron
(d) Vitamin C and calcium

Q39. Why must some food be coated before deep-frying?
(a) Protect the flesh
(b) Make food attractive
(c) Speed up cooking process
(d) Ensure food is cooked safely

Q40. Which of the following would accompany fillet of fish caprice style?
(a) Sweet and sour sauce
(b) Grilled banana halves
(c) Mustard sauce
(d) Parsley butter

Q41. What temperature should fish be deep-fried at?
(a) 180°C
(b) 120°C
(c) 150°C
(d) 200°C

Q42. How long should a hard boiled egg be cooked for?
(a) 3 to 4 minutes
(b) 6 to 8 minutes
(c) 8 to 10 minutes
(d) 12 to 15 minutes

Q43. What is the correct cooking method for scrambled egg?

(*a*) Shallow fry on a high heat

(*b*) Braise over a low heat

(*c*) Poach over a high heat

(*d*) Stir over a low heat

Q44. Which ONE of these is a root vegetable?

(*a*) Cabbage

(*b*) Broccoli

(*c*) Courgette

(*d*) Carrot

Q45. How long should medium sized new potatoes be steamed for?

(*a*) 15 to 20 minutes

(*b*) 1 to 2 minutes

(*c*) 30 to 40 minutes

(*d*) 10 to 12 minutes

Q46. What is the maximum length of time sandwiches should be stored for in a refrigerator at 5°C?

(*a*) 2 hours

(*b*) 12 hours

(*c*) 24 hours

(*d*) 48 hours

Q47. Which foods does a Florida cocktail consist of?

(*a*) Lemon, orange, apple

(*b*) Melon, grapefruit, pineapple

(*c*) Banana, orange, apple

(*d*) Grapefruit, orange, pineapple

Q48. Which ONE of these is a compound salad?

(*a*) Russian

(*b*) Cucumber

(*c*) Tomato

(*d*) Beetroot

Q49. What is the dressing for Caesar Salad?

(*a*) Lemon juice, garlic oil, raw egg yolk

(*b*) Raw egg yolk, olive oil, seasoning

(c) Lime juice, olive oil, blue cheese ☐
(d) Lemon juice, vinegar, mustard ☐

Q50. Which ONE of these is an entrée?
(a) Roast pork ☐
(b) Grilled kidneys ☐
(c) Chicken chasseur ☐
(d) Smoked fish ☐

Q51. Which gas does yeast produce during fermentation?
(a) CO ☐
(b) H_2O ☐
(c) SO_2 ☐
(d) CO_2 ☐

Q52. What colour should fresh yeast be?
(a) White ☐
(b) Fawn ☐
(c) Yellow ☐
(d) Grey ☐

Q53. Which Vitamin is found in wholemeal flour?
(a) D ☐
(b) A ☐
(c) B ☐
(d) E ☐

Q54. What is Naan Bread?
(a) Unleavened bread ☐
(b) Shallow fried bread ☐
(c) Leavened bread ☐
(d) Deep fried bread ☐

Q55. What flour is suitable for puff pastry?
(a) Wholemeal ☐
(b) Strong ☐
(c) Plain ☐
(d) Soft ☐

Q56. What are the correct proportions of flour to fat for short pastry?
- (a) 4:2
- (b) 4:1
- (c) 2:4
- (d) 2:5

Q57. What is Coupe Alexander?
- (a) Stoned cherries/vanilla ice cream/melba sauce
- (b) Orange segments/lemon sorbet/whipped cream
- (c) Fruit salad/strawberry ice cream/whipped cream
- (d) Banana/vanilla ice cream/chocolate sauce

Q58. At what temperature should coffee be held
- (a) 5°C
- (b) 75°C
- (c) 85°C
- (d) 100°C

Q59. Which of the following should be served with coffee?
- (a) White sugar/milk
- (b) Brown sugar/cream
- (c) Lemon/cream
- (d) Salt/white sugar

Q60. How is a scald caused?
- (a) Ice
- (b) Dry heat
- (c) Wet heat
- (d) Chemical

Q61. What does the expression "going the extra mile" mean?
- (a) Having a sense of humour with customers
- (b) Making an extra effort for your customers
- (c) Trying out an unusual type of food
- (d) Walking around the kitchen all day

Q62. Detailed list of formal education, general knowledge, technical knowledge etc. needed for receptionist is called:
- (a) Job analysis
- (b) Job specification
- (c) Job list
- (d) Job description

Q63. The important duty of front office clerk is:
(*a*) Reception
(*b*) Registration
(*c*) Room Allocation
(*d*) Reservation

Q64. A mandatory document used at the time of registration of guest is:
(*a*) Passport
(*b*) Reservation card
(*c*) Guest history card
(*d*) Guest registration card

Q65. The majority of international reservations received by a hotel are through:
(*a*) Letters
(*b*) Telephones
(*c*) Fax
(*d*) E-mail

Q66. A guest who has refused accommodation in spite of confirmed reservation is called:
(*a*) Turn in
(*b*) Turning a guest
(*c*) Turning down the guest
(*d*) No Show

Q67. Safe deposit boxes are located in the:
(*a*) Lobby
(*b*) Back office
(*c*) Concierge desk
(*d*) Reservations

Q68. In front office, internal control involves:
(*a*) Verifying accounts entries and balance
(*b*) Tracking transaction document
(*c*) Guest Problems
(*d*) Day to day reports

Q69. Difference between total payment and total charges is called:
(*a*) Account receivable
(*b*) Account balance

(c) Account allowance
(d) Accounts Book

Q70. A programme designed towards marketing a hotel is called:
(a) Video check out system disputed bill
(b) Front office follows through at check out
(c) Web Check-In and Check-out
(d) Fidelio

Q71. Beer bottle with a cork:
(a) Biére de garde
(b) Hife
(c) Budweiser
(d) Arctic Pills

Q72. Egg noggs consists of:
(a) Liquor + Egg +Soda +Nutmeg + Ice + Castor Sugar
(b) Liquor + Egg +Soda +Lime Juice +Sugar
(c) Liquor + Egg +Soda +Nutmeg +Sugar
(d) Liquor + Soda +Sugar +Lime Juice + Bitter

Q73. Grain Formula used in the manufacturing process of Dry Gin is:
(a) Equal parts of barley, corn and rye
(b) 75% corn, 15% barley and 10% other ingredients
(c) 75% corn, 15% maize and 10% Rye
(d) 75% barley, 15% corn and 10% maize and rye

Q74. The term 'Mother's Ruin' is related to:
(a) Whisky
(b) Rum
(c) Gin
(d) Wines

Q75. Jamaican rums are made from slow fermentation, which lasts up to:
(a) 1 Week
(b) 3 Weeks
(c) 2 – 3 Days
(d) 1 Month

Q76. Sweet Mash whiskey is made from:
- *(a)* Freshly developed cultured yeast ☐
- *(b)* Intense and character in flavour ☐
- *(c)* By Sour mash distillation process ☐
- *(d)* Mixture of straight and other whiskies ☐

Q77. California's blush wines are made from:
- *(a)* Melbec ☐
- *(b)* Sémillon ☐
- *(c)* Zinfandel ☐
- *(d)* Sangiovese ☐

Q78. Which country other than Ireland spells its whiskies with an 'e'?
- *(a)* Scotland ☐
- *(b)* US ☐
- *(c)* Japan ☐
- *(d)* Canada ☐

Q79. Seville coffee is served with which of the following liqueur?
- *(a)* Tia Maria ☐
- *(b)* Benedictine ☐
- *(c)* Crème de cassis ☐
- *(d)* Cointreau ☐

Q80. Evian, pure still table water is from:
- *(a)* Italy ☐
- *(b)* Holland ☐
- *(c)* Belgium ☐
- *(d)* France ☐

ANSWER SHEETS

Exercise–1

Q.No.	Answer	Q.No.	Answer	Q.No.	Answer	Q.No.	Answer
1.	c	21.	c	41.	b	61.	a
2.	a	22.	c	42.	b	62.	c
3.	c	23.	a	43.	d	63.	b
4.	c	24.	d	44.	b	64.	a
5.	a	25.	b	45.	b	65.	a
6.	d	26.	d	46.	a	66.	c
7.	a	27.	a	47.	d	67.	a
8.	a	28.	b	48.	a	68.	c
9.	b	29.	a	49.	b	69.	b
10.	b	30.	d	50.	c	70.	a
11.	b	31.	a	51.	c	71.	a
12.	a	32.	b	52.	d	72.	d
13.	d	33.	d	53.	a	73.	b
14.	d	34.	d	54.	d	74.	a
15.	d	35.	a	55.	a	75.	d
16.	c	36.	a	56.	c	76.	b
17.	c	37.	c	57.	a	77.	b
18.	a	38.	b	58.	c	78.	d
19.	a	39.	d	59.	d	79.	c
20.	d	40.	a	60.	a	80.	a

ANSWER SHEETS
Exercise–2

Q.No.	Answer	Q.No.	Answer	Q.No.	Answer	Q.No.	Answer
1.	b	21.	b	41.	a	61.	b
2.	d	22.	c	42.	c	62.	a
3.	d	23.	a	43.	d	63.	b
4.	b	24.	a	44.	d	64.	d
5.	b	25.	a	45.	a	65.	b
6.	d	26.	b	46.	c	66.	a
7.	a	27.	d	47.	d	67.	a
8.	b	28.	a	48.	a	68.	b
9.	b	29.	a	49.	a	69.	a
10.	d	30.	b	50.	c	70.	a
11.	d	31.	d	51.	d	71.	a
12.	d	32.	d	52.	b	72.	a
13.	a	33.	b	53.	c	73.	b
14.	a	34.	a	54.	c	74.	c
15.	d	35.	b	55.	b	75.	c
16.	d	36.	a	56.	c	76.	a
17.	c	37.	a	57.	a	77.	c
18.	d	38.	c	58.	c	78.	b
19.	d	39.	a	59.	b	79.	b
20.	b	40.	b	60.	c	80.	d

BRAIN TWISTER

1. King of cheeses?
2. Porter house steak is larger than T-bone steak, true or false?
3. English equivalent of Dahi?
4. 'Enchiladas' belong to which cuisine?
5. Which spice is associated with cooking of apples?
6. Two main sources of sugar?
7. Does salt retard the function of yeast?
8. Feta is a cheese from Athens?
9. _____Is the word used for fish stock?
10. Clotted cream is a specialty from which country?
11. Mousse is lighter than a soufflé true or false?
12. Spell–boulangerie?

ANSWERS

1.	Stilton	2.	True
3.	Yogurt	4.	Mexico
5.	Cinnamon	6.	Beet, Cane
7.	Yes	8.	Greece
9.	Fumet	10.	England
11.	False	12.	BOULANGERIE

CHECK YOUR KNOWLEDGE

1. What is the other name for wine butler?

2. Name 2 types of inventory evaluation system?

3. Elevenses is a tea coffee with snacks served around:
   (a) 9am.
   (b) 11am.
   (c) 1pm.
   (d) 11pm.

4. Which spirit is used in preparation of a flambe dish "crepe suzette"?

5. What would be the appropriate height of the hostess desk?
   (a) 4ft.
   (b) 5ft.
   (c) 5.5ft.
   (d) 3ft.

6. What is a fine champagne?
   (a) sparkling wine from grand champagne region
   (b) armagnac
   (c) cognac
   (d) sparkling wine from rare champagne region

7. Size of a meat or dinner plate is:
   (a) 11 inches diametre
   (b) 10 inches diametre
   (c) 8 inch diametre
   (d) 9.5 inches diametre

8. What is the study of wines known as?

9. Size of soup plate is?

10. The capacity of a normal beer bottle is?

11. Capacity of a red wine glass is:
    (a) 6 oz.
    (b) 7 oz.
    (c) 8 oz.
    (d) 9 oz.

12. Alcohol percentage of sparkling wines is:
    (a) 10-13%
    (b) 14% or less
    (c) 15-20%
    (d) 14-24%

13. Capacity of juice glass or pony tumbler is:
    (a) 3 oz.
    (b) 4 oz.
    (c) 5 oz.
    (d) 7 oz.

14. During fermentation sugar breaks up into alcohol and ___by the action of yeast.

15. Term E.P.N.S. stands for:
    (a) electro plated new silver
    (b) electronically plated nickel silver
    (c) electro platinum nickel silver
    (d) electro plated nickel silver

16. Mead is a spiced fermented juice of___.

17. Which one of these is not a kind of menu?
    (a) typical menu
    (b) a la carte menu
    (c) speciality menu
    (d) table de hote

18. Which herb is used for flavouring gin?

19. Which is the first course of French classical menu?

20. Is it true that the alcohol cannot be digested by our body as the foods are?

21. Name any 2 kinds of dressings used in cold horsdoeuvres?

22. Alcohol is broken down by:
    (a) brain
    (b) kidney
    (c) intestines
    (d) none of these

23. What is French name for snails?

24. Liver breaks down the alcohol at a rate of:
    (*a*) 15ml per hour
    (*b*) 30ml per hour
    (*c*) 45ml per hour
    (*d*) 60ml per hour

25. Out of these which one is generally served as an accompaniment with caviar?
    (*a*) mint sauce
    (*b*) horseradish sauce
    (*c*) blinis
    (*d*) roast gravy

26. Cabernet sauvignon is a famous pre dominant grape of red wines of bordeaux region. True or false?

27. What is pate de foie gros?

28. Out of these which one is a white grape?
    (*a*) pinot
    (*b*) merlot
    (*c*) chardonnay
    (*d*) syrah

29. Where has ministroni soup originated from?
    (*a*) England
    (*b*) Italy
    (*c*) France
    (*d*) Hungary

30. What is the mash/juice of grapes known as before going through the process of fermentation?

31. What is french term for eggs?

32. Which laboratory yeast is commonly used for prepration of wines?

33. Lasagne is a kind of:
    (*a*) soup
    (*b*) pasta

(*c*) horsdoeuvres
(*d*) none of these

34. What is the procedure of adding extra sugar to grapes mash is known as?

35. American service is:
(*a*) platter to plate service
(*b*) preplated service
(*c*) buffet service
(*d*) blue moon service

36. Champagne brut is a dry wine. True or false?

37. Give english name for product fromage?

38. Kabinett, spatlese, auslese all are wines from which region?

39. K.O.T. stands for?

40. Chablis is a white wine from Italy. True or false?

41. Whats the appropriate space requirement for a cover at a deluxe restaurant:
(*a*) 23" × 18"
(*b*) 23" × 17"
(*c*) 24" × 18"
(*d*) 24" × 17"

42. Service temperature for red wines is:
(*a*) 18-21°C
(*b*) 18-21°F
(*c*) 10-12°C
(*d*) served frozen.

43. O.D.C. stands for?

44. Aperitifs should be___(dry/sweet) in nature?

45. I.T.D.C. stands for:
(*a*) Indian Tourism Development Corporation.
(*b*) Indian Travellers Development Corporation.
(c) Indian Trade Development Corporation.
(*d*) International Tourism Development Corporation.

46. Fish dishes are well suited with chilled sweet white wines. True or false?

47. Plate du jour means?

48. Tonnic water is colourless and:
    (*a*) ginger flavoured
    (*b*) junipper flavoured
    (*c*) quinnine flavoured
    (*d*) thyme flavoured

49. Which wine compliments with most dishes?

50. Lager beers are bottom fermented beers. True or false?

51. Dry beers were first produced and marketed in:
    (*a*) Japan
    (*b*) England
    (*c*) France
    (*d*) Italy

52. Corona is a beer from:
    (*a*) USA
    (*b*) Mexico
    (*c*) Netherlands
    (*d*) Germany

53. Heineken is a beer from which country?

54. What are the 2 types of stills used for distillation?

55. Patent still method is also known as coffey stll method. True or false?

56. Brandies are aged in oak casks for a minimum of:
    (*a*) 6 months
    (*b*) 1yrs.
    (*c*) 2yrs.
    (*d*) 5yrs.

57. What does V.S.O.P. stands for?

58. What does X.O. stands for?

59. Brandy is a distilled juice of:
    (a) rice
    (b) grapes
    (c) barley
    (d) grains

60. Rum is a spirit distilled from diluted___?

61. The most famous rums come from:
    (a) India
    (b) West Indies
    (c) Russia
    (d) Japan

62. Name any one popular brand of white rum?

63. Coruba is a popular Jamican___(white/dark/golden) rum?

64. Tequila is a spirit developed in:
    (a) Pakistan
    (b) France
    (c) Mexico
    (d) Armagnac

65. There are 2 varieties of Tequila - white and ___?

66. Name any three brand names of vodka?

67. Whisky is obtained by distillation of a fermented mash of ___?

68. Name any 2 brands of bourbon whisky?

69. Jack daniels is best known___whisky distiller?

70. Name 1 popular brand of Irish whisky?

71. Arrack is a aniseed flavoured spirit. True or false?

72. Calvados is an___flavoured brandy?

73. Kirsch is a cherry brandy from which country?

74. ___is a Japanese rice wine?

75. Advocat is a liqueur from:
    (a) Italy
    (b) France
    (c) Holland
    (d) Ireland

76. Cointreau is a___flavoured liqueur:
    (a) almond
    (b) aniseed
    (c) honey
    (d) orange

77. Curascao is from:
    (a) Holland
    (b) France
    (c) Scotland
    (d) Italy

78. D.O.M. in context to liqueurs stand for?

79. Kummel is a which coloured liqueur:
    (a) green
    (b) white
    (c) brown
    (d) golden

80. What is the alcohol percentage of liqueur tia maria:
    (a) 32%
    (b) 37%
    (c) 41%
    (d) 42%

81. Liqueurs are generally served after or before meals?

82. What is 1 jigger?

83. White lady is a cocktail based on:
    (a) vodka
    (b) white rum
    (c) gin
    (d) tequilla

84. Bloody marry is generally served in:
    (a) high ball
    (b) cocktail glass
    (c) old fashioned
    (d) none of these

85. Colorado maduro is the strongest cigar. True/false?

86. Give 2 brands of international cigarettes?

87. Best cigars come from:
    (a) Germany
    (b) Hawana
    (c) India
    (d) Italy

88. Cigar will keep well in their own boxes known as___?

89. Accompaniments for puree soup would be?

90. Accompaniments for roast beef?

91. What is the technical name given to copper wire on a sparkling wine bottle?

92. What provide bitterness to beer?

93. What is the bottom of sparkling wines bottle known as?

94. What is clarets?

95. What is the purpose of slip cloth on a table?

96. ITC stands for?

97. Which of the following is a rest course:
    (a) sorbet
    (b) roti
    (c) releve
    (d) entremet

98. Whats the difference between entremet and dessert?

99. What is a lime cordial?

100. What is said to be the centre point of a table?

ANSWERS

Ans1. Sommelier.

Ans2. *(a)* Physical inventory *(b)* Perpetual inventory.

Ans3. (b) 11a.m.

Ans4. Brandy.

Ans5. (a) 4ft.

Ans6. (c) cognac.

Ans7. (b) 10 inches diameter.

Ans8. Oniology

Ans9. 8 inch diametre.

Ans10. 650 ml.

Ans11. (b) 7 oz.

Ans12. (b) 14% or less.

Ans13. (c) 5 oz.

Ans14. Carbon dioxide.

Ans15. (d) Electro plated nickel silver.

Ans16. Honey.

Ans17. (a) Typical menu.

Ans18. Juniper berries.

Ans19). Horsdoeuvres.

Ans20. Yes, true.

Ans21. *(a)* American dressing *(b)* Acidulated cream
(c) English dressing *(d)* French dressing
(e) Lemon dressing *(f)* Mayonnaise dressing
(g) Vinaigrette dressing *(h)* Thousand Island dressing.

Ans22. (d) None of these.

Ans23. Escargots.

Ans24. (a) 15ml per hour.

Ans25. (c) Blinis.

Ans26. True.

Ans27. Paste of goose liver.

Ans28. (c) Chardonnay.

Ans29. (b) Italy.

Ans30. Must.

Ans31. Oeuf.

Ans32. Sacromycis elipsoidus.

Ans33. (b) Pasta.

Ans34. Chapatalization.

Ans35. (b) Preplated service.

Ans36. True.

Ans37. Cheese.

Ans38. Germany.

Ans39. Kitchen order ticket.

Ans40. False.

Ans41. (c) 24" × 18".

Ans42. (a)18-21°C.

Ans43. Out door catering.

Ans44. Dry.

Ans45. (a) Indian Tourism Development Corporation.

Ans46. False.

Ans47. Plate or speciality of the day.

Ans48. (c) Quinnine flavoured.

Ans49. Champagne or sparkling wines.

Ans50. True.

Ans51. Japan.

Ans52. Mexico.

Ans53. Netherlands.

Ans54. (1) Pot still, (2) Continuous still.

Ans55. True.

Ans56. (b) 2 yrs.

Ans57. Very superior old pale.

Ans58. Extra old.

Ans59. (b) Grapes.

Ans60. Sugar molasses.

Ans61. West Indies.

Ans62. Bacardi.

Ans63. Dark.

Ans64. (c) Mexico.

Ans65. Golden.

Ans66. Smirnoff, Wyborowa, Limonnaya.

Ans67. Barley.

Ans68. 1. Jim beam gold label, 2. Wild turkey.

Ans69. Tennessee.

Ans70. Jamesons.

Ans71. True.

Ans72. Apple.

Ans73. Germany.

Ans74. Sake.

Ans75. (c) Holland.

Ans76. Orange.

Ans77. (a) Holland.

And78. Deo optimo maximo.

Ans79. White.

Ans80. (a) 32%.

Ans81. After.

Ans82. 45 ml.

Ans83. (c) Gin.

Ans84. (d) None of these.

Ans85. False.

Ans86. Camel/555/dunhill.

Ans87. (b) Hawana.

Ans88. Humidor.

Ans89. Croutons.

Ans90. Yorkshire pudding, horse-radish sauce and roast gravy.

Ans91. Agrafe.

Ans92. Hops.

Ans93. Punt.

Ans94. Red wines from Bordeaux region.

Ans95. To avoid pilferage to touch the table cloth.

Ans96. Indian Tobacco Company.

Ans97. (a) Sorbet.

Ans98. Entremets is a sweet course while dessert is fruit and nut course.

Ans99. Concentrated lime juice.

Ans100. Bud vas.

CHECK YOUR KNOWLEDGE
Multiple Choice

1. Record of all charges by the guest during his stay is called:
   - Guest folio
   - Registration form
   - Movement list
   - C-form

2. Room with special design for disabled such as extra wide door for wheel chair are:
   - Special needs facilities
   - Barriers free facilities
   - Additional facilities
   - Corporate facilities

3. The "Holiday Inn" comes under which parent company:
   - Bass
   - East India Group
   - Marriott
   - Regency

4. An example for guest operated interface would be:
   - Call accounting system
   - In room movie system
   - Sales terminal
   - Telephone interface

5. Which of the following is the form not used in pre arrival stage:
   - Reservation record
   - Letter of confirmation
   - Reservation rack slip
   - Registration form

6. When a guest room is scheduled to be vacant after the following days check out, the room status is:
   - Due out
   - Unchanged
   - Occupied
   - Skipper

7. Description of the room available or unavailable for immediate occupancy of a short term:
   - Reservation status
   - Housekeeping status
   - Occupied room
   - Changed room

8. Maximum amount of credit card charges hotel can accept without special authorization:
   - Card limit
   - Floor limit
   - House limit
   - Credit limit

9. Hotel practice of extending credit to the guest by agreeing to bill the guest or the guest company for charges is called:
   - Direct billing
   - Account voucher
   - Voucher charges
   - Folio well

10. When meals are priced separately from rooms in a hotel, it is referred to as:
    - A.P.
    - E.P.
    - M.A.P.
    - Bermuda plan

TRUE OR FALSE

1. When a mail arrives for a guest who has not registered, it should be immediately returned to the sender.
2. Because of high visibility front desk agents are frequently the first to learn of a guest complaints.
3. For security reasons most hotels use only one type of guestroom keys.
4. Safe deposited should be located in limited access area.
5. In its simplest written form an account is recorded as a T account.
6. The P.O.S. describes the time and location at which goods and services are purchased.
7. An account allowance occurs when one guest offers to pay charges posted to another guest folio.
8. Cash voucher is an amount assigned to a cashier to handle various transactions that occurs during particular work shift.
9. In computer based automated front office the audit is called update.
10. The night auditor begins when the business day begins.

ANSWER IN ONE WORD

1. "P.A.T.A" stands for?
2. "I.A.T.A" stands for?
3. What does "F.H.R.A.I" stands for?

4. What is the currency of China, Germany, Japan, Australia, Italy, and France?

5. Name the International Airport for the following (New Delhi, Kolkatta, Mumbai, Washington, San Francisco, Singapore).

6. What does D.C. stands for in Washington?

7. Name any two Scandinavian countries?

8. Which place holds the Pushkar festival?

9. What does G.M.T. stands for?

10. Name the International Airlines for the following countries coming to India: (Netherlands, Germany, Canada, Japan, Russia, U.K., U.S.A., Hongkong, Sri Lanka, U.A.E.).

CAPITALS

1. Mizoram:
2. Sikkim:
3. Name any four union territory:
4. Afghanistan:
5. Bhutan:
6. Bolivia:
7. Scotland:
8. Bulgaria:
9. Mexico:
10. Canada:

CHAPTER 22

Rapid Knowledge Gainer

Q1. What is the temperature of heat when a matchstick is burnt?
Ans. 1000 degree celcius.

Q2. All juices contain which acid?
Ans. Ascorbic Acid.

Q3. How many kilo calorie of energy is obtained from 100gm of eggs?
Ans. 147.

Q4. Culinary term for deep fat frying?
Ans. Friture.

Q5. In what three colour broccoli found?
Ans. White, green and purple.

Q6. Beef rib steak is known as?
Ans. Entrecote.

Q7. A natural vegetable based fibre derived from the coconut?
Ans. Coir.

Q8. "Faluda" used to accompany KULFI, is made up of?
Ans. Corn flour.

Q9. Small round tomatoes popularly been used in Italian cookery is known as?
Ans. Cherry tomatoes.

Q10. Mornay sauce is a derivative of?
Ans. Bechamel sauce.

Q11. A famous Japaneese preparation which involve use of raw fish?
Ans. Sushi.

Q12. The suspension of two ingredient that do not usually mix?
Ans. Emulsion.

Q13. Term used for food cooked on skewer?
Ans. Brochette.

Q14. The best known accompaniment for chicken satay?
Ans. Peanut sauce.

Q15. Whipped egg white and sugar is?
Ans. Maringue.

Q16. Fat around the kidney known as?
Ans. Suet.

Q17. Uniform size of vegetable cuts is known as?
Ans. Payassane.

Q18. Farnacious dishes include?
Ans. Pasta and rice.

Q19. Well known Law of Muslims for killing and preparation of meat?
Ans. Halal.

Q 20. Two other name of Lady Finger?
Ans. Okara and gombus.

RAPID KNOWLEDGE GAINER

1. Pile is a Cut of?—Fish
2. Beer is Manufactured From?—Barley
3. Who Invented Champagne?—Dom Perignon
4. What is the Currency of Brazil?—Real
5. What is Mistelle?—Fortification of Vermouth
6. Petit Stands for?—Small
7. What is Madera Called in French?—Madere
8. Spell the Word Gnocchi?—Gnocchi
9. Capacity of Champagne Sucer is?—6 Ounce
10. Hock and Mossel Originates from which Country?—Germany

11. Standard Shiping Cask for Sherry is Known As?—Butt
12. Salsa is the Spanish Word for?—Sauce
13. Fruit Cocktail is Garnished with?—Cherry
14. Expand the Term F.T.E.?—Full Time Employees
15. What are Calenders?—Ironing Machine
16. What do You call Cafe in English?—Coffee
17. What Spirit Can be used for Removing Paints?—Methylated Spirit
18. Name the City with Maximum Number of Vehicles on Road?—New Delhi
19. Wine Waiter is also Known as?—Sommeliar
20. Saki Belongs to which Country?—Japan
21. Expand the Term V.D.U.?—Visual Display Unit
22. R.D.M. Stands for?—Room Division Management
23. KLM Airlines Belongs to which Country?—Netherlands
24. Which Spirit is used in Preperation of Flambee Dishes?—Brandy
25. The Capital of Bhutan is Kabul, is it True or False?—False
26. All Sparkling Wines are Champagnes, is it True or False?—False
27. What is the French for Snails?—Escargots
28. Which Ham is Consumed Raw?—Parma
29. Consommes Celestines the Garnished with?—Juliennes of Pancake
30. Who Coined The Term Privitisation?—Peter Ducker
31. Stock in Hand is Also Known as?—Inventory
32. What is the French name for Eggs?—Oeufs
33. What is the Capital of Bolivia?—La Paz
34. Aroflot is the Airlines of which Country?—Russia
35. What is the Liver of Goose Called?—Pate De Foie Gras
36. What is Pain?—Bread
37. Meat Contains which Protein?—Myosin

38. Which is Served first Dry Wine or Sweet Wine?—Dry
39. Taka is the Currency of?—Bangladesh
40. Who Invented Reumage Process?—Madame Clicquot
41. The Only Red Wine Served Chilled is?—Lambrusco
42. Enhancing the Colour is known as?—Bluing
43. Strogonoff Word Corresponds to which Country?—Russia
44. Expand the Term P.V.C.?—Poly Vinyl Chloride
45. J.F.K. Airport is Located at which City?—New York
46. Kahalua Liquer is Flavoured with?—Coffee
47. Fortran Stands For?—Formula Translation
48. Who are Connaseurs?—Who Judge Wine and Cigars
49. Poivre is the French Name for?—Pepper
50. A Room having attached Kitchen is Called?—Efficiency Room
51. Roquefort is what Type of Cheese?—Blue Vein Cheese
52. Ratio of Water to Pasta when Boiling is?—10 is To 1
53. Lettable Room are Known as?—Saleable Room
54. Crib Rates are Applicable to?—Children Below 5 Years
55. What is Danish Blue?—Cheese
56. Expand the Term A.L.U.?—Arithmetic Logical Unit
57. What is Mur?—Ripe
58. What is Trocken?—Dry
59. What is Juslie?—Thickened Gravy
60. What is Adam?—Semi Hard Cow Cheese
61. Le Petit Dejeuner Means?—Breakfast
62. Red Wine Compnies with Lamb is it True or False?—True
63. Expand The Term P.I.A.?—Payment in Advance
64. What is the Meaning of Emince?—Minced

65. French Name for Oyster is?—Les Huitres
66. Experiment of Illumination is Conducted by?—Hawthorne
67. Spell the Word Savoury?—Savoury
68. Gazpacho is a Cold Soup is it True or False?—True
69. Fermented Juice of Pear is Termed as?—Perry
70. The Term Block Refers as?—Reserved
71. American Name for Chef De Rang is?—Captain
72. Twill is the Name of what?—Weave
73. Expand the Term T.O.D.?—Time of Departure
74. What do you understand by Fino?—Dry Sherry
75. Pasanda is Taken From?—True
76. Which is the Oldest Tea Producing Country?—China
77. Largest Coffee Producing Country is?—Brazil
78. Liquid Salt Solution is Known as?—Brine
79. Expand the Term E.D.P.?—Electronic Data Processing
80. Study of Wines As?—Oniology
81. Whiping of Egg White with Sugar is Called?—Merigue
82. Chicken Marengo is Invented by?—Chef of Napolean the Great
83. Expand the Term G.M.T.?—Greenwich Mean Time
84. What does D.C. Stands for in Washington?—District of Colombia
85. Champagne is Dry or Sweet?—Dry
86. Lasagne is a Type of?—Pasta
87. A.P.C. in Indian Cuisine Stands for?—Achaar, Pickle and Chutney
88. How much Brain does a Computers has?—Nil
89. What is the Capital of Scotland?—Edenberg
90. Evening Service is also known as?—Turn Down Service
91. **Who is the Father of Indian Hotel Industry?—Rai Bahdur Mohan Singh Oberoi**

92. Triple O Stands for?—Out of Order
93. Expand the Term P.O.P.?—Plaster of Paris
94. Which Place Holds the Famous Pushkar Festival?—Pushkar
95. Expand the Term T.V.P.?—Textured Vegetable Protein
96. The Guest who Skips out is known as?—Skipper
97. What is the Logo of Nestle?—The Bird Sitting on the Nest
98. Give the Other Name for Chinese Parsley?—Cilantro
99. Sorbet is a Rest Course, is it True or False?—True
100. Corona is the Beer From which Country?—Mexico
101. Which City is Named as the City of Flyovers?—New Delhi
102. Lager Beers are top or Bottom Fermented?—Bottom
103. What is the Capital of Argentina?—Buneous Aries
104. What is the Standard par for Uniform?—3
105. Dal Panchratan is the Combination of How many Dals?—5
106. Shredded Spinach is also known as?—Chiffonade
107. Alsace Wines Take their name from?—Chataeus
108. How much is 1 Jigger?—45 M.L.
109. How much is 1 Pint?—375 M.L.
110. What is the Vegetarian Substitute for Gelatine?—Agar-Agar
111. The term Service Console is known as?—Side Station
112. Sales Recaptulation Report is also Termed as?—Transcripts
113. Who is the Father of Nouvelle Cuisine?—Paul Bocuse
114. What are Sekts?—German Sparkling Wines
115. What are Astu Spumante?—Italian Sparkling Wines
116. Reward and Prestige Power is known as?—Formative Power
117. Glen Mist is the Liquer Flavoured with?—Honey
118. Yellow Connective Tissue in meat are?—Elatin

119. Expand the Term M.I.P.S. in Computers?—Million Instructions Per Second
120. Expand the Term R.C.I.?—Resort Codiminium International
121. What is the Currency of Japan?—Yen
122. Jack Danniels is Best Known as?—Tennese
123. Managers Report in Front Office is Termed as?—Daily Operational Report
124. Expand the Term F.M.C.G.?—Fast Moving Consumable Goods
125. Accompaniment for Roasted Duck is?—Orange Sauce
126. The Room Assigneds to four People is Termed as?—Quad
127. Expand the Term C.R.T.—Cathode Ray Tube
128. Saccrometer is Used for?—To Measure the Density of Sugar
129. Smoked Salmon Originates From?—Sandinavian Countries
130. Who is the Founder of Park Hotels?—Swraj Paul
131. Who is the Father of Computers?—Charles Babbage
132. Expand the Term G.D.S.?—Global Distribution System
133. Earlier Vodka Were Known as?—Gorzalla
134. Afri Coco is what Flavoured Liqueur?—Coconut
135. Plate Du Jour is Known as?—Speciality of the Day
136. Varnish Made from Alcohol and Lac is Known as?—Shellac
137. Artichoke is Tuber or Bulbous?—Tuber
138. Cigar Boxese Known as?—Humidor
139. Roti in English Means?—Roasted
140. What is the Staple Food of West Bengal?—Rice
141. What is the Capital of Bulgaria?—Sofia
142. Name the Capital of Canada?—Ottawa
143. Blancs Means?—White
144. What do you Mean by Noir?—Black
145. What are Chateus?—Vineyards

146. Expand the Term P.O.S.?—Point of Sale

147. Puree Soups Are Accompanied with?—Croutons

148. Roasted Beef is Accompanied with?—Horse Raddish Sauce and Yorkshire Pudding

149. What is the International Airways of Canada?—Air Canda

150. The Book used to Maintain Daily Schedules is Known as?—Log Book

151. Name the Dish Prepared under the Moon Light?—Nimish

152. Expand the Term N.A.S.A.?—National Aeronautics Space Authority

153. What are Pernod?—Aniseed Flavoured Liqueur

154. Juniper Berries are use for?—Flavouring Gin

155. Drambuie is what Flavoured Liqueur?—Herb

156. Where is the Famous Hewthrow Airport Located?—London

157. Roasted Pork is Accompanied with?—Apple Sauce

158. Expand the Term H.T.M.L.?—Hyper Text Mark up Language

159. Hotel with Gambling Facility are Termed as?—Casino

160. Bottom of Sparkling Wines is Termed as?—Punt

161. Expand the Term I.C.F.?—Indian Culinary Forum

162. What are two Types of Distillation?—Pot and Patent Still

163. Basic Principles of Management are Designed by?—Henry Fayol

164. The Word Crustaceans is Associated with?—Fish

165. Small Hooks on Both Ends are Termed as?—Helical Hooks

166. Ozone Depletion is Caused Due to?—Chlorofloro Carbons

167. What is the Currency of Egypt?—Egyptian Pound

168. Name the City on Waters?—Venice

169. Which is the City of Canals?—Amstredam

170. International Airport of Hongkong is?—Kowloon International

171. Which Wine Compliments with Mostly Dishes?—Sparkling Wines

172. What is the Other Name for Chinese Parsley?—Corriander
173. What is the Capital of Ethopia?—Addis Abbaba
174. What is the Capital of Australia?—Cannebera
175. What Provides Bitterness to the Beer?—Hops
176. Shukto Originates from which State?—West Bengal
177. The Term Offloading is Associated with?—Overbooking
178. Contreau is what Flavoured Liqueur?—Orange
179. Expand the Term P.A.T.A.?—Pacific Area Transport Association
180. Tiramisu is what Flavoured Desert?—Coffee
181. Who is the Father of Fast Food Industry?—Ray Kroc of MC. Donalds
182. What is Gigot?—Leg of Mutton
183. Coffee with Rum is Called as?—Carreabean Coffee
184. Bloody Mary Without Vodka is Known as?—Virgin Mary
185. Screw Driver Without Vodka is?—Plain Orange Juice
186. Pale Pink Gills is the Sign of?—Old or Stale Fish
187. Which is the Oldest Tea Producing Country?— China
188. What is Mumbai Duck?—A Fish
189. Salt Used for Frosting Glass?—Celery Salt
190. Tail of Fillet is Called ?—Fillet Mignon
191. French for Underdone Meat is?—Au-Bleu
192. What are Crapinnetes?—Flat Sausages
193. Is Full Garnish Used in Mocktails?—Yes
194. Name the Steak Served Raw?—Tartere Steak
195. What is Spit Roasting?—Open Fire Roasting
196. Bolognaise is the Famous Salami, is it True or False?—False
197. What is Semolina in Hindi?—Sooji
198. Coffee with Brandy is Called?—Cafe Royale

199. Coffee with Vodka is Called?—Russian Coffee
200. Matured Bacon is Called?—Green Bacon
201. What is Barron?—Complete Back of Bacon
202. Perrier Belongs to which Country?—France
203. Evian is Sparkling water from France, is it True or False?—False
204. Hind Leg of Mutton is Known as in India?—Raan
205. Irish Coffee Includes Cream, is it True or False?—True
206. In which Method the Throat is Cut and Bleed?—Halal
207. Fat Deposited Between Muscles Fibers is Called?—Marbelling
208. White Connective Tisues are Called?—Collagen
209. European Slauter House Are Called?—Abbotoire
210. Resting Place for Animals Before Slaughtering is Called?—Pens
211. French Term for Head of Pork is?—Tete
212. An Enzymes Found in Raw Papaya is?—Papain
213. Is Fashinable Straw a Part of Full Garnish?—No
214. Black Pudding is Made from Chicken, True or False?—False
215. Tomacino, Circelli etc. are Associated to?—Sausages
216. Is Cafe Complete Also Known as Complete Breakfast?—Yes
217. Coffee is Produced from which Tree?—Genuscoffea
218. Who is Termed as the Father of Cookery?—Aughuthus Escoffier
219. Meat Called Immediately After Slaughtering?—Pantelante
220. Beverage is Derived from which Latin Word?—Bevere
221. What is the Eresoulution Rigor?—Action of Enzymes on Flesh
222. What is Fermented Cactus Juice Called?—Pulque
223. What are Wine Atsters Called?—Connasieurs
224. Expand the Term LBV?—Late Bottled Vintage
225. Angustra Bitter Belong to which Country?—Trinidad

226. What is Agrfe Clip?—Clip on the Champagne Cork
227. Sercial, Verdelho are Associated with?—Madera
228. Underberg Bitter Belongs to which Country?—Germany
229. What is Bortgis?—Oble Rot Disease
230. To Which Country Does Tokey Belongs?—Hungry
231. Cava is the Sparkling Wine of?—Spain
232. Remuage Bottles are Dipped into which Soloution?—Brine
233. Expand the Term C.S.I.?—Computer Society of India
234. What is W.A.N.?—Wide Area Network
235. Fernet Brance is the Bitter from which Country?—Italy
236. What is Butt?—Standard Shipping Cask
237. What does D.O.M.?—De Optimo Maximo
238. Pol Rigor is Brand Name of What?—Champagne
239. Soler Process is Associated with what?—Sherry
240. Sweet Red Wines are Served Chilled, is it True or False?—False
241. Dimensions of Fish Plate are those to Soup Plate is it true of False?—True
242. Barley is involved in which Alcoholic Beverage?—Beer
243. Zinfadel Grapes Belongs to which Place in U.S.A.?—Calfornia
244. What is Flavoured with Hops in Brew Kettle?—Filtered Wort
245. The Word Small in French Means?—Petit
246. Derivative of Hollandaise is?—Maltaise
247. Tia Maria is Flavoured with?—Coffee and Rum
248. Define Fonde De Cuisine?—Basic Kitchen Stock
249. Remoulade is the Derivative of?—Mayonnaise
250. The Standard Par for Blankets is?—1.5
251. How Many Portions Does 1 Liter of Soup Yiels?—5
252. How Many Fillets form a Lemon Sole?—4

253. Are Geen Potatoes Edible?—No

254. Stains of Paints can be Removed By?—Methylated Spirit

255. Is Magnesite a Semi Hard Loor?—No

256. Name two Basic Category of Carpets?—Woven and Non-Woven

257. Blue and Yellow gives Birth to which Colour?—Green

258. Name the Fat used for Pot Roasting?—Butter

259. How much Space Does a Floppy Disk Has?—1.44 M.B.

260. The Opposite of Debit Card is?—Credit Card

261. Expand Spatt?—Special Attention Guest

262. Which Cheese of Italian Takes 2-3 years to Mature?—Parmeasan

263. Give the Other Name for American Service?—Preplated Service

264. What is Fermented Spiced Honey?—Mead

265. Bistol Cream is a word Associated to?—Sherry

266. Name the Famous Fortified Wine of Italy?—Portugal

267. From which Country does Saki Belongs?—Japan

268. What is the Meaning of Trancheur?—Carver

269. What is the Capcity of C.D.?—700MB

270. What is Augartin?—Sprinkled

271. What is the Meaning of Le Ris?—Sweat Bread

272. Stimulant in Tea is Called?—Thiene

273. From Which Country Still to Cheese Belong to?—England

274. What Accompaniment is Given with Sweet Juices?—Castor Sugar

275. French name for Eed is?—Anguille

276. French Term for Lamb is?—Agneau

277. Thickened Gravy is Called?—Juslie

278. German for Dry is Known as?—Trocken

279. What is Mollet?—Soft

280. What is the First Version of Windows?—Win 3.1
281. What are Weps?—Leakage of Wine Through Cork
282. Potted Shrimps are from?—England
283. Word Kasher is Synonimus with which Style of Cookery?—Jewish
284. What is Voiler?—To Cover with Spun Sugar
285. What is The French Name for Scarambled Egg?—Oeufs Brouille
286. What is Chambre?—Room Temperature
287. Frappe Means?—Chilled
288. Expand the Term W.T.O.?—World Trade Organisation
289. What Olorosis?—Types of Sherry
290. What do you Mean by CRU?—Growth
291. Expand the Term MDP?—Marquise De Pompadouve
292. The Word CTC Stands for?—Cutting, Tearing, Crushing
293. What is Pomac?—Fermented Apple Juice
294. Name the Worlds Tallest Building?—Empire Estate New York
295. French Name for Fish Liquid is?—Cout Bulillon
296. What are Agraz?—Almond Sorbets
297. Who Invented Charcoal Filtered Cigarettes?—Phlip Morris
298. Which is the Worlds Largest Hotel?—Excalibur
299. In which Suite Did—Mr. Bill Clinton Stayed
300. Which Hotel has the Biggest Convention Centre in India?—Jaypee Palace, Agra

RAPID KNOWLEDGE GAINER

What is Slave's Drink?	Rum
What is the Capital of Cuba?	Hawana
What is the Correct Method of Cooking Spinach?	Blanching
What Protien is Present in Wheat?	Gluten
White Fat Present in Lamb?	Marble Fat
Name the Country, Which Produces Maximum Number of Wines?	Italy
Foyot Sauce is a Derivative of?	Hollandaise
Doux are What Type of Wine?	Sweetest Wine
What is the Spiced Fermented Honey Known As?	Mead
What is Saunth?	Dry Ginger Powder
What is English Term for Champignons?	Mushroom
What is Fermented Rice Extract Known as?	Sake
What Agent Gives Orange Colour to Carrot?	Carotene
Which Restaurant Introduced Tandoor in India?	Moti Mahal
What is the Controversial Step in Serving Wine Involving Pouring Wine out of it's Bottle in to Another Container?	Decanting
What is the Mixture of Black Coffee and Vodka?	Russian Coffee
Boullabaise is a National Soup of Which Country?	France
In Which inn was the Boston Tea Party Decided?	Green Dragon Town
Who is the Founder of Hilton Hotels?	Conrad N. Hilton
Japanese Inns are Known as?	Ryokan
KLM is the National Airlines of which Country?	Netherlands
Correct Service Temperature Range for Hot Sauce	True is 80-85ºC?
Chinois is known as Conical Strainer?	True
Birds Nest is the Name of one of the Speciality Soup?	True

What is Weps?	Leakage of Wine through Cork
What is the English Term for Aracyides?	Peanuts
What is Turkey Called in French?	Dinde
What is Ravioli?	Stuffed Pasta Packets
Traditional Accompaniment of Roast Turkey?	Cranberry Sauce
When was the I.T.D.C. Formed?	1965
From which Part of the Saffron Plant is the Saffron Collected?	Flower/Stamen
Normande is a Derivative of?	Veloute Sauce
What is a Mignon?	Fish Cut
What is a Fool?	Sweet Dish Made with Sieved Fruit
What is Estouffade?	Brown Stock
Expand the Term CPR?	Cardio Pulmonary Resuscitation
What is the Capital of Scotland?	Edenburgh
What is the Accompaniment of Roast Lamb?	Mint Sauce
What is the French Name of Pig's Belly?	Poitune
What is Name of the Travel Agency of Oberois	Mercury Travels Group?
What is the Capital of Bulgaria?	Sofia
What is the Traditional Kashmiri Banquet Known as?	Wazwan
What is Plant Du Jour?	Dish of the Day
White Connective Tissues in Lamb are Called?	Collagen
Yellow Connective Tissues in Lamb are Called?	Elastin
Murukku is a Dish From Which Cuisine?	Tamil

What are the Traditional Indian Accompaniments?	A.P.C. (Achar, Papad, Chutney)
Which Country Produces Limburgur Cheese?	Belgium
Accompaniment for Grape Fruit During Service?	Castor Sugar
Jardiniere Cut is in the Shape of?	Baton Shape
Japonnaise is a Type of?	Fruit Based Salad
What is the Currency of Germany?	Deustchmark/Euro
Size of a Joint Plate?	10 Inches
What are Bon Bons?	Sweet or Sugar Candies
What is Ham Called in French?	Jambon
What is Chambre as a Process?	Bringing Red Wine to Room Temperature
Sony Ericsson Originates from which Country?	Sweden
Broadway is a Type of?	Sandwich
What are Shams?	Decorative Pillow Covers used on Bed
What is the National Soup of U.S.A.?	Manhattan Clam Chowder
What is Mignonette?	Coarsely Ground Pepper
What is the Capacity of Champagne Tulip?	6-8 oz
What is the Capacity of Liqueur Glass?	4 oz
What Accompanies Minestrone Soup?	Grated Parmesan Cheese
Chetelaine Corresponds to What?	Meat Based Salad
Expand the Term I.M.F.?	International Monetary Funds
Expand the Term F.E.R.A.?	Foreign Exchange Regulation Act

Expand the Term P.O.P.?	Plaster of Paris
What is Farin?	Fine Potato Flour
Absolut Vodka Comes from Which Country?	Sweden
Who is the Founder of Jay Pee Hotels?	Mr. J.P. Gaur
What is Pomac?	Fermented Apple Juice
What is the % of Carbon Dioxide in Beer?	0.4%-0.5% by Vol.
Which is the Flavouring Agent in Malibu Rum?	Coconut
What is a Canard?	Duck
Ideal Dry Storage Temperature us?	15°C-18°C
At which Temperature Perishable Food Items are Stored in Refrigerator?	4-7°C
Approximate Ratio of What to Vegetables when	10:1 Blanching us?
The Ratio of Water While Cooking Pasta is?	10:1
Expand the Term U.N.E.S.C.O.?	United Nations Educational, Scientific and Cultural Organization
Expand the Term E.P.A.B.X.?	Electronic Privatised Automatic Branch Exchange
Expand the Term I.H.A.?	International Hotel Association
Expand the Term R.S.V.P.?	Respondez Sil Vous Plait
Expand the Term I.A.T.A.?	International Air Transport Association
Expand the Term I.A.T.O.?	International Association of Tour Operation

Room Shown as Occupied, But is Vacant, What is the Room Called?	Sleeper
Speed of Computer is Measured in?	MHz Mega Hertz
Expand the Term P.M.S.?	Property Management System
What is the Botanical Name of Tea Plant?	Camellia Sinesis
Name the Natural Yeast Present in Grapes?	Saccaromyces Ellipsoides
Master Chef in Kashmiri Cusine is Known as?	Vasta Weze
Freshly Gathered Grape Juice is known as?	Must
Fermented Apple Juice is Known as?	Cider
Fermented Cactus Juice is?	Pulque
Sediments of Red and White Wine are known as?	Lees
What does Brut Means?	Extra Dry
Expand the Term F.R.R.O.?	Foreingner's Regional Registration Office
Name the Accompaniment of Roast Duck?	Orange Sauce
Egges are Graded According to their Weight?	True
Au Nature Refers to Simply Cooked Food Items?	True
The Ratio of Oil and Vinegar in French Dressing is?	3:1
The Ratio of Oil and Vinegar in American Dressing is?	1:1
Poaching Liquor is Known as?	Court Bouillon
French Term for Poultry is Known as?	Volaille
Expand the Term T.Q.M.?	Total Quality Management
What is Sec?	Dry
Soup in Which Blood Used as Thickening Agent?	Grand Vernier
What is the Capital of Philipinnes?	Manila

What is Polenta?	Corn Meal
Cherry Based Syrup used in Flavouring of Liqueors	Cerise
Cigars which can be Opened from both Sides?	Pantella
Which of the Following is the King of Liqueurs?	Benedictine
Who Invented Remuage Process?	Nicole Cliquot
Which of the Following has a White Wine Base?	Vermouth
Which One is Irish Whisky?	Jameson
What is Zuppa?	Italian Soup
What are Chinese Snacks Known as?	Dim Sums
What is the Unit of Light?	Lumens
What is the Alcohol Percentage of Tia Maria?	32%
Name the Person who Barks the Order in Kitchen?	Aboyer/Barker
Which of the Following is Correct?	8 Bit = 1 Byte
What is the Capital of Turkey?	Ankara
What is the Height of a Bar Stool?	30 Inches
Expand the Term MPEG?	Moving Pictures Expert Group
Expand the Term N.H.A.I.?	National Highway Authority of India
American Plan Includes Room Rent, Breakfast, Lunch or Dinner?	False
English for Maitre D' Hotel is Senior Captain?	True
Osetrova is a Type of Caviar?	Ture
Dry Sherry is Added to Turtle Soup	True
Consomme Xavier is Garnished with Threaded Egg?	True
Approximate Size of Single Bed Sheet?	36 × 75 Inches
Expand the Term YMCA?	Young Men's Christian Association
Expand the Term I.L.O.?	International Labour Organisation

Expand the Term DNA?	Did Not Arrive
What is the National Emblem of India?	Ashoka Pillar
How Many Lion does Ashoka Pillar Have?	4 (3 In Front & 1 at the Back)
Expand The Term DOS?	Disc Operating System
What is Jus Lie?	Thickened Gravy
What is Edam?	Semi Hard Cow Cheese
Le Petit Dejeuner Means?	Breakfast
Poivre is the French Name For?	Pepper
The Proof of Whisky can be Tested by using Gun Powder?	True
Chillies can be used as a Flavour Enhancing Agent in Vodka?	True
Heiniken Beer is From Germany?	False it is from Holland
Cigars can not be Served in the Sorbet Course?	True
Vodka can be Stored in Refregirators?	True
A Room Having Attached Kitchen is Called?	Efficiency Room
Meat Contains Which Protein?	Myosin
Which Wine is Served First? Dry Wine or Sweet Wine?	Dry
The only Red Wine Served Chilled is?	Lambrusco
J.F.K. Airport is Located at which City?	New York
What is Kahlua Liqueur Flavoured with?	Coffee
Who are Connossieurs?	Who Judge Wine and Cigars
Crib Rates are Applicable to?	Children Below 5 yrs.
What is Danish Blue?	Cheese
Which Group Runs the Restaurant Ghain Croissants?	Ambassador

What is Baba?	Yeast Sponge or Bun
White Stew are Known as?	Blanquettes
What is Wild Marjoram Known as?	Oregano
The Mash, Herbs, and Sugar is Called?	Wort
What is Holland's?	Type of Gin Distilled in Holland
Give the French Name for 'Cooked in Over'?	Au Four
What is Irish Mist?	Liqueur from Irish Whisky
Chinese Cooking Pan used for Stir Frying?	Wok
Which Country Does Stilton Cheese Belong To?	England
What Accompaniment is given with Sweet Juices?	Castor Sugar
French Term for Lamb is?	Agneau
What is the First Version of Windows?	Windows 3.1
Word Kosher is Synonimous with which Style of Cookery?	Jewish
What Do You mean by Voiler?	To Cover with Spun Sugar
What Does Frappe Mean?	Chilled
What is Olorosis?	Type of Sherry
What is MDP?	Marquise De Pompadour
The Word CTC Stands for?	Cutting, Tearing, Crushing
Which is the Most Popularly used Software for F&B Service Operations?	Micros
What is Americano?	Black Coffee
Word "Vitreous" is Associated with?	Chinaware
What Type of Cheese is Gorgonzola?	Blue Cheese

The Word Smorgasbord is Associated to which Kind of Service?	Buffet Service
The Word Dijon is Associated with What?	Mustard
What is Spiral Part of Waiter's Friend Known as?	Worm
With which Type of Service are Dome and Cloche Associated?	Room Service
Effervescence in Aerated Water is Due to Presence of which Gas?	CO_2
Pre-Dinner Drinks Are Known As?	Aperitifis
Word "Francaise" "Verte" "Saison" is Associated with what?	Salads
What are Tisanes?	Flavoured Tea
Cleaning Procedure Starts from the Floor Towards Ceiling?	False
Blank Inventory Sheets to be Made Available to Linen Keeper?	True
The Lost and Found Procedure Means that House Keeping Staff can Retain all Items Found in the Room/Public Areas?	False
Stains Caused By Oil, Grease, Wax, Paint, Tar can be Removed by use of Solvent Such as Carbontetrachloride?	True
Garnish Used while Serving Campari?	Twist of Lemon Peel
What is the Flavour of Tonic Water?	Quinine Flavoured
Skin of Grape is Known as?	Narc
Who Invented Charcoal Flavoured Cigarettes?	Phillip Moris
What is Meth Uselah?	Champagne Bottle (6LTS.)
What Type of Fermentation is Prefered for Softer Wine Taste?	Malolactic Fermentation
What is the Protective Covering over the cork of the Wine Bottle Known as?	Capsule, Made of Tin & Lead

Give the Term used for French Ware Houses used for Storing Wines	Chai
Expand the Term C.Q.?	Ccork Quality Council (Setup in USA in 1992)
French Word for Wines that are Highly Acidic?	Dur
The Product Obtained After the Ist Distillation in the Pot Still Process is?	Low Wines
Process of Turning Starch in the Cereals into Sugar Ready for Fermentation is?	Saccharify
From Which Civilization Beer is Originated?	Mesopotamia
Flattened Armagnac Bottles are Known as?	Basquaise
Which Gin is Suitable for Cocktails?	London Dry
Name Aniseed Flavoured Spiritfrom Turkey?	Raki
Drying of Tobacco Leaves is Known as?	Curing
How can you Avoid the Burn Sensation in Brandy?	By using Luke Warm Water
Tequila is Obtained from which Plant?	Blue Agave
Which Spirit is used in Preperation of Flambe Dishes?	Brandy
What is the Capital of Bhutan?	Timphu
What is the French for Snails?	Escargots
Which Ham is Consumed Raw?	Parma
Consommes Celestines are Garnished with?	Juliennes of Panchake
Stock in Hand is Also Known as?	Inventory
What is Pile?	Cut of Fish
Who Invented Champagne?	Dom Perignon
Give the other Name for Chinese Parsley?	Cilantro
Lager Beers are Top or Bottom Fermented?	Bottom

What is the Capital of Argentina?	Beunes Aires
Shredded Spinach is also Known as?	Chiffonade
What is the Capital of Australia?	Canberra
What Provides Bitterness to the Beer?	Hops
Shukto Originates from which State?	West Bengal
The Term Offloading is Associated with?	Overbooking
What is Gigot?	Leg of Mutton
Coffee with Rum is Called as?	Carreabean Coffee
Bloody Mary without Vodka is Known as?	Virgin Mary
Sales Tax on Hard Drinks in Delhi is?	20%
How Many Mother Sauces?	6
Scientific Name of Yeast in Wine is?	Saccaromyces Ellypsoidus
What does Insipid Means?	Tasteless
Expand the Term S.I.C.O.M.?	State Industrial and Corporation of Maharashtra
Andhra Pradesh is the Biggest Producer of what?	Chillies
Sediments in Wine are Called?	Leese
Grape Juice without Skin is Called?	Must
Adding of Extra Sugar in Wine is Called?	Chaptalization
Which is the Protein Present in Pulses?	Legumin
Stage of Sugar at 119 Degree Celcium is Called?	Ball Stage
Whipped Egg White and Sugar is Called?	Meringue
Which is the Strainer used for Straining Stocks called?	Chinois
What is the Holding Temperature for Emulsion Sauce?	30°C–37°C
Scotch Egg is Derivative of?	White Sauce
What Room thought to be Occupied but is Vacant?	Sleeper

What are Castors Called?	Wheels
What does Manual Press Cooking is Called?	Dum Cooking
What was Delightful Poisson Later Called?	Wine
What is Fermented Apple Drink is Called?	Cider
What is the Fermented Drink Obtained from Cactus Called?	Pulque
What are Sweetened Flavoured Spirits Called?	Liqueurs
Tip of the Knife is Called?	Tip
Hotel for Motorist is Called?	Mote
What is the size of table cloth?	72 Inches x 72 Inches
Expand the Term V.P.P.?	Value Payable Post
Highest Runs Scored in one Ball Ever?	50 Run
Expand the Term G.R.E.?	Guest Relative Executive
Expand the Term G.S.E.?	Guest Service Executive
What is the Time for Baggage Down?	10 Mins
English Name for Arbi?	Colocasia
What is Jamun Known in English?	Jambul Fruit Java Pulp
What is Depouiller?	To Skim
What are all Red Wines from Bordeaux Called?	Clarets
Name the Cheese whose name means Cheese on House	Wensyldale
Back Caciocavallo which Cheese Accompanies Apple Pie?	
Giang Style of Cooking is Known for what?	Hot Salad
Expand the Term S.B.R.?	Styrene Butadiene Rubber
What is Reduced Stock Known as?	Glaze
What Types of Food are Whiting and Winkle?	Sea Food
What is the Full name of Founder of Reuter News Agency?	Paul Julius Reuter
What is the Meaning of "Ould Out"?	Room not Available
A List of all Accounts in a Ledger is Known as?	Trial Balance

What does Another Term for Work Shift is Known as?	Watch
What does Afolding and Portable Bed is Known as?	Z-Bed
Name the Types of Budgets Prepared in Hotel?	Zero Budget and History Budget
What is the Scientific Name for Wild Yeast?	Saccaromyces Ellipsoidos
What are Vats?	Place Where Wines are Stored
White Sports Found on Grape's Skin are Called?	Bloom
Salt Solution used to Make Mine is Called?	Prine
Give Another Name for Spirits?	Distilled Drinks
Starch are Basically Known as?	Carbohydrates
Name the Types of Wines?	Still Wines and Sparkling Wines
Name 3 Glasses to Serve Champagne?	Saucer, Tulip and Fluit Champagne
What is the % of Living Yeast Cell in Wines?	Not Less than 90%
Who Makes Duty Roasters in House Keeping?	Assistant Executive House Keeper
Expand the Term R.S.O.T.?	Room Service Order Taken
Expand the Term K.O.T.?	Kitchen OrderTicket
Expand the Term U.M. in House Keeping?	Under Maintenance
Who Wrote Gora?	Rabindra N. Tagore
Who Wrote Shakuntla?	Kalidas
What is the Currency of Italy?	Lira
What is the Capital of Italy?	Rome
What is the Currency of Vietnam?	Dong
What is the Capital of Peru?	Lima
Expand the Term H.R.A.C.C.?	Hotel & Restaurant Approval Classification Committee

Which is the Greatest Waterfall in the World?	Angel Falls (Venezuela)
Expand the Term B.P.L. in Electronics?	British Physical Laboratory
What is the Capital of Algeria?	Algiers

REFERENCES

- Theory of catering "Ronald, Victorceserani and David Foskett."
- Larousse gastronomique "Hamlyn."
- Chef book of formulas and yield and sizes "SCHMIDT."
- Food and hygiene "Roday."
- The food and wine "Dean and Deluca."
- Hotel housekeeping operations and management "Oxford Publisher."
- Cookery for the hospitality "Dodgshun and Peters."
- Dietetics "B. Sri Lakshmi."
- Theory of cookery "K.L. Arora."
- Basic hotel front office procedure "Petter Renner."
- Front office operation "Dix Bard."
- Hotel front office operation "Baker Huyton Bradley."
- Food and beverage "Davis Lock Wood Stone."
- Food and beverage "Andrews."
- Food and beverage "Jagmohan Negi."
- The waiter handbook "John Fuller and A.J. Currie."
- The bar and beverage book "Costas Katsigris and Mary Porte, Joh Wiley and Sons."
- The world guide to whisky, "Michael Jacksons."
- Hotel Housekeeping and operation "Andrews."
- Environmental management "N.K Uberio."
- The books of cocktail "Salamander."
- Encyclopedia of wines, spirits and beer "Hamlyn."
- www.vegas and today .com
- www.travellandleisure.com
- www.fhrai.com
- www.indiainfoline.com
- www.hotel-online.com/news
- www.hotelnewresource.com
- www. Hotelinterctive.com